Taking Back the United Methodist Church
by
Mark Tooley

Taking Back The United Methodist Church
©Mark Tooley
Published by Bristol House, Ltd.

First Printing, March 2008
Second Printing, June 2010, Updated

ISBN: 978-1885224-67-5
Printed in the United States of America.

Design by Larry Stuart
Cover art by Doug Hall

BRISTOL HOUSE, LTD.
1201 E. 5th St., Suite 2107
Anderson, Indiana 46012
Phone: 765-644-0856
Fax: 765-622-1045

To order call: 1-800-451-READ (7323)
www.bristolhouseltd.com

Table of Contents

In memory of my grandmother,
Lucille Harris Gilmer (1914-2001)

CHAPTER   ONE

BEGINNINGS

It was Veterans' Day 1989 and we were on an early morning chartered bus heading for a confrontation with the United Methodist General Board of Global Ministries (GBGM) in New York City!

There were 30 of us, mostly lay people inexperienced in the intricacies of church politics. In response to my letter to the bishop of Virginia, the Arlington District in Northern Virginia had organized the expedition for us to speak face to face with GBGM executives for a full day at the famous Interchurch Center on New York's Upper West Side.

Global Ministries! They were the Goliath of The United Methodist Church. With a budget of $100 million, assets several times that and a headquarters staff of more than 400, GBGM was not typically trifled with. Pastors, district superintendents and even bishops often bowed before its power.

But GBGM had always been controversial and troubling to well-informed evangelicals within United Methodism. Decades ago, Methodism had once dispatched more than 2,000 missionaries overseas. By the 1980s, the full-time career missionary force was down to only about 400. (Today it's fewer than 200.)

In the 1960s and 1970s, GBGM had shifted from a traditional evangelistic focus to liberation theology. This new theology claimed the church's role was social and political revolution, and it even sometimes called the church to support armed insurrection. No longer was saving souls the primary emphasis. Now the main objective was overthrowing political and economic systems perceived to be unjust. If eternity or the afterlife were concerns at all, GBGM was primarily universalist. If heaven existed, everybody was automatically going there, no matter what one's beliefs or behavior. All religions were essentially equal attempts at the same truth.

Unconcerned about eternity, GBGM was zealously focused on changing the here and now, partly through non-controversial relief and social work, but increasingly also through highly divisive political action of the far left.

In 1983 *Good News* magazine, in "Missions Derailed" by Jim Robb, described GBGM's grants to far-left political action groups. Robb's sensational exposé received the United Methodist Communicators top award for that year, but the powerful and impervious GBGM mostly chose to ignore the slight.

Robb had built on the report that United Methodist layman and labor union official David Jessup distributed to the 1980 General Conference about GBGM and other church agencies. Jessup, who belonged to a United Methodist church in suburban Maryland outside Washington, D.C., was the AFL-CIO's liaison to overseas trade unions. He was expert in steering these unions away from Marxist ties and toward democratic movements. Unsurprisingly, Jessup was suspicious when his children returned home from Sunday school collecting money for GBGM missions. The causes described in the GBGM materials sounded eerily like some of the groups against which Jessup warned away his foreign labor union contacts.

Jessup was a committed liberal Democrat and an anti-communist with strong opinions about international human rights. He launched his own investigation about GBGM's "missions" causes and grants to outside groups. And Jessup was increasingly aghast as he learned that GBGM was granting hundreds of thousands of dollars to groups supportive of, and often closely tied to, radical and openly Marxist causes.

Recipients of GBGM's generosity included groups support-ing Nicaragua's Marxist Sandinista regime, which increasingly was persecuting Nicaragua's Roman Catholics and evangelicals, among others. One GBGM group, CEPAD, was a relief group in Nicaragua that was a virtual partner of the Sandinistas, even distributing Sandinista Marxist propaganda that repeated the themes of liberation theology. Other recipient groups were sup-porting the Marxist rebels in neighboring El Salvador. The Com-mittee in Solidarity with the People of El Salvador, one grantee, helped organize radical demonstrations in the U.S. that not only called for a cut off of U.S. arms to El Salvador but also praised the FMLN guerrillas there.

Other GBGM recipients were praising the Communist re-gimes of Southeast Asia. Church World Service, the relief arm of the National Council of Churches and generously supported by GBGM, was even partnering with Communist Vietnam's "New Education Zones," which were essentially concentration camps for opponents of the totalitarian regime.

Elsewhere in Asia, GBGM was funding groups that were apol-ogists for North Korea's nightmarish Stalinist government, while pushing for the withdrawal of U.S. troops from South Korea. Other groups getting GBGM funds were apologists for the Mao-ist New People's Army in the Philippines.

In the Middle East, GBGM was funding groups that support-ed the Palestine Liberation Organization (PLO), while ignoring the PLO's active terrorist activities and close ties to the Soviet Union.

In Africa, GBGM was funding groups that openly espoused armed revolution and often were Marxist. Often these grants were channeled through the Geneva-based World Council of Churches' Program to Combat Racism, which funneled money to the guerrilla insurgencies that became the Marxist regimes of Mozambique and Angola, and eventually tyrannical Robert Mugabe's regime of Zimbabwe. GBGM also funded the SWAPO and African National Congress insurgencies in Namibia and South Africa, when those groups were still aligned with local Communist parties and the Soviet Union.

Perhaps most troubling, GBGM was funding groups like Christians Associated for Relationships with Eastern Europe (CAREE), which was affiliated with Finland-based World Peace Council, an open Soviet front group that received KGB money to advocate for Western disarmament. CAREE was even housed in the Interchurch Center in New York, where GBGM was based! Other radical groups funded by GBGM were housed in the United Methodist Building in Washington, D.C., which is owned by the United Methodist General Board of Church and Society.

These radical groups receiving money from the United Methodist Church's missions agency cared little to nothing about spreading the gospel of Jesus Christ. Just the opposite, they were focused on grabbing political power in the name of empowering the oppressed. Particularly troubling to David Jessup, a long-time proponent of democracy and human rights, was church support for causes that were decidedly non-democratic and sometimes even totalitarian.

Jessup single-handedly distributed his 40-page report to the 1,000 delegates meeting at the United Methodist General Conference in 1980. The report raised ecclesial eyebrows. But the delegates took no decisive action to change GBGM's policies, except that all church agencies from thereon would have to report publicly their grants to outside groups. Jessup's report did lead to the creation of the Institute on Religion and Democracy (IRD), for which I now work.

Troubled by these radical political grants by GBGM, but even more distressed by GBGM's lack of concern for evangelism, evangelical leaders within United Methodism had for years been in dialogue with GBGM officials. The dialogue effectively ended in 1983, when GBGM appointed Peggy Billings as head of its World Division missionary force. A former GBGM missionary to South Korea, Billings was proponent of "Minjung Theology," which was a Korean version of liberation theology.

Evangelicals realized that with Billings as head of United Methodism's missionary force, there was little to no prospect of any emphasis on evangelism. And the politics would become even more extreme. In 1984 evangelical leaders created the Mission Society for United Methodists, which would attempt to supply the evangelism-focused missionaries for the church that GBGM was refusing to do. The Atlanta-based Mission Society, initially headed by former GBGM official H. T. Maclin, today has more than 223 missionaries around the world.

Back in 1989 the Mission Society was still a small organization with an uncertain future. With or without its eventual success, many of us newly awakened to GBGM's radical policies were not content to allow GBGM to walk away from Christian missions altogether.

Our small, GBGM-bound delegation of Virginia United Methodists had left the church parking lot at 5:30 a.m. on Veterans Day 1989. In the sleepy darkness, I could recognize friends from at least 10 other churches in the Arlington District. With us too were our district superintendent, the district's United Methodist Women's president and the district's former United Methodist Men's president.

We arrived on schedule at the massive, 1950's era Interchurch Center on New York's scenic Riverside Drive at 10 a.m. sharp. The Rockefeller family had built the office building, overlooking the Hudson River and Grant's Tomb, to house ecumenical and mainline church offices at discounted rates. It was conveniently located next to Union Seminary and the Rev. William Sloane Coffin's cathedral-like Riverside Church. All three structures— the center, the church and the seminary—had been flagships of

once-ascendant liberal mainline Protestantism in America. Indeed, then Secretary of State John Foster Dulles, a former ecumenical official himself, was present for the center's dedication.
But by the 1980s, and even much earlier, all three were stages for
radical theologies and political movements that would have been
unrecognizable even to many of their liberal founders.

Walking through the marble lobby of the Interchurch Center,
we saw inscriptions on the wall dedicating the building to the
"glory of God." We were curious as to whether our meetings up-
stairs with GBGM officials would live up to that promise!

Our Arlington district superintendent introduced us to the
GBGM executives as lay and clergy people, two-thirds of whom
were critical of GBGM's policies and one-third of whom were
more supportive. GBGM's executives were led by World Division chief Bob Harman, who had succeeded Peggy Billings. Harman was cordial and soft in tone. But as we would learn, his
views were not very dissimilar to those of the far-left Billings.

Central to our discussion with GBGM was my citation of
GBGM's questionable spending policies in a letter to then Bishop
Robert Blackburn in 1988. In a 15-page report, somewhat similar to David Jessup's report of eight years earlier, I listed several
dozen radical and most non-church related groups that GBGM
had funded over the previous decade.

My letter, which my local church's administrative board had
authorized, also noted with concern that GBGM spent nearly
one-third of its budget on headquarters expenses, while only 20
percent of its budget gave direct support to missionaries. (Today,
less than 12 percent of GBGM's budget supports missionaries.)
And I had noted that GBGM had more than 400 headquarters
staffers, which meant there was roughly one bureaucrat for each
of GBGM's overseas missionaries. (Today GBGM has fewer than
200 full-time, career overseas missionaries. Its headquarters staff
is about 250.)

All of those facts had shocked members of my local church

when I first began to inform them after becoming my church's missions chairman. Recently graduated from college, I was anxious to serve the congregation that I had continuously attended since my earliest childhood. While still a college student, I had represented my church as a lay member of the Virginia Annual Conference. Even there, I had gotten a troubling whiff of the politics and theology that often guided the elites, if not the members, of our denomination.

Resolutions from Virginia's Committee on Church and Society were often left-wing, urging that the U.S. unilaterally disarm, and expressing disapproval of U.S. efforts to foster democracy against Marxism in Central America and elsewhere. Meanwhile, the Virginia Conference, like the rest of United Methodism, had continuously lost members since the 1960s.

After becoming missions chairman for my local church, I immediately began to read everything I could about GBGM. I got a copy of its two-inch-thick budget disclosure document, listing its hundreds of grants, many of them benign, but dozens of them to radical political groups. I read its monthly magazine, *New World Outlook*, which often echoed the radical political themes of liberation theology. I even read the 1986 book, *Betrayal of the Church*, by United Methodist evangelist Edmund Robb who had joined with David Jessup to found the Institute on Religion and Democracy in 1981. Robb's book described how GBGM and other mainline Protestant agencies had betrayed their church members by advocating far-left, and even Marxist, political causes in place of the gospel.

All of this information about GBGM was infuriating and almost incomprehensible! This was not the United Methodism in which I had grown up. It did not represent my local church or any of the United Methodists I had known.

Ironically, when I became mission chairman and investigated GBGM's policies, my church was pastored by a staunch evangelical who preached blood and thunder salvation sermons. It seemed very incongruous. My pastor proclaimed the need to be born again in Jesus Christ for the sake of eternity. Meanwhile, the missions board that we were supporting with our collection plate money ignored the need for personal salvation and instead advocated a sort of communal salvation through political action.

My local United Methodist church was located in an aging but soon to be redeveloped neighborhood of Arlington, Virginia, right across the Potomac River from Washington, D.C. It was a wonderful and also very typical United Methodist congregation. Central United Methodist Church had several hundred mostly older people, a majority of whom had been in our church for decades. Some of them even dated back to the church's founding in the 1920s. They were very dedicated. But our church, like most of United Methodism, was failing to win new converts, especially among young people.

I had grown up at Central United Methodist Church with a dozen others my age. But by the time I had finished college, I was virtually alone in my age group. Most of my fellow church members were of my grandparents' generation. We desperately needed to focus on evangelism. Yet our church's missions agency was adrift as a social and political action agency, clueless about the beliefs and needs of local United Methodist churches.

Central Church was full of pillars of the community. It was also, for all its imperfections, full of people who believed in the Bible and in the centrality of Jesus Christ. In typical United Methodist fashion, the message we heard from our pulpit was often mixed. We had had liberal and conservative pastors. But our beliefs, thanks to the hymns, Sunday school and the liturgy, remained fairly fixed.

When I shared my findings about GBGM with my church's administrative board, they were horrified. "It's been going on for years!" exclaimed one exasperated church pillar, recalling the *Reader's Digest* and *Sixty Minutes* exposes of the early 1980s, when mainline church agencies were scandalously shown to support overtly Marxist revolution. My findings, composed in a letter to the bishop, were also mailed to the mission chairs of the 50 other churches of the Arlington District, as well as to the district superintendent. I wanted to make sure we got a response!

Within 24 hours, the district superintendent angrily phoned my pastor to complain about the letter's wider distribution. My pastor explained that the letter came from the church's administrative board, and it was not his role to stop it. "It's started!" my pastor told me, understanding that I was launching a long-term campaign to reform our denomination's missions agency.

Bishop Blackburn, soon to retire, replied that he, as a bishop, had no authority over GBGM's policies. But his successor, Bishop Thomas Stockton, would be more responsive. After hearing from other churches in the Arlington District that were indignant over GBGM, and after my church hosted several district-wide meetings to address the GBGM controversy, Bishop Stockton organized our trip to New York City.

"That's the Devil's territory," one local pastor had smilingly warned us about the meeting with GBGM in New York. Many of us were apprehensive, but we were not afraid. Reassuringly, Bob Harman and other GBGM executives who greeted us were attentive and friendly. But as the hours went by, and as we delved into the details of GBGM's funding for radical groups, the meeting became more and more tense.

Specifically, we objected to GBGM's funding for guerrilla movements that were engaged in armed revolution. "Surely, you understand that the vast majority of United Methodists, if they knew about these grants, would object?" I asked.

"Yes, we do understand that," replied GBGM's long-time treasurer Stephen Brimigion. "But years ago, most in the church did not support our activism in the civil rights movement. We can't follow majority opinion; we have to follow our consciences," he explained.

At least he was honest. And liberal church activists had indeed been right about civil rights during the 1950s and 1960s, when most in the church were silent or even actively opposed. But did that history justify GBGM's perpetually ignoring the informed consent of the denomination's members who paid their bills? If GBGM's executives have such strong consciences, should they not spend their own money on these controversial causes?

Bob Harman, at first so soft spoken, launched into a very long monologue on why GBGM must stand with "brothers and sisters in Christ" around the world. By "brothers and sisters," he implicitly was referring to the armed guerrilla groups to which we were objecting. He was clearly a true believer in liberation theology, which often equated revolutionary violence against perceived oppression with the work of the gospel.

Before the meeting was over, Steve Brimigion launched a personal attack on me, asserting that GBGM had serious concerns about my own professional background and sources of information. He was referring to my then employment with the CIA. I responded that all of my sources about the radical groups that GBGM funded were in fact publicly-available information. Ed Robb's *Betrayal of the Church* and David Jessup's report for the 1980 General Conference were clearly examples of that.

The meeting with GBGMs executives ended sourly. As we left, Steve Brimigion shook my hand and said he meant no personal insult to me. I replied that perhaps we would be in agreement when we both got to heaven, but probably not before! The long bus ride home down I-95 to Northern Virginia was mostly quiet, as the 30 of us digested what we had seen and heard. Few minds were changed.

But those of us who were troubled by GBGMs lack of accountability knew that GBGM would not easily change policies because of public criticism by a few churches in Virginia. A wider part of the United Methodist Church had to learn that our missions agency had, whatever their intentions, betrayed our church and, on some level, betrayed the gospel!

Within weeks, many of us were busily at work preparing resolutions for the 1990 Virginia Annual Conference that demanded greater accountability by GBGM. We called ourselves "United Methodists for More Faithful Ministry" (UMFMFM), and we mailed our reports on GBGM to more than 1,000 churches in Virginia.

Our resolutions, calling for restrictions on GBGM funding of secular, non-church groups, were defeated. District superintendents and other officers of the conference spoke against them, affirming the integrity of the church's missions agency, while avoiding any detail. But we had created a stir. We had to turn many away from our crowded luncheon featuring Dr. Ernest Lefever, founder of the Ethics & Public Policy Center in Washington, D.C., and a well-known author about radicalized mainline churches. And the *Richmond Times-Dispatch* ran a front-page article about our resolutions. "Attack on Methodist Missions Rejected," the headline screamed. But it helpfully and lengthily recited our information about GBGM's funding practices.

Shortly after the Virginia Annual Conference, Bishop Stockton phoned me. He was forming what would become the Bishop's Working Group on Mission, to engage us in dialogue about the GBGM controversy. The two-year-long committee would include four persons from UMFMFM and conference officials, plus Dr. James Logan, who was both a theologian at Wesley Seminary and a director on GBGM.

With Dr. Logan's help, the Bishop's Working Group on Mission agreed on several resolutions for the 1992 General Conference that would restrict GBGM's grants and require GBGM to give "priority" to funding of missionaries. "How could these possibly be controversial," we wondered. The 1991 Virginia Annual Conference ratified our resolutions, after a robust floor speech by Dr. Logan.

In April 1992 after I took a week off from work and went to Louisville, Kentucky, to be part of the Good News monitoring team at the General Conference, I sat in on the legislative committee for Global Ministries to advocate for and observe the handling of our Virginia Conference resolutions.

Whenever our resolutions came before the full committee for a vote, a GBGM executive, usually Bob Harman, was invited to address the committee and argue against the resolutions. Mandating priority support for missionaries would potentially devastate GBGM funding for the overseas central conferences, he and others implausibly argued. Invariably, all legislation that challenged GBGM was defeated. But the debate was robust, and often 40 percent of the delegates in committee voted for our resolutions. "They've never seen a meeting like that before," Dr. Logan assured me about the GBGM executives, who were often accustomed to deference.

The 1992 General Conference went on to ratify the church's official teachings about homosexuality. And it adopted a new biblically-sound mission statement for the church, which Dr. Logan had helpfully crafted through our Bishop's Working Group on Mission. But clearly the General Conference was not willing to assert itself against GBGM. The only exception was a vote to study possibly moving GBGM out of expensive New York City. But even that predictably would be defeated at the 1996 General Conference, when a stacked study committee recommended moving GBGM to Washington, D.C.

How could GBGM be reformed, if not directly by the General Conference? Clearly, a church-wide campaign must be mounted to inform the church's millions of laity about where their church dollars were going. But how to do that?

In 1994 the answer came. Diane Knippers asked if I would consider leaving my government employment to join the staff of the Institute on Religion and Democracy (IRD) as its new director of United Methodist activities. Herself the daughter of a United Methodist navy chaplain, she was the new president of IRD whom I had often invited to speak at events in the Virginia

Conference. My response was unhesitant. Naturally I would join the IRD!

IRD had been founded by fellow United Methodists David Jessup and Rev. Edmund Robb specifically to challenge radicalized mainline church agencies. Importantly, IRD's goal was not to tear down, contrary to the charges of its many critics. IRD's objective was to reform and renew America's mainline churches, believing that they continue to have a providential role in America's religious fabric, despite their spiritual and demographic decline.

In November 1994 I entered the Washington, D.C., offices of IRD, right across the street from New York Avenue Presbyterian Church where Abraham Lincoln had worshiped and famed Rev. Peter Marshall had pastored. The challenge before me was one of the most exciting I could imagine: the reclamation of the United Methodist Church for Christ-centered biblical beliefs.

CHAPTER   TWO

THE PRESIDENT'S PASTOR

It was my first assignment in the new job. IRD President Diane Knippers asked if I could do an "exposé" of Rev. Dr. J. Philip Wogaman. He was a renowned United Methodist ethicist who had taught for years at Wesley Theological Seminary, and who, since 1993, was pastor to Bill and Hillary Clinton at Foundry United Methodist Church in Washington, D.C. He was also extremely liberal and an outspoken advocate for overturning United Methodism's disapproval of homosexual practice.

In many ways, Wogaman's views embodied what had led United Methodism and the mainline denominations astray: denying or minimizing historic Christian doctrines about Christ and the Bible while substituting for them the advocacy of left-wing political causes. The author of many books and articles, as well as a prominent delegate at General Conference, Wogaman was an intelligent and formidable proponent of liberal, social-gospel Methodism.

But in early 1995 I was hardly familiar with Wogaman, though he had prominently served on the Committee to Study Homosexuality that had recommended to the 1992 General Conference that *The Discipline's* disapproval of homosexual behavior be deleted. Before starting my research through Wogaman's voluminous writings, I several times attended services at Foundry

United Methodist Church.

The Gothic, stone church, built in the late 19th century, stands in what was then a transitional neighborhood about one mile north of the White House. Franklin Roosevelt had taken Winston Churchill there for Christmas in 1941, and it is where the British prime minister first heard "Silent Night." Harry Truman once stopped for services at Foundry but was irritated by the pastor's effusive attention. Abraham Lincoln had visited Foundry when it was at a different site, and President Rutherford B. Hayes was a member.

By the mid-1990s, Foundry's neighborhood was gradually gentrifying, and many of the new residents were homosexuals attracted to the area's architectural charm and night life. The Clintons' limousine ride there on a Sunday morning probably took no more than five minutes. But the presidential couple was not at the early morning service I attended in January 1995. Instead, Red Cross President Elizabeth Dole, wife of Senator Majority Leader Bob Dole, was by herself in a middle pew. Wogaman was urbane and cerebral as he presided elegantly over the service, welcoming Mrs. Dole back after her back surgery. His sermon was non-controversial. But during the announcements, Wogaman noted that former Supreme Court Justice Harry Blackmun, a United Methodist and author of the *Roe vs. Wade* abortion rights decision, was to have spoken at Foundry the previous Sunday. Wogaman regretted that pro-life demonstrators outside the church had caused Blackmun to cancel. The pastor, quoting from the church bulletin, also alerted parishioners that materials about the Republicans' "Contract with America" were available in the church social hall.

Having in recent years become a decidedly liberal church, Foundry's social concerns committee had compiled talking points against the "Contract with America," upon which Republicans had seized control of Congress the previous November, helping to elevate Bob Dole from U.S. Senate minority to majority leader. "Some provisions have potentially devastating effects on the weakest elements of our society: e.g. removal of the safety net, eliminating environmental regulations, widening the income gap between rich and poor, to name a few," warned the church bulletin of January 29, 1995. "Concerned members should study the issues and relay their views to legislators and the White House."

It was the last time Elizabeth Dole would worship at Foundry United Methodist, which she and her husband had attended for many years. The *Washington Times*, on February 2, 1995, quoted me as reporting this: "Elizabeth Dole warmly shook hands with Reverend Wogaman after [the] service, but the Doles are rumored to be shopping for a new church." Having been approached by a relative of Mrs. Dole's a year before, I knew that the Doles, especially Elizabeth, were unhappy with Foundry United Methodist Church's increasingly liberal direction under Dr. Wogaman. Both were lifelong Methodists, and she had seriously renewed her Christian faith during the 1980's, under the ministry of the Rev. Ed Bauman, Foundry's previous pastor. But Dr. Wogaman's outspoken political and theological views were probably more suited to the Clintons than to the Doles.

Wogaman and official United Methodist publications denied that the Doles were unhappy at Foundry Church. The Christian faith "can transcend political differences," he insisted to *Newscope* on February 17, 1995. "I've always had a cordial response from the Doles even if I've said something with which they might disagree." *Newscope*, noting that the *Washington Times* had reported the Doles might be church shopping, curtly denied the rumor. "There is not a shred of information to confirm that conjecture."

The Clintons typically attended Foundry Church twice a month, usually at the 11 a.m. service. I was present at least once during their attendance, and their presence was surprisingly unobtrusive. Parishioners had to walk through a metal detector. The Clintons were the last to be seated, sitting in a front pew, with secret service agents quietly sitting around them. Bill Clinton always carried a large Bible, a habit more common to Baptists like himself than to United Methodists, who more regularly rely on the Bibles in the pew racks. A few news media were always standing outside the church.

Frequently commenting to the media as pastor to the presidential couple, Wogaman told the *United Methodist Reporter* that the Clintons were "obviously church people" and have "deep spiritual roots" that they show by both being "gracious and forgiving." He described thinking "warmly" of the Clintons and the Doles, who, despite their political differences, could still "join together in Christian fellowship and Christian community."

But the Doles would soon very publicly separate themselves from Foundry Church because of Wogaman's controversial views.

After pouring through Dr. Wogaman's many books and articles, my exposé of him appeared in IRD's *Faith and Freedom* newsletter in April 1995. My article pointed out that Wogaman as both Christian ethicist and pastor had for decades advocated a greater welfare and regulatory state as Christian imperatives, questioned key Christian doctrines like the Virgin Birth, disputed scriptural admonitions against homosexual behavior and supported abortion rights.

Economics had been a chief focus for Wogaman. In 1992, after Soviet communism had collapsed, he urged that free markets in the U.S. "must not prevent us from using aspects of socialism." In 1990 he warned that, "Unrestrained laissez-faire capitalism," had created "drug abuse, murder, unethical business practices, family breakups and homelessness." Socialism's "critique" of the free market's "brutalities and idolatries" needs "to be heard," he further insisted. In 1989 he had written that the U.S. would not become socialist in the "foreseeable future" but needs to "reverse the decline towards greater inequality." He recommended higher tax rates, "more generous" welfare to reverse Ronald Reagan's "abandonment of the poor" and "public responsibility" for health care.

Wogaman criticized Reagan in 1985 for not using tax rates to promote social change and for "over-reliance on the free market." Socialism "can claim modest but real economic success" in China and Cuba, he affirmed. In 1978, Wogaman wrote, "We live in a time when the socialist question needs to be pressed. Why should not the oil companies be nationalized?" Wogaman insisted that he had never been "greatly tempted by communism" but both Marxism and capitalism were "seriously flawed." He urged avoiding "closure on the great debate between democratic forms of socialism and mixed-economy socialism."

Despite his anti-communism, Wogaman noted in 1967 that, "The USSR is characteristic of the more tolerant communist arrangements for religion." He said, "It is highly questionable whether Christians in Russia or China are treated any worse than Marxists in the United States." He suggested that "world government" may be the answer to global conflict."

On abortion, Wogaman had saluted the U.S. Supreme Court's 1973 abortion rights ruling for its "humane spirit and practical wisdom." He wrote, "In many cases (and not just those involving the health of the mother or deformity of the fetus) abortion may be faithful obedience to the God of life and love." For some years, Wogaman had publicly urged the church to accept homosexual practice: "Many [homosexuals] manifest the fruit of the Spirit among us without a hint of scandal."

Hinting about his own liberal theology, Wogaman alleged in 1994 that pastors do not tell the "truth" about the latest biblical "scholarship," for fear of upsetting their parishioners' faith. "Human limitations" in the Bible, such as claims of a "literal" virgin birth have "injured" good people, he asserted. "We create stumbling blocks for people who are thoughtful enough to see moral and factual errors in those Scriptures for themselves."

"There are parts of the Bible no longer consistent with deep convictions of faith and moral life that we now share," Wogaman sermonized. "The Word of God can't be contained in any document." He rejected the Virgin Birth as essential. "There is something much deeper about the divinity of Christ than that."

Noting that Foundry Church comprised predominantly white, upper middle class and wealthy people, I wrote that most United Methodist pastors do not have either Wogaman's sophisticated polish or an equally affluent and liberal urban audience to support them. "They do have seminary educations that imbued them with the doctrines that Wogaman preaches," I concluded in my article. "And they have dwindling, aging congregations that are perplexed as to why opposing the latest Republican policies is more important than defending the Virgin Birth."

Only weeks after my article appeared in the Spring 1995 IRD newsletter, nationally syndicated columnist Cal Thomas repeated my report on Wogaman in newspapers across America. He described Wogaman's left-leaning politics as giving "moral nurture" to President Clinton's policies and helping to explain the decline of The United Methodist Church. "Once Methodism was America's largest denomination," Thomas concluded. "Now, it is declining faster than any other."

The following Sunday (April 30, 1995), with Hillary Clinton in the congregation, Wogaman asserted from his pulpit that Cal Thomas and I were not simply after him, but after the President as well. "I think much of this was a political attack aimed at getting at President Clinton through the practice of his religion," he said, faulting the negative coverage on "the climate of the times in which we live." In a subsequent newspaper op-ed, Wogaman hyperbolically linked negative articles about his ministry to the kind of mentality that had fueled the recent Oklahoma City bombing.

"Might there be a connection between corrosive words and destructive actions?" Wogaman asked ominously in his op-ed. "People in the media don't plant bombs," he wrote. "But if they plant hatred and division, doesn't that affect the behavior of un-stable hearers or readers?"

Although frequently addressing hot button issues, Wogaman had usually preferred to be known as a conciliator. Clearly he was stung to be labeled as deeply controversial, with left-wing views on politics and theology. He referred to the Thomas column an "unmitigated slam dunk," and called the quotes attributed to him "accurate but desperately out of context." More troubling, Woga-man claimed to the United Methodist News Service that neither Thomas nor I had ever approached him for comment. "There was no contact with me at all," he asserted. "Absolutely none."

In fact, I had faxed my article to Wogaman well before pub-lication, asking for his comment. He would acknowledge this later, in 2004, when he published his memoir, *An Unexpected Journey*. He then wrote: "I was sent a copy of the [Tooley] article for corrective comment by its author, which I ignored. It came at an unusually busy time; I really didn't have time to attend to the many errors and distortions in the article." But Wogaman admitted that he regretted "that I [referring to himself] didn't take the time, no matter how busy I was, to go through the article patiently and offer corrections."

Several weeks after the Thomas column, the *New York Times*, the *Washington Post* and the Associated Press all carried stories from a "person close to the Doles" who said that the Republican couple was searching for a church that would "more accurately reflect their traditional Christian beliefs." Wogaman declined to comment, though he later admitted that he had "grieved over their departure."

For a while, at the recommendation of IRD President Diane Knippers, the Doles worshiped at Clarendon United Methodist Church in nearby Arlington, Virginia, whose pastor was theo-logically orthodox. Curious as to whether the Doles were still attending, I asked my 81-year-old grandmother, who lived near the church, to check on the Doles' possible presence. Dutifully, my grandmother did so, spotted a woman she believed to be Elizabeth Dole and followed her to her car writing down her tag number! Over Sunday lunch at my parents' house, my grandmother asked my father, a retired Arlington policeman, to have the tag number traced so as to confirm Elizabeth Dole's identity. My father declined.

In an interview with *World* magazine about his church attendance, Bob Dole later commented; "No doubt about it, the Foundry Church was quite liberal. All that talk about reconciliation, that's important to a lot of people, but more important is just getting basic religion based on the Bible, listening to the message." The Doles went on to attend the National Presbyterian Church, to which Elizabeth transferred her membership from Foundry. Bob kept his membership at a United Methodist church in his native Kansas. "Rev. Wogaman's a very fine man, felt badly about us leaving," Dole said. Wogaman would later speculate that the Doles had left Foundry because of Dole's need for conservative Christian votes in his upcoming presidential bid!

After five years of discussion, and at Wogaman's strong urging, Foundry's administrative board voted by a narrow 52-46 in October 1995 to become "Reconciling," i.e. supporting the practice of homosexuality despite the United Methodist Church's official stance. Many long-time members began to leave. Among the departing was a former homosexual who had become celibate because of his Christian faith. "I need neither man nor woman to make me happy," he said. "I know Him." But the hostility of Foundry's large homosexual membership, and lack of support from the pastors, persuaded him to leave. Predictably, homosexual causes became increasingly prominent in the church. In November 1995, Foundry hosted a "Sharing Our Rainbow of Light" conference, sponsored by PFLAG (Parents and Friends of Lesbians and Gays).

The featured speaker was radical Episcopal Bishop John Shelby Spong of Newark, who predictably speculated in a speech at

Foundry that St. Paul was homosexual and then charged that "our primary understanding of God's grace came from a self-hating gay man." Spong mocked various Bible stories. "If a star led the wise men to the baby Jesus, then why couldn't King Herod find him?" Spong asked a laughing audience. "I don't think Isaiah, Jeremiah or the Psalmist anticipated the life of Jesus of Nazareth," Spong continued. "People can't predict future events. It's a magical view of the Bible."

It was too much for some even in Foundry's liberal audience. "I am a gay, Jewish Christian, convicted by the biblical prophecies and in my heart," responded one distressed attendant. "Don't the Hebrew Scriptures point in the direction of Jesus?" Spong reacted with a scoff. "Jews might be safer if we took evangelical Christianity away. Converting Jews to Christianity is not on the radar screen." The angry bishop insisted that the Virgin Birth and Resurrection of Jesus were not literal events but just "interpreted" that way. Likewise, Jesus' earthly father Joseph and the disciple Judas were merely fictional characters whom the early church created, Spong surmised.

Later in a conference workshop, Wogaman enthused: "Bishop Spong's remarks this morning were so stimulating," as he described his own similar concerns about a "literalistic" view of the Bible. "I'm not sure what to do with Bishop Spong's thoughts on St. Paul being gay," Wogaman said. "But I am touched by the relationships of gay couples in this church." Asked about the possibility of Jesus Christ being depicted in art as a "drag queen," Wogaman responded, "I don't condemn it. I just don't know. I'll have to think about it some more."

Wogaman's nonchalant response to the Jesus-as-Drag-Queen proposal ignited considerable controversy after IRD published a report about "Sharing our Rainbow of Light." In an interview with the *Nashville Banner*, Wogaman explained: "The question caught me by surprise and I didn't seek to be controversial so I replied in a polite way that I would have to think about that. Personally, I would find the idea offensive but I didn't say so. I didn't want to be discourteous to the speaker in the workshop, so in the tone of my voice I tried to distance myself from this idea."

Less restrained than Wogaman, Bishop Spong wrote me two angry letters about my coverage of his remarks at Foundry. "I have seldom seen an article that was more distorted, filed with half-truths and misleading statements than this," he fumed on February 12, 1996. "There are two conclusions I can draw," the bishop continued. "One is that you were so ignorant you did not understand the issues at all, a conclusion that I seriously doubt. The other is that you are so malevolent that you are willing to distort in order to gain points for your particular point of view." He concluded: "You really ought to be ashamed."

I responded by asking the bishop to specify the inaccuracies of which I was guilty and to clarify his own views on whether or not the wise men, Joseph and Judas, along with the biblical prophecies about the advent of Christ, were really just fables. On February 21, 1996, Spong responded: "I thought the primary issue was malevolence when I read your article, but from your questions I think the primary issue is ignorance. Your questions are framed in such a way as to be almost nonsensical except to the most extreme biblical fundamentalist."

Spong chastised me for belonging to the "Pat Robertson, Jerry Falwell, Oral Roberts school of American Protestant Christiani-ty," and he suggested that I needed to be "educated about biblical scholarship in the last 150 years." Explaining that he would not respond further, Spong concluded, "I do regret that ignorance combines with a political agenda to do to Christianity what people like you seem to be doing."

I responded to Spong that his disagreements appeared not to be with Jerry Falwell or Oral Roberts, but with the biblical apostles and prophets, along with every self-described Christian body of the last 2,000 years. "How do you justify accepting a senior posi-tion and generous salary from an organization whose core beliefs you publicly assail and ridicule," I concluded by asking, realizing there would be no response.

At least Bishop Spong had responded directly to me. Wogaman had never attempted to communicate directly with me, even when I had asked for his comment. We did not meet directly until May 1996 at the United Methodist General Conference in Denver. In the convention center hallway I was talking to James Holsinger, the former Virginia Conference lay leader who would later join the United Methodist Judicial Council and be nominated by President Bush as U.S. Surgeon General. "I'm going to introduce you to Phil Wogaman!" he told me with a mischievous smile. He and Wogaman had served together on the 1988-1992 Committee to Study Homosexuality, from which Holsinger had resigned to protest the committee's impending report hostile to the church's teachings.

"So you're Mark Tooley?" Wogaman said to me with a frozen smile, as Holsinger drew us together. "You've been terribly unfair to us." He cited my report about the "Rainbow of Light" conference. I responded by asking how he could have invited to his pulpit a man such as Bishop Spong who denied every central doctrine of Christianity. "Every doctrine?" Wogaman asked. "But he believes in the grace of God." I responded that Spong's understanding of grace was not centered on Jesus Christ's work on the cross.

Our conversation was civil, if tense, and Wogaman said I was welcome to attend his church any time. In fact, IRD's office had coincidentally moved right across the street from his Foundry Church in July 1995. Friends and critics suggested that we had wanted to monitor Wogaman and his church on a nearly full-time basis! But actually we had simply found very nice space in an old mansion previously used by the Soviet Embassy and now owned by a graduate school. If present on Sunday mornings, you could look outside our windows and watch the Clintons walk up the steps of Foundry Church. I never had occasion to return to

Foundry after the "Sharing our Rainbow of Light" conference.

In his memoir, Wogaman never mentioned having met me personally. But he did write that IRD had revealed its "basic character" in its coverage of the "Sharing our Rainbow of Light" event, which thanks to IRD, he recalled had taken on a "life of its own throughout the Bible Belt." Wogaman also wrote: "I have to thank Mr. Tooley for helping to sharpen my perspective on the ethics of journalism, even though mostly by illustrating its abuses."

Wogaman's public profile would rise even higher in the wake of Bill Clinton's 1998 scandal with White House intern Monica Lewinsky. Rumors had longed stalked Clinton about his womanizing, and the sexual harassment suit by Paula Jones was the legal tripwire that led to the eventual disclosure of Clinton's ties to Lewinsky. Amusingly, sometime in 1997, one of our young IRD staffers happened to be seated near Wogaman and fellow United Methodist ethicist Alan Geyer in a neighborhood Thai restaurant. They were discussing the sexual harassment allegations against Clinton, wondering if they could be true!

In the immediate aftermath of the Lewinsky allegations, Wogaman was publicly supportive of Clinton and his denials. On the first Sunday after the revelations, the Clintons were at Foundry Church, and Wogaman deliberately stepped outside to be photographed with the Clintons after the service, in a signal of "pastoral support." Wogaman took to the airwaves to defend Clinton throughout the scandal, defending him as a "moral man" with "deep well-springs of morality and love." The pastor urged that character be understood beyond just sexual morality to include Clinton's "commitments to poor people and to persons of ethnic minorities." Meanwhile, he condemned the investigation by special prosecutor Ken Starr, whose conduct was a "moral outrage." Coincidentally, Starr, himself once United Methodist, had served on the board of Wesley Seminary while Wogaman was a professor there.

Not surprisingly, Clinton invited Wogaman to be one of his three pastoral counselors in the wake of the Lewinsky scandal. Wogaman recounts in his memoir that Clinton once asked him publicly to describe Clinton's own remorse for his behavior. Obligingly, Wogaman did exactly that on an interview on MSNBC, where one reporter accused him of being "used" by Clinton. The pastor admitted that perhaps he was "used," but he insisted that publicly explaining Clinton's contrition was a public service.

On Sunday, January 7, 2001, Clinton gave a farewell speech at Foundry Church. He thanked the church for its "kindness and courage [toward] gay and lesbian Christians, people who should not feel outside the family of God." And he thanked Wogaman for "being my pastor and friend, my counselor and teacher." He noted that "for more than two years now, he and two other minister friends of mine have shared the burden of meeting with me on a weekly basis. It has been an immense blessing to me and to my service as President." With Clinton's departure from Washington, D.C., Wogaman retired from Foundry Church. He occasionally teaches at Wesley Seminary and served as an interim president at United Methodist Iliff Seminary in Denver. Although now in his late 70s, Wogaman remains active in the activist Methodist Federation for Social Action, still attends General Conference as a lobbyist and is as outspoken as ever on homosexual advocacy.

Before he retired, Wogaman and I occasionally would pass each other in our neighborhood, even working out at the same local gym, where he swam regularly, and where I played racquetball. He was courteous if not effusively friendly. As he was "thankful" to me for illustrating the "abuses" of journalism, so I too was thankful to him for helping to illustrate, however unintentionally, the theological and political ills that have fueled 43 years of United Methodist decline.

Surprisingly, there was one area of agreement between Wogaman and me. Both he and I had submitted legislation to the 2000 General Conference that would specifically acknowledge that war for Christians is regretfully justified in some circumstances. I specifically cited tyranny, genocide and aggression as possible justifications for war. The General Conference merged my language with his into the Social Principles of the *Book of Discipline*. I have always enjoyed mentioning that Wogaman had been my silent partner in making this historic addition to our church's teachings.

CHAPTER   THREE

HOMOSEXUAL HIGH TIDE AT GENERAL CONFERENCE 1996

At the United Methodist General Conference of 1996 in Denver, Colorado, 15 of the church's bishops publicly disagreed with the church's teachings on homosexuality. They got an oblique endorsement from Hillary Clinton, who became the first First Lady to address a General Conference. And 40 percent of the delegates agreed with them, which turned out to be the high water mark for the homosexual cause within United Methodism.

Meanwhile, I met Dr. Philip Wogaman for the first time, as the previous chapter describes. I also met United Methodist ecumenical official Jeanne Audrey Powers, who had become the seniormost church official to "come out" as lesbian. Paradoxically, I also met a conservative lay delegate from the Alabama-West Florida Conference named Jeff Sessions, who was Attorney General of Alabama and would soon become a U.S. Senator.

Interspersed throughout these many encounters in the hallways were tense legislative committee meetings, sometimes acrimonious plenary sessions and a plethora of rancorous demonstrations and press conferences. The whole future of United Methodism was at stake over the course of 10 days. And somehow the mountain air and severe beauty of the Rockies as a backdrop only added to the heavy drama of it all!

For years the most tense moments of every General Conference have been the debates over homosexuality. It has been the chief battle-flag issue for both conservatives and liberals in the church and the one issue that potentially could ignite a formal schism within United Methodism. Homosexuality has been debated at every General Conference since 1972, when language describing homosexual practice as "incompatible" with Christian teaching was first added to the Social Principles. Subsequent General Conferences added specific prohibitions against ordination for practicing homosexuals, church funding for homosexual causes and celebration of same-sex unions.

In July 1995, the Rev. Jeanne Audrey Powers had publicly declared, "I have been a lesbian all of my life," at a Minneapolis convention for Reconciling Congregations (now called Reconciling Ministries Network), the main caucus group fighting to overturn United Methodist teaching on marriage and sex. She was the associate general secretary of the General Commission on Christian Unity and Inter-religious Concerns, based in New York. Calling her announcement a "political act," Powers said she was offering "resistance to false teachings that have contributed to heresy and homophobia within the church."

Powers further declared: "As long as the phrase 'homosexuality and the Christian faith are incompatible,' and 'celibacy in singleness' continue to stand in our Discipline, no matter how these phrases are introduced or framed, our church is on record as perpetuating heterosexism in its life and homophobia in its teaching." But coyly, Powers referred to her "partner," while still refusing to say whether she was "practicing" her lesbianism. "No one has the right to know intimate details of any other person's loving sexual practices," she insisted, even as she was making a very public speech and doing news releases about her lesbianism. She added that "practice" was not the issue as "identity is a matter of 'being,' not 'doing.'" She said she would not give up her ministerial credentials, although her retirement was already in sight. Advocating a "subversive strategy" within the church on

behalf of homosexual causes, Powers likened herself to resisters of
Nazism and to the Hebrew midwives who saved the baby Moses
from Pharaoh. "I'd like to come right out and say that perhaps
there are times when lying, deception and operating under false
pretenses is the most life-giving action, the most faithful response
for Christians." In Powers' supportive audience in Minneapolis
was Bishop Roy Sano of Los Angeles, president of the Council
of Bishops.

Minnesota Bishop Sharon Brown Christopher later hailed
Powers as a "distinguished ecumenist" and a "respected leader"
in United Methodism. The chief of Powers' agency, Bruce Robbins, likewise commended Powers for doing "a courageous thing
by being truthful with people." He was joined by West Virginia
Bishop William Grove, board president of Powers' agency, who,
in a joint news release with Robbins, hailed her "courage" and
defended her right to "disagree with church teaching." In fact,
their agency had already voted to become "Reconciling," endors-
ing the pro-homosexuality cause.

Few United Methodist officials were willing to criticize Powers
in public, and doubtless many bishops and other senior church
bureaucrats quietly supported her challenge to the church's policies. Where church prelates were silent, IRD's UM*Action* program spoke out. We did a news release urging Powers' ouster.
And we mailed a letter to thousands of supporters declaring:
"Powers Must Go!" We asked the question: "Why is United
Methodist money subsidizing a senior, well-paid official to use
OUR CHURCH to promote her sexual/political agenda? Why
are bishops supporting Powers instead of defending the church's
doctrines and integrity?"

Our letter concluded: "If church officials will not lead, then
we ordinary churchgoers must act!" The letter went to 50,000
United Methodists. Bruce Robbins, with whom IRD President
Diane Knippers had a friendship, wrote to complain to her about
my letter's "innuendo and incorrect statements" that would fuel

"ill-will" and "polarization" across the church. Disputing my assertion that Powers would take her pro-homosexuality campaign to the 1996 General Conference, Robbins insisted that Powers had given him a written statement pledging not to speak publicly about homosexuality. Obviously, the statement was not retroactive to Powers' very public speech just a few months before! In fact, Powers had repeated her lesbianism declaration at a speech to a United Methodist Clergywomen's Consultation in Atlanta in August of 1995. Clearly, Powers had no plans for silence. Robbins, always courteous and very capable, was himself an opponent of the church's sexuality teachings, but he was less aggressive than Powers in promoting that opposition.

The flap over Powers was only a foreshadowing of the battles at the 1996 General Conference. IRD organized two luncheons for delegates in Denver. At one Bruce Robbins would discuss issues of religious liberty with Diane Knippers. Robbins made clear that he would not share the podium with me, but Diane was acceptable! Powers attended the lunch and, always the extrovert, enthusiastically introduced herself to me. Our other lunch featured a debate between United Methodist theologian Tom Oden, who later would join IRD's board, and Commission on the Status and Role of Women (COSROW) General Secretary Stephanie Hixon. Sparks flew as Oden inveighed against the radical theologies of United Methodist seminaries and targeted the United Methodist Women's Division's support for "killing the unborn." Avoiding the specifics of controversial issues, Hixon smoothly appealed for amiability within the church. COSROW has long been a radicalized agency that advocated feminist theology. But a 1992 vote that narrowly rejected the abolition of COSROW had persuaded the agency at least to appear more moderate. Our IRD lunches were a microcosm of the larger spiritual and political conflict within that General Conference.

Setting the crisis tone early on for the whole General Conference, 11 active and four retired United Methodist bishops, in a

news release disseminated in Denver, publicly declared their opposition to the church's teachings on homosexuality. "It is time to
break the silence," which they asserted was "hurting and silenc-
ing thousands of faithful Christians." The bishops said they were
bound to abide by church law, even if it "pained" them and "contradicted" their personal convictions. They urged churches "to
open the doors to gracious hospitality" to "gays and lesbians." In
fact, "Open the Doors" was the official theme of the pro-homosexuality caucus groups at General Conference that year. Their
activists stood at the convention hall doors and opened the doors
for delegates to illustrate their ostensible hospitality and make
their political points.

Possibly I played a small, if inadvertent role, in persuading
some of the 15 bishops publicly to reveal their pro-homosexuality views. Less than two months before, I had noticed that Reconciling Congregations' annual report listed their major donors,
which included most of the 15 bishops, along with numerous
church agency executives and seminary professors. I wrote all of
them to confirm their identity in preparation for a public article. Most did not reply. At least one retired bishop, Jesse Dewitt,
asked me not to publicize his name. But less than two months
later, he had signed on with the other 14 bishops in their very
public declaration. Realizing that their names were soon to be
publicized anyway, had these bishops decided preemptively to
announce themselves? Perhaps.

The dramatic announcement by the 15 renegade bishops forced
the full Council of Bishops into a three-day closed session. But
the tepid resulting statement from the council merely stated that,
"serious differences" exist among United Methodists about sexuality. "These differences are also reflected within the Council of
Bishops. We have been praying together and have been talking
with one another in a new spirit of honesty and openness that is
both painful and hopeful." The bishops vaguely acknowledged
that they were committed to "teach and uphold our church's doc-

trine and discipline."

The orthodox bishops were largely silent in public, with some exceptions. The two bishops of Georgia, Richard Looney and J. Lloyd Knox, released a statement: "We are confident that the church's present position on homosexuality is solidly based on Scripture and Christian tradition and that it does reflect God's love incarnate in Jesus Christ." They continued: "All persons are of sacred worth but not all practices are consistent with Christian teaching." Bishop Robert Morgan of Kentucky similarly called the church's stance on homosexuality "consistent with Scripture, tradition, man and experience."

But the 15 dissident bishops were bold in not backing down. Bishop Mary Ann Swenson of Denver told the *Denver Post*, "We shouldn't be fearful of controversy," and she rejoiced that their declaration had been "freeing." Announcing her own support for "gay marriages," she suggested: "We need to make the barriers between us visible, so we can overcome them."

In a further boost to the "Denver 15," one of their number, Bishop Judith Craig of West Ohio, was scheduled to deliver the official Episcopal Address on behalf of the Council of Bishops. "We yearn for a holy community that embraces sexuality as a good gift of creation rather than something about which to be embarrassed or to interpret and define in ways that exclude persons from full participation in the life of the church." Her comments were hardly veiled.

Craig continued: "We affirm the sanctity of marriage. At the same time we are called by a gracious Christ to live with a spirit of welcome for persons of many realities and persuasions." Earlier, Craig had joined Bishop Don Ott, another of the "Denver 15," in a pro-homosexuality rally outside the convention center. Bishop Fritz Mutti of Kansas led a protest worship service called "Friends, Allies, Lovers and Saints," sponsored by "Affirmation," the caucus that spawned Reconciling Congregations. He denounced church leaders who disapproved of homosexual ordination as "mean-spirited" because they will not "share the light" with homosexuals.

At the largest rally of all, at least seven of the 15 attended a convocation for the Methodist Federation for Social Action (MFSA), where they were rapturously applauded by more than 500 supporters. "I've always had a loving quarrel with my church," Bishop Melvin Talbert of San Francisco told the crowd. Jeanne Audrey Powers, having evidently forgotten her written promise to Bruce Robbins to be quiet about homosexuality, took the rostrum to salute the bishops' "historic moment." She likened them to courageous ancestors who had opposed segregation and fought for female ordination.

In the most flamboyant moment at the MFSA rally, Garrett Seminary professor Barbara Troxell placed her hands on Powers and blessed her in the name of "Sophia," a feminine name for God favored by radical feminist theologians. Both women shook as Troxell shrieked the name of her goddess. Powers afterwards urged the ecstatic crowd to "take your holy rage and stick it." A "gay" choir also performed. The next day, Powers asked me whether I had enjoyed the spectacle. I responded that I thought the music was good. She good-naturedly laughed and asked my views about her speech. I said she was very charismatic. She smiled and replied that I must mean that "The Spirit" was with her. I responded that I thought "a spirit" was definitely with her. "You mean the Holy Spirit, don't you?" she asked. "No," I said. "Just a spirit." Powers chuckled as she walked away. The repartee was amusing but sad. An unholy spirit had indeed been present at the MFSA event, and through much of the General Conference of 1996. Fortunately, the Holy Spirit is more powerful than any alternative spirits.

There was more drama to come. First Lady Hillary Clinton was to speak on the eighth day of the General Conference, briefly and probably not coincidentally before the crucial votes on homosexuality. Herself a lifelong Methodist, she received an adulatory welcome from the delegates. She was effusively introduced by Bishop Richard Wilke of Arkansas, who hailed her as the "First Lady of the world." He had been "thrilled" for Clinton to serve as the official "church attorney" for his conference when she lived in Little Rock. And he fondly recalled a Suday school picnic that she hosted on the lawn of the Governor's Mansion. Wilke praised Clinton's book about children, *It Takes a Village*.

"I have not been this nervous with 150 bishops since I read my [childhood] confirmation essay on what Jesus means to me in my home church," Clinton responded. "For me, the Social Principles of the Methodists have been as much a description of our history as a prod for my future action," she affirmed. Sharing the podium with Clinton was her pastor, J. Philip Wogaman. Earlier, a delegate from South Carolina had proposed that a Republican woman, Elizabeth Dole, also be invited to address the conference. The motion was defeated by a 562-301 vote. The delegate had argued that inviting Dole was "one way to avoid sending confusing signals" during an election year.

Instead, the conference voted to send a letter of greeting to Dole, whom Bishop William Grove called "a faithful United Methodist." Wogaman later took the floor to announce that Dole in fact no longer attended Foundry Church but had transferred to a Presbyterian congregation. He did not mention that Dole and her husband had left Foundry because of its "liberal theology." Wogaman urged prayers for both the Clintons and the Doles.

Wogaman must have been pleased when Clinton's speech was more than simply an ode to her Methodist upbringing. She concluded by exclaiming into the microphone, "Throw open the doors of our churches and welcome in those who John Wesley sought out!" Recognizing their own "Open the Doors" slogan, hundreds of pro-homosexuality activists vigorously clapped and shouted their approval of the First Lady.

But even the First Lady's not very subtle words of support for pro-homosexuality forces were not sufficient for victory. The delegates voted by a 60 to 40 margin in favor of the church's current teaching that homosexual practice is "incompatible" with Christian teaching. They also ratified a specific new prohibition against the celebration of same-sex unions.

As usual, the Church and Society legislative committee had recommended overturning the church's stance on homosexuality. It proposed instead that the church declare itself "unable to arrive at a common mind on the compatibility of homosexual practice with Christian faith." A liberal delegate from Iowa, the Rev. Merlin Ackerson, a member of that committee, told the General Conference during the homosexuality debate that Jesus, and not the Bible, was the Word of God. The scriptural condemnation of same-gender sex could therefore be ignored in favor of seeking the "mind and spirit of Christ."

But delegates from overseas, who represented 13 percent of the conference, led the way in countering Ackerson's argument for separating Jesus from scriptural authority. "We love them [homosexuals]," said Sul Nawej of what was then called Zaire but now is The Congo. "But we want to say to them, 'Go, and do not sin any more.'"

Trying to sound conciliatory rather than polemical, Wogaman subtly argued the pro-homosexuality cause. "The church must be careful not to condemn when it doesn't have a really clear basis," he said. "My friends, we need one another. We need healing on this issue." For him, "healing" meant overturning the church's teaching that sex is for marriage only. Mexican delegate Luis Travino responded that the church in Mexico would never accept homosexual practice. "Methodism is not only yours. Don't make us ashamed to be Methodists."

The debates over homosexuality were not the only potential cause for embarrassment by United Methodists. With little open debate, the General Conference, as is its tradition, ratified dozens of controversial political statements, many of them originating with the Board of Church and Society or the Methodist Federation for Social Action. Conservative delegates reserved their energy for the sexuality battles, usually saying little about the political resolutions, which endorsed the following:

- Calling for the U.S. President to pardon 14 Puerto Rican "political prisoners" who were involved in numerous bombings and other acts of terrorism during the 1970's on behalf of a "socialist" Puerto Rico freed from U.S. "imperialism."
- Calling for a withdrawal of U.S. forces from Panama, payment of U.S. reparations for the 1989 invasion of Panama, investigation of CIA "crimes" in Guatemala, while blaming multinational corporations for poverty in Central America.
- Affirming the "right" of homosexuals to serve openly in the U.S. military.
- Retaining United Methodist membership in the pro-abortion rights Religious Coalition for Reproductive Choice.
- Supporting affirmative action programs for minority groups while rejecting arguments against racial and sexual preferences as "specious."
- Calling for the U.S. to lift its embargo on Cuba and reinstate diplomatic and economic relations with Fidel Castro's regime.
- Affirming the United Nations and condemning "media promoted falsehoods" about the UN's operations, while affirming the United Methodist Office at the United Nations.
- Reaffirming United Methodist support for socialized medicine.

These results were not surprising given who many of the delegates were. A poll by the Council on Ministries showed that there was a firm liberal majority of the delegates, or at least among the U.S. delegates. More than 60 percent of the clergy delegates said they were liberal on political and social issues. More than 53 percent called themselves liberal on religious issues. More than 51 percent of the lay delegates said they were liberal on political and social issues, and 48 percent said they were liberal on religious issues.

In their political preferences, delegates favored Democrats over Republicans. Among clergy, 62 percent vote Democrat, while only 15 percent vote Republican. Among laity, 48 percent vote Democrat, with 29 percent voting Republican.

By contrast, a 1996 study by the Pew foundation found that Methodists as a whole favor Republicans over Democrats by 34 percent to 33 percent with 30 percent calling themselves independent. A 1992 Council on Ministries study found that 69 percent of United Methodist laity at large are conservative.

In the 1996 poll of delegates, 38 percent of lay delegates and 22 percent of clergy delegates believed that the Scriptures are God's word. Twenty-nine percent of laity and 48% of clergy thought the Bible was "authoritative for Christian faith" but not a book of science or history. Twenty-nine percent of laity thought the Bible "contains some errors reflecting limitations of the authors," while 28 percent of the clergy agreed.

Clearly, and not surprisingly, the delegates more often represented liberal church elites rather than average local church people. The culture of the General Conference, as of the United Methodist bureaucracy in general, is very different from the typical local church culture. The battle to legitimize homosexual behavior was mostly a cause for liberal church elites, who viewed the church as an engine for radical social change and interest-group empowerment rather than God's instrument for the salvation of the world.

Frustratingly, the 1996 General Conference vividly illustrated what has plagued United Methodism. Both conservatives and liberals shy away from debating the real issues that have divided United Methodism for decades: scriptural authority and the identity of Jesus Christ. Conservatives believe that the Bible is God's wholly reliable, revealed authority. They believe that Jesus Christ is the unique Son of God, the supernaturally born son of a Virgin who was bodily resurrected, the Savior of the whole world, who was dispatched by God the Father to redeem fallen humanity. Liberals, in contrast, see the Bible as human stories that illustrate humanity's search for God. For them, Jesus is a social liberator, giving hope to oppressed peoples, much as Martin Luther King and Gandhi did.

Oddly, the delegates to General Conference rarely discuss these core theological differences openly. Instead, most of these differences are subsumed under the homosexuality debates. Conservatives see homosexual behavior as a consequence of humanity's innately sinful nature. For conservatives, Jesus Christ is the Good News, who can break the bondage of all sin. Liberals see people as basically good, and therefore sexual preference is God-ordained and meriting affirmation. For liberals, good people do not need salvation from a Savior so much as affirmation from a Liberator. The differences between the two worldviews are vast and ultimately irreconcilable. Hence, the stakes for our church are very high. And one side or the other ultimately will prevail.

Except on the issue of homosexuality, liberals seemed to win on most issues at this General Conference. Revealingly, the General Board of Global Ministries (GBGM) successfully defeated attempts to be relocated out of New York City. The 1992 General Conference had narrowly approved the move. But the Task Force Site Selection Committee was stacked with liberal supporters of GBGM, who disingenuously ruled that expensive Washington, D.C., would be the best new locale. Although the 1992 General Conference had estimated that a re-location would cost $9 million, the Task Force decided that the actual cost would be $72 million. Efforts to examine other less expensive sites were dismissed, and the whole re-location idea collapsed. The GBGM bureaucrats in New York City had won!

Having first entered the maelstrom of church politics because of the radicalism and bureaucratic waste of GBGM's New York City headquarters, this was to me a grievous but not unexpected defeat. There would be other battles to come! And there were new friends to make, who would assist in the future work of church reformation. At the 1992 General Conference, Mary Ellen Bullard of Montgomery, Alabama, had courageously argued in the Global Ministries legislative committee for restrictions on GBGM's ability to disburse grants to non-church groups. GBGM staff lobbied against her, and the proposal was defeated. But she was a gallant warrior, and she would attend future General Conferences.

Early in the 1996 General Conference in Denver, Mary Ellen Bullard introduced me to Jeff Sessions, who was serving as a lay delegate. He was Alabama's attorney general and was running for U.S. Senator. A lifelong United Methodist, he is a dedicated churchman with a passion for the reformation of his church. In future years, he would become occasionally outspoken about United Methodism, even gently admonishing the bishops about their need to show restraint in their political pronouncements.

I left Denver exhausted but hopeful about future General Conferences and battles yet to be fought. On the plane home to Washington, I sat by happenstance next to a fellow Northern Virginian who belonged to Centreville United Methodist Church. He had been reading the Denver newspaper coverage of the General Conference. "I can't believe how liberal our church is getting!" he exclaimed to me, without knowing that I would be sympathetic. We commiserated together about our church's plight.

Neither of us realized that the 1996 General Conference would come to be remembered as the high water mark of liberalism within United Methodism. History, demography and the Holy Spirit were all at work, slowly pushing our church back toward the timeless truths of orthodoxy.

CHAPTER   FOUR

HERESY AMONG THE BISHOPS?

At the 1996 General Conference, the 15 dissident bishops who openly supported actively homosexual clergy had ushered in a new frontier for United Methodist controversies. But a new bishop would be elected later in 1996 who would push still further in questioning Christian teachings. But this time, the questions were not just about sexual ethics but about the very identity of Jesus Christ.

Bishop J. Joseph Sprague, the new Bishop of Northern Illinois, would become possibly the first United Methodist bishop publicly to dispute the full and eternal deity of Jesus Christ. A long-time liberal pastor in the West Ohio Conference, Sprague uttered in public what many United Methodist seminary professors had long taught, and what doubtless many liberal bishops had long believed, at least quietly.

Theological liberalism in Methodism is NOT new. United Methodist Boston University School of Theology was strategically injecting liberalism into the northern Methodist Episcopal Church by the 1890s. Probably most if not all of Methodism's seminaries, both north and south, were predominantly liberal by the 1920s. But for much of the 20th century, many liberal clergy, including bishops, did not publicly preach what they actually believed, or disbelieved, about the Bible.

The recent years of debate over homosexuality are not ultimately about sexual ethics but about biblical authority, the nature of humanity and the identity of Jesus Christ. Exasperatingly, both liberals and conservatives often prefer to avoid core doctrines in favor of debate about the outer issues.

Bishop Sprague scandalously disregarded his vows to uphold United Methodist doctrines when he denied the full and eternal deity of Jesus Christ. But he also helpfully revealed the unstated theology of many liberal bishops. And his explicit challenge to Christian orthodoxy would precipitate another first: direct public disagreement among United Methodist bishops over doctrine.

Not timid, Sprague was only a few months into his first term as bishop before publicly challenging historic Christian beliefs about Jesus Christ. He was reviewing *Meeting Jesus Again for the First Time*, by Marcus Borg, a Jesus Seminar author and self-described "panentheist" who denies the existence of a personal deity. Sprague was effusive about the book in his "Books-Between-Bites" talk at the Batavia United Methodist Church in northern Illinois during Advent of 1996.

"Jesus didn't believe himself to be the messiah or the son of God," reported the *Kane County Chronicle* of December 20, 1996. "That message came not from an atheist, nor some rabble-rousing leftist radical," it continued. "This portrait of Jesus was presented on Thursday by a high-ranking clergyman of a mainstream Protestant denomination."

The clergyman from a mainstream denomination was Bishop Sprague.

"Sprague agrees with Borg's thesis, which is that believing in Jesus means giving one's heart to God, not literal belief in events described in the Bible," the newspaper reported. "It was the church that made Jesus a messiah," Sprague reportedly insisted. "It is important to separate the historical Jesus from the Jesus presented by the writers of the New Testament."

Sprague reportedly identified with Marcus Borg, who recounted that children reared in Christianity learn "rigid doctrine about Jesus which isn't believable when they reach adulthood." When older, they become "closet agnostics." Sprague described himself as once caught between "ignorant fundamentalism and vapid liberalism." Noting that he does not "believe in every miracle described in the Bible," Sprague echoed Borg in describing Jesus as still a "remarkable healer" whose healings do not need to be entirely "explained away."

On February 4, 1997, I wrote Bishop Sprague to ascertain the accuracy of the *Kane County Chronicle* report and asking him to elaborate about his views. In a February 25 letter, Sprague described the newspaper account as a "mixture of what I said, of what I reported that someone else (Borg) said, and what a reporter heard." He referenced his latest column for the North Illinois Conference newspaper about Borg. And he commended Bishop John Shelby Spong's newly published *Liberating the Gospels*, which more polemically than Borg denied the historicity of the Gospels.

"I would only ask that you and others in The Institute on Religion & Democracy read the Borg book and my response to it before 'coming after me,'" Sprague implored.

In his February 14, 1996, column for the *Northern Illinois Conference United Methodist Reporter*, Sprague heartily agreed with Borg's views. "New Testament scholarship has been clear about this reality for nearly 200 years," the bishop insisted, echoing Borg's assertion that the Gospels are only the early church's "memories" of Jesus and not direct reports. "The shame is that too few preachers who knew the reality well, have had the courage or energy to help the laity see this truth and the wonderful affirmation it contains about the power of the Risen Christ's life-giving presence in the early Church," Sprague wrote. "We need not protect the laity from reality!"

Sprague would devote much of his next eight years as bishop to foisting this "reality" on ostensibly uninformed laity whom less courageous clergy had failed to enlighten about the latest biblical "scholarship." The Winter 1997 issue of our *UMAction Briefing* headlined our story about Sprague's remarks: "UM Bishop Denies Deity of Christ." The bishop responded with a May 9, 1997, column:

"I received a short stack of accusatory, hostile letters and faxes," Sprague began. "A few were well written, most were not. Most assumed that the writers knew all that was needed to attack, cajole, even slander." All of this "nonsensical" correspondence had been provoked by publicity about his remarks on Marcus Borg, including the "inflammatory" *UMAction Briefing*, which had "alleged" that Sprague had denied Christ's deity.

Sprague explained, perhaps for the first time publicly as bishop, that his Christology was of the "relational (as opposed to the substantial) tradition, which has a rich, valued place in the history of Christian thought." According to this ostensible tradition, as Sprague described, Jesus as "fully human" experienced such "at-one-momentness with God," through his "radical and complete trust in and commitment to the God he called 'Abba,'" that he "revealed in and through himself the very heart, the essential nature of God." Accordingly, Jesus was "fully God, fully human – not by some trans-human altering of his genetic code, but my relationship with God, Neighbor and Self."

The bishop acerbically noted: "If only Good News or IRD had cared enough or were fair enough to ask." Having evidently forgotten about my own letter to him, he speculated about the reasons for supposedly not asking. "Does an attack, full of erroneous assumptions and half-truths, excite the faithful, open bank accounts and expedite check writing to keep the Good Folks going?" For Sprague, as for many in the liberal church hierarchy and bureaucracy, the only logical explanation for concerns about liberal theology has to be fundraising for conservative groups. "I trust that the Northern Illinois Conference and the whole Church finds me transparent, non-defensive, candid in my beliefs and commitments," he concluded.

Although Sprague has claimed that he believed that Jesus is "fully God," his understanding of that deity seemed considerably less than apostolic. On May 16, 1997, I again wrote the bishop, asking him to clarify his views on Christ's deity. "Was Jesus divine before achieving His 'complete trust' in God, and when did He achieve it?" I asked. "Could someone other than Jesus trust in God so completely so as also to become 'fully God?'" And "Did all three Persons of the Trinity exist prior to Jesus' attaining his 'at-one-momentness' with God?"

Sprague never directly responded to my questions. But on May 27, 2007, he wrote a seven page explanation of his views to an Illinois pastor and sent me a copy. Sprague alleged that the *UMAction Briefing* coverage of his original remarks about Borg had "scrambled Borg and Sprague like an undifferentiated egg and eggbeater omelet." He described the article as "close to slander, given the vows I have taken, vows which I seek to uphold." He further asserted that "to allege that I deny the deity of Christ because I do Christology, relationally, 'from below' and, hence, do not meet someone's litmus test for orthodoxy is arrogant at best and close to slander at worst." With frustration he noted that IRD appears to "reject, even to find unfaithful" this "from below" Christology.

Insisting that he affirms the "historic doctrines, such as the Virgin Birth," Sprague explained that such "imagery" must be "interpreted theologically for today." He warned that "to freeze God's revelation in ancient texts" would suggest an inactive God who is not constantly "refilling" the believing community. Sprague explained that his "relational" Christology understands that Christ's deity resulted from his "radical trust relationship in and through which the very heart of God, the essence of deity, was made fully manifest in Jesus of Nazareth." He alleged that IRD's "theology from above" denies a fully human Jesus because this Jesus would be "devoid of a genetic code, some amalgam of divine substance, as if God were a person who sent a part of himself, a chip off the old block." In a quote from a favorite theologian, Sprague acknowledged that "classical Christology was a christology 'from above,'" mentioning the Nicene Creed as such a theology.

"I shall not engage further in letter writing with Good News or IRD," Sprague concluded. "I view such activity to be of questionable value," preferring "face to face dialogue and debate." True to his word, I did not ever hear again directly from Bishop Sprague. But the church would continue to hear from Bishop Sprague, with often dramatic consequences.

In January 2002, Sprague expounded on his "Christology from below" with much more salacious detail than before. This time he was speaking at United Methodist Iliff Seminary's "Week of Lectures" in Denver. Typically I ordered the tapes of this annual event every year but would not have time to listen to them until several months later. So it was not until summer 2002 that IRD disseminated the details of Sprague's latest salvo against Christian orthodoxy, which he denounced as "idolatry."

Called "A Fully Human Jesus," Sprague's Iliff speech would, he candidly admitted, "offend" some. His previous theological assertions had elicited complaints of "heresy," he said, by a few "neo-literalists" who "fail to understand the symbolic nature of religious, theological language."

But Sprague declared he wanted to help "confused believers" who cannot believe the "stilted Christological language of the ancient creeds." Gospel writers Matthew, Mark and Luke were writing theology, not history or biography, he insisted. Sprague excluded the Gospel of John altogether from his remarks since, he explained, Jesus "simply did not preach, teach, or describe himself as John suggests."

Sprague described the Virgin Birth as a "theological myth" that was not "intended as historical fact" but simply a poetical truth that the early church experienced. "To treat this myth as a historic fact is to do an injustice to its intended purpose and to run the risk of idolatry itself," Sprague warned.

The bishop affirmed that Jesus was born as the human son of Joseph and Mary, through "natural procreation," and "did not possess trans-human, supernatural powers." According to Sprague, Jesus was not born the Christ but became the Christ as he achieved his "at-oneness" with God.

"I believe in the resurrection of Jesus, but I cannot believe that his resurrection involved the resuscitation of his physical body," Sprague explained. The "inconsistent reports" in the New Testament regarding the resurrected Jesus confirm this point of view, he said. Rather than a literally resurrected Jesus, Sprague spoke of a more abstract "resurrected Jesus power" that "reconciles and renews, drives history towards justice, drives creation's evolution, and is the foundation of the new age that both is and is to come."

"But resurrection, including that of Jesus, does not include bodily resuscitation. God does not work this way." Linking resurrection with bodily resuscitation is to "make a literal religious proposition of a metaphorical symbolic expression of truth itself." Sprague called this "the kind of idolatry from which I dissent."

Sprague also said he must "dissent from Christocentric exclusivism which holds that Jesus is the only way to God's gift of salvation," which is "arrogant." He warned against "castigating other religions as being inferior." These religions may be "more circuitous, bumpy even, but I trust God to call the family home by whatever means," Sprague said.

The bishop also rejected the traditional Christian notion that Christ died on the cross for the sins of humanity.

"Obviously, such an understanding of atonement leaves no room for me to affirm the substitutionary atonement theory that portrays Jesus' blood on the cross as satisfying an angry deity through one majestic sacrificial human death, much like sacrifices of sheep and goats in ancient Israel were understood to appease God and atone for the sins of all," Sprague argued.

This idea of Jesus dying on the cross for the sins of others drives many away from following God, Sprague insisted. "How much more blood sacrifice is needed in a world saturated with blood and famished for a different understanding of salvation?"

"The concept of a blood sacrifice is superstition at best and an idolatrous allegiance to a non-Jesus methodology of God," Sprague warned. He urged "progressives" to offer other, more positive theories of atonement to persuade people to do good. And he urged "neo-literalists" to abandon their "idolatry" of literal belief.

Sprague asserted that Jesus was still unique in his "relational commitment" to God. But he admitted his belief in the uniqueness of Jesus was his "Achilles tendon," since he could not fully explain why Jesus can or should be unique.

In response to a question, Sprague admitted that he would have to "leave the possibility open" that there could be others like Jesus, but at this point he would stick with his affirmation that Jesus was unique in his "trust and obedience."

At Iliff, it was not clear whether Sprague believes in a personal deity or in a more abstract life force. "God is not a supreme being out there in the beyond," he said. "Rather, the word 'God' is the sound image we humans employ to point to the every essence of it all that is both in our midst and yet beyond the boundaries of time and existence. Symbolically, if we employ the spatial metaphor developed by Paul Tillich, 'God is not the being up there or down there, but the foundational ground of all being not limited by time or space, history or creation.'"

Besides the IRD website and my article in *Good News* magazine, news about Sprague's remarks were transmitted through Christian radio and the liberal *Christian Century* magazine, along with secular media, including the *Washington Times* and eventually the *Chicago Sun-Times*, whose headline was "The Bishop who Denied the Virgin Birth." The Rev. Don Wildmon of the American Family Association wrote every United Methodist bishop in the U.S., asking for comment about Sprague's remarks. Almost all declined or did not even bother to answer, except for newly elected Bishop Timothy Whitaker of Florida.

"Do you or any United Methodist bishop you know plan to bring charges against Bishop Sprague?" Wildmon, a United Methodist minister had asked each bishop. Whitaker responded that theological differences in the church should be addressed through debate rather than "judicial means." But in his six-page response, a copy of which he sent to Sprague, the Florida bishop said he disagreed with Sprague. In a detailed critique, Whitaker described Sprague as continuing the "Protestant Liberal project of relating to modernity," which is "an antiquated project."

In an elaborate but gentle six-page critique that Whitaker would soon make public and mail to his fellow bishops, he called Sprague "a person of deep faith," whose comments at Iliff on the divinity of Jesus were "incoherent." Noting that Sprague had contradicted the Nicene Creed affirmation of Christ as "eternally begotten of the Father," Whitaker wondered if Sprague had fallen into the ancient heresy of "adoptionism," which denied Christ's eternal deity. He challenged Sprague's "Christology from below," asking whether it didn't twist the Incarnation 180 degrees by positing Jesus as "the human being who ascended to God rather than God who descended to human being."

Whitaker said the Virgin Birth was "integral to the Christian faith" and characterized Sprague's rejection of it as a "commonplace point of view among Protestants who are captive to the presuppositions of the Enlightenment."

"I propose that an intelligent explanation of the virginal conception of Jesus as a free creative act of God as part of the drama of the incarnation is as plausible in this or any age as is any rejection of it," Whitaker wrote. He suggested that in a postmodern culture, the Virgin Birth of Jesus was an opportunity to "challenge . . . the naturalistic reductionism of the Enlightenment."

Regarding the physical resurrection of Jesus, Whitaker suggested that Sprague's notion of a merely psychological or spiritual resurrection would leave the church with a much weaker gospel. "If Jesus' body was not involved," Whitaker said, "then the so-called resurrection meant only that Jesus survived death, not that he overcame it." He concluded: "It is important today to confess the resurrection as a sign of God's purpose to transform nature and history because this victory gives us hope as we seek to care for God's creation and to witness to a coming kingdom of justice and peace."

Responding to Sprague's rejection of Christ's death as a substitutionary atonement for the sins of the world, Whitaker said that such a belief is "embedded in the apostolic witness that Jesus died 'for' us or 'instead of' us. . . ." The Florida bishop added, "I can appreciate his [Sprague's] objection to a concept of a blood sacrifice to appease God, but I do not think that the notion of sacrifice can be removed from the church's teaching about the mystery of the cross because its meaning is embedded in Jesus' own words of institution of the Eucharist at the Last Supper."

Whitaker also defended the traditional Christian understanding of Jesus Christ as the only Savior of the world, which Sprague had questioned. He disagreed with Sprague's contention that Christology is uniquely divisive within the church. The debate over Jesus is old, he observed, and is largely carried on by university scholars who are "still in captivity to the presuppositions of the Enlightenment."

"The apologetic task as it has been practiced often by mainline Protestants during the 19th and 20th centuries has exhausted its usefulness," Whitaker wrote. He charged that "the accommodation to the Enlightenment in Protestant apologetics has contributed to the church's loss of confidence and an enervation of its mission to make disciples of Jesus Christ." An appeasing reductionist rationalism, if it were ever justified, is certainly unnecessary today. "Postmodern people have awakened to the realization that there is more to reality than what is presupposed by the claims of the Enlightenment," the Florida bishop asserted. "Postmodern people are more open than modern people to the assumptions of traditional Christian affirmations of divine revelation, mystery and miracle."

Whitaker declared that the church's future depends "upon a faithful transmission of the apostolic witness and the universal faith by the power of the Holy Spirit." If Sprague believes that the language created by the ancient church creeds to describe the Trinity and the person of Jesus Christ is "merely poetic imagery," then he is mistaken, Whitaker wrote. "I am of the opinion that he is not as careful about attending to the directions and boundaries of beliefs established by the councils and creeds as he should be, particularly in his reflections on the divinity of Jesus Christ."

Sprague is "valiant" in trying to find new ways to express "ancient truths," Whitaker said. "Yet one wonders why he thinks his new ways are more relevant than the language of the councils and creeds of the church."

In a cover letter that Whitaker sent to all other United Methodist bishops, he explained that he was releasing his statement "because I have deep convictions about Christology, and I want to differentiate my views from his [Sprague's]." Whitaker added that "United Methodists want to know how other bishops think and if Bishop Sprague represents their views."

Almost no other bishops were as bold as Whitaker in publicly challenging Sprague's heterodoxy. One exception was Bishop Marion Edwards of the North Carolina Conference, who explained to his assembled clergy in October 2002 in Raleigh why he "profoundly disagrees" with Sprague.

"For me, the most serious lapse in Bishop Sprague's address . . . was to diminish the reality of the Holy Trinity," Edwards said. He feared that Sprague's Son of God was merely a "great hero" and not the "eternal fullness of the second person of the Trinity."

Edwards warned that Sprague was potentially "diluting the Trinity by making the Son of God a kind of 'johnny-come-lately' to the godhead." He accused Sprague of teaching the second-century theory of "adoptionism," which taught that Jesus became divine through adoption, and which orthodox Christianity rejected.

Sprague has "omitted" from his conversation the "authority of the canon of Scripture," Edwards noted. According to Methodism's founder John Wesley, the "biblical canon is the authority of the church," Edwards said. Sprague's problems with the Virgin Birth, resurrection of the body and the atonement "may spring from not always letting all of Scripture speak to the rest of Scripture," Edwards observed.

"I believe that the stronger and clearer teaching of the New Testament is the Christian hope for the resurrection of the body," Edwards said, expressing concern that Sprague's understanding of eternal life may be vague. He also accused Sprague of creating a "straw man" by denying Jesus' body was physically resuscitated.

"The biblical teaching of the resurrection is a teaching about a new body, not a resuscitation of the old body," Edwards said. "'New,' which redeems the 'old,' is the biblical word which I find missing from a consideration of Bishop Sprague's resurrection theology."

Edwards implied Sprague created another straw man by criticizing the atonement of Christ as a blood appeasement of an angry deity. "The death [of Christ on the Cross] is not to make God happy; the death is the sad pay for sin," Edwards explained.

Reacting to Sprague's assertion that the Virgin Birth is merely a "truthful myth and not a historical fact, Edwards said the Virgin Birth, though not "traditionally a core doctrine," is nonetheless "a teaching of the Church."

According to Edwards, "Its truth [the Virgin Birth] is clear: God was active in the birth of Jesus, not simply in the miracle of conception, but in the incarnation of what God had to say to us: the Word became flesh."

"In his zeal to make the faith understandable to modern ears, the bishop seems to have accommodated too much to the culture," Edwards declared about Sprague.

Edwards reminded his audience that a pastor's obligation, according to *The Book of Discipline*, is "ensuring faithful transmission of the Christian faith." He also quoted the *Discipline* in describing the responsibility of a bishop to "guard, transmit, teach, and proclaim, corporately and individually, the apostolic faith as it is expressed in Scripture and tradition, and, as they are led and endowed by the Spirit, to interpret that faith evangelically and prophetically."

"I truly believe the Church has been given the faith of the apostles" Edwards concluded. "This faith I have received. This faith, and no other, I truly believe."

In the church's encounter with today's "cultured despisers" of religion, Edwards said the church need not fear. "The faith of the Church is too intellectually powerful, too grand, too splendid, too life-giving for us to be guided by fear."

Edwards' words were as bold as Whitaker's were brilliant. But almost no other bishops followed them in open critique of Sprague. And Sprague himself largely declined to comment about the reactions of his fellow bishops. Instead, he preferred to point at IRD as the culprit for the negative publicity. After I called for Sprague's resignation in an August 2002 news release, Sprague reacted angrily. "IRD is grounded not in the Christian gospel but in a rigid political/economic persuasion that consistently misuses Christian language to legitimize its cause," Sprague opined. "There is a great distance between the vision espoused by the IRD and the eternal kingdom that Jesus of Nazareth came to announce and inaugurate."

A little defensively, Sprague rattled out a final touché that Mark Tooley "can follow a secular program if he so chooses, but I will continue to follow the call of Jesus Christ while remaining an active and faithful member of the Council of Bishops."

Strangely, very few United Methodist bishops publicly defend-

ed Sprague. One exception was South Carolina Bishop John Mc-
Cleskey. Speaking to the "Bishop's School of Ministry" in Myrtle
Beach in October 2002, he "unequivocally" rejected the sugges-
tion that Sprague resign.

McCleskey credited Sprague with having "affirmed the orthodox position of Jesus as fully human and fully divine." But the
South Carolina bishop added that Sprague has "denied the Virgin Birth as a biological fact," preferring to regard it as a "concept
. . . used to express the deeper theological truth of the special
nature of Jesus."

Sprague "has offered his own interpretation of how Jesus is both
human and divine," said McCleskey, who hailed this as "the stuff
theological and doctrinal dialogue is made of!" McCleskey then
described "two widely divergent theological perspectives." One
is "literalism," which insists that the Bible is "literally true," that
the world was created in "seven 24-hour days," that evolution is
fiction, that the Virgin Birth of Jesus was a biological fact and
that Jesus' resurrection means his physical body was "resuscitated
in the same form as before his crucifixion."

At the other end of the spectrum is "rationalism," which insists
that an affirmation must make sense scientifically or is otherwise
not true.

"These two perspectives often fall into the same trap," McCleskey remarked. "Literalism says that the Virgin Birth is biologi-
cally true and that the resurrection of Jesus means his physical
body was resuscitated," he said. "Extreme commitment to such
literalism says that those who do not affirm these perspectives are
unfaithful and should get out of the church."

Meanwhile, rationalism rejects non-literal doctrines. "Both
have closed the door to symbol and to mystery and put more
stock in and understanding of 'fact' than in faith," McCleskey
insisted. "These extreme views fail to understand the nature of
theological and creedal language, and they thus close the door on
genuine exploration of the difference between essential doctrine

and theological opinion."

The ancient church creeds that affirm Jesus was born of the Virgin Mary simply mean that Jesus "originated with God" and was "born to a human mother," McCleskey said. "They were never intended to be biological statements." The bishop claimed that in the ancient world the concept of virgin births was not limited to Jesus but included Buddha, Zoroaster, Plato and Augustus Caesar, who were supposedly born "supernaturally." The bishop also noted that a modern child conceived by in-vitro fertilization could be born to a virgin mother, but would not be "religiously unique."

For McCleskey, the "essential thing" about Jesus is not a "biological claim" but his identity as "fully human and fully divine," the "interpretation" of which is a "matter of opinion." The "biological interpretation" of the Virgin Birth has "certainly been one of the interpretations of his nature through the centuries." But it has never been the "unquestioned, required interpretation," the South Carolina bishop claimed.

Christ's resurrection should simply be understood as an "affirmation of God's victory over sin and death," McCleskey said. The rest is a matter of opinion. "If resurrection is only the resuscitation of the physical body," he asked rhetorically, "then what will distinguish the resurrection of Jesus Christ from the resuscitation of the bodies of those persons who have been put in deep freeze until medical science can find a cure for the diseases that killed them?"

"In the Wesleyan tradition it has never been the purpose of doctrine to provide a litmus test to determine who are the real Christians," McCleskey asserted. Theology is not about doctrinal purity, he said, but about "bringing to bear on human life the grace of God which finally touches the evil and pain and brokenness of the world with goodness and caring and wholeness."

"It is time for us United Methodists to lay to rest theological perspectives which are focused on gaining, keeping, or reclaiming

power and control—whether in the local congregation, the annual conference, or the general church," he charged.

McCleskey's defense of Sprague was heroic but lacked Bishop
Whitaker's intellectual breadth. His comparison of the Virgin
Birth to invitro-fertilization was facile, and his constant reference
to "fundamentalist" beliefs in Jesus' physical "resuscitation" was
simply inaccurate, as both Bishops Edwards and Whitaker had
explained that Christ's bodily resurrection was considerably more
than an emergency-room style reviving of a dead body.

More emotively than McCleskey, Bishop Charlene Kammerer
of Western North Carolina defended Sprague before a gathering of her clergy in February 2003. "Stirred up" over the IRD's
effort to "pit one bishop against the next," she insisted that her
"brother" Sprague was not a "heretic."

"I am weary as one bishop of our church of being monitored,
of being evaluated, of being looked at by caucus groups in our
church who are waiting to trip me up or my brother or my sister up," Kammerer complained. "It is using ideology for a particular purpose and we must speak against this." Avoiding any
of the substance of Sprague's theology, she instead focused on
the Council of Bishops as a "family" that rightfully defends itself
from outside criticism.

"The Council of Bishops is not about finding out among us
who is the heretic and who is not," she implored, rambling on
somewhat incoherently. "You don't talk about my momma when
you talk about the United Methodist Church. Well, you and
your people don't talk about other bishops to me as if somehow
one is bad and one is good. No, no that is not how we act as
the Christian community. So I am stirred up over that. You can
tell." Apparently Kammerer was not interested in any thoughtful
exchange.

By the end of 2003, the controversy over Sprague's Iliff speech
had largely died down. A feature in the *Chicago Sun-Times* in November 2003 quoted me calling him the "most vocal prominent

active liberal bishop in Protestantism today." Sprague responded in the article by denying he is liberal. "I consider myself a radical," he instead insisted.

Sprague told the newspaper that other humans have the potential to attain the same transcendence that Jesus did, though none has. "As a Christian, I would say that [Jesus] is the unique and normative revelation," he explained. "Have I experienced persons who approached that? Has history seen persons who have? I would say yes. Gandhi. Martin Luther King? Yeah."

During his eight years as bishop, four formal complaints were filed against Sprague for his failure to affirm United Methodist beliefs. As the *Chicago Sun Times* described, "One was dismissed out of hand, and the others were basically dismissed with the understanding that Sprague restate his 'belief in historic Christianity.'" The bishop said he had asked for at least one trial to facilitate a fuller debate, but it never happened.

Sprague's book, *Affirmations of a Dissenter*, outlined his previously declared heterodoxies and was published in late 2002. Rather than serve another final term as bishop, for which he was eligible, he retired in 2004. "No one's forcing me out," he insisted to the Chicago paper. "I don't want the right wing to think that they've run me out. One of the things that I've had to be prayerful about—and I mean that very seriously—was my ego saying, 'Stay. The hell with them. They're not going to drive me out.'"

Not surprisingly, Sprague's good-bye was hardly quiet. The Board of Church and Society had sought to install Sprague as a "chaplain in residence" in the United Methodist Building in Washington, D.C. Sprague publicly looked forward to being "the front-runner on certain issues" while leading weekly worship services on Capitol Hill. A one-million-dollar endowment fund was to have subsidized the bishop's chaplaincy, which doubtless would have included outspoken political advocacy. But after being publicized, the appointment became controversial, not enough money was raised, and Sprague withdrew from consideration.

My young and very capable assistant John Lomperis, along with 400 others, attended Sprague's retirement banquet in August 2004 in the Chicago area. The large banquet was publicly advertised as "open to all," and John went as a reporter. He was seated at a table with the bishop's family. They were cordial, but doubtless it was somewhat awkward for them, as it was for John.

Toward the end of his brief farewell speech, Sprague acknowledged John's presence: "IRD is here and I want them to print this." He then announced, "I intend, God being my helper, to continue, through a new and flexible venue soon to be cobbled together from several options, to speak, write, and engage the demanding justice and peace issues which confront the church, the world. . . ." The speech was then interrupted by resounding applause.

Sprague graciously shook John's hand, but *North Illinois Conference United Methodist Reporter* editor Linda Rhodes angrily confronted John about why he was there. She afterwards published an editorial about John's supposedly provocative presence. "It shocked many of us attending Bishop Sprague's retirement dinner when this blatant enemy of everything Bishop Sprague has stood for throughout his ministry 'crashed' this final farewell for the Bishop's friends and family." Rhodes' headline for her story was "Crashing the Party," above a large photo of John.

It seemed like a predictable and even suitable farewell for United Methodism's most controversial bishop.

CHAPTER   FIVE

IRD'S CRITICS

Imagine my surprise when I was sitting at the directors meeting of the General Board of Church and Society, and the presiding bishop announced: "We shall now consider a resolution on the Institute on Religion and Democracy."

It was the evening of October 3, 1998, and the directors were meeting at Gallaudet University in Washington, D.C. A school for the deaf, the campus was naturally very quiet! But the resolution condemning IRD from United Methodism's official D.C. lobby office would loudly echo through much of the church.

"We call on all United Methodists to reject IRD's efforts to undermine the Board," the statement declared. "We particularly decry the efforts of *United Methodist Action* to discredit the financial campaign to renovate the United Methodist building in Washington, D.C, and thereby undermine the church's stewardship of a unique United Methodist treasure."

The statement called UM*Action* a "privately funded, self-appointed, secular lobbying group based in Washington, D.C. that attacks the Bible-based prophetic efforts officially authorized by the General Conference."

What had provoked this condemnation? Probably it had been years of criticism of the Board from IRD, since IRD's 1981 founding, but certainly since the creation of IRD's UM*Action* program in 1994. UM*Action* had always highlighted the United Methodist lobby office as the Religious Left's chief base in the nation's capital, largely unaccountable to the church's membership and displacing more traditional Christian ministry.

Specifically, the Board was reacting to UM*Action's* September 21 fundraising letter sent to 65,000 United Methodist homes. "The UM Building is well known as the headquarters of radical church groups," our letter had reported. "They are united in a rigid political agenda that is often more secular and political than it is UM. Space is rented to other left-wing religious lobby groups, such as the National Council of Churches." We also noted that the Board is "not accountable to the church's members, to traditional Methodist beliefs, or to the Bible." The letter cited the Board's support for the legality of partial-birth abortions, for homosexual causes and the Board's uncritical attitude towards Fidel Castro, among other dictators.

Our letter highlighted the Board's drive to raise $7 million to renovate its headquarters building on Capitol Hill. Majestically located across from the U.S. Capitol and the U.S. Supreme Court, the white marble edifice was built by Methodism's Old Temperance Board to advocate Christian virtues. If only the old temperance activists could see today what their building had become!

Bishop Charles Wesley Jordan of Iowa, as president, presided as the Board approved the anti-IRD statement by a vote of 42-2, accompanied by a standing ovation for the Board's long-time General Secretary Thom White Wolf Fassett. Earlier in the meeting, Fassett has boasted of his recent meetings with Fidel Castro and Yassir Arafat. "IRD is attacking head-on," complained Bishop Melvin Talbert of Sacramento, in opposing any moderating amendments to the statement. "We fail our people by not telling the truth."

Phil Granger, a North Indiana district superintendent, was one of the two directors who opposed the statement. "There's an agenda by IRD, Methodist Federation for Social Action, Confessing Movement, Good News and every agency of this church," he noted. "We all have our say. Let's not demonize one another."

The other "no" vote was from North Carolina layman C.A. Dillon, who proposed a motion for the Board to dialogue with IRD. "They love the Lord as much as we do. We agree on our love for Jesus Christ. Let's invite one another for the next meeting." Dillon's proposal was supported by Bishop Talbert, who said, "We can have honest dialogue." The vote was unanimous. But the Board's staff never implemented the motion, and the approved dialogue with UM*Action* never occurred. Accompanying the Board's resolution was a four page "fact sheet" that ostensibly responded to IRD's critique. "To eliminate the General Board of Church and Society would mute a remarkable history of the long-standing witness and advocacy the church has maintained for decades," the fact sheet insisted.

Although prone to ignore UM*Action*, official United Methodist publications like *Newscope* and United Methodist News Service eagerly reported the Board of Church and Society's unprecedented condemnation. As I sat in the conference room with the Church and Society directors after their vote, I sensed that some of them, especially the staff, felt a sense of exultation. But for IRD, this kind of criticism from a prominent church agency was always helpful to spreading our message of church reform to a larger audience.

Surprisingly, less factual in reporting about the Board's attack on IRD was in an October 23, 1998, editorial by the *United Methodist Reporter*. It alleged "significant inaccuracies" in IRD's critique of the Board but failed effectively to describe any. The editorial did "confess that sometimes the prophetic social justice role of Mr. Fassett and the Church and Society staff makes us uncomfortable too. We don't always like hearing what they have to say, either." But the editorial asserted that the "function of prophets is to call the community to account for its actions in light of the biblical witness to God's emerging reign on Earth."

It was difficult to see the Board's staff members as "prophets" faithful to God's Word when they advocated unrestricted abortion rights or homosexual causes, or defended dictators known for persecuting Christians. The *United Methodist Reporter* hailed the Board for agreeing to "discuss criticisms face to face" with UM*Action*, and it quoted my own agreement to dialogue. But of course, the Board never implemented its own resolution.

In an ad that UM*Action* paid $5,000 to place in the *United Methodist Reporter*, we responded to the editorial's claims of "certain inaccuracies" by IRD. "UM*Action* proposes to replace the failed Board with a Wesleyan social witness that reflects the informed consciences of United Methodists," we declared. And we urged a new social witness for the church that would "unite Christians rather than divide," and "focus on key issues where there is a clear biblical teaching."

IRD's board and UM*Action's* Steering Committee convened for their biannual gathering just a few days after the Board of Church and Society's official denunciation. The IRD board presented UM*Action's* Chairman David Stanley and me with a special certificate of "distinguished recognition and conspicuous loquaciousness," for having been "formally rebuked by the General Board of Church and Society for 'deceptive claims' which 'undermine the church's stewardship of a unique United Methodist treasure.'"

IRD Board Chair Helen Rhea Stumbo, a United Methodist lay woman, laughingly presented the "award" to me. In the spirit of the moment I pledged to work in the future for official denunciations of UM*Action* by the Board of Global Ministries and the Council of Bishops. We were joking, but those goals would almost be achieved!

Earlier in 1998, there were other official United Methodist reactions to IRD/UM*Action*. Bishop Bruce Blake of Oklahoma published a column in his conference newspaper on May 8,

1998, responding to an April 19 op-ed I wrote for Oklahoma City's newspaper, the *Oklahoman*. My column's headline was "Divisions Plague United Methodists."

Bishop Blake, who unsuccessfully tried to get his response published in the *Oklahoman*, insisted that United Methodists "believe Jesus went to the cross, not critical of others, but representing those fruits of God's presence in his life." Blake blandly avoided specifics, asserting that Bishop Sprague "is a faithful servant of Jesus Christ," claiming that the Council of Bishops would "uphold the doctrinal positions of the Church," and insisting that "diversity does not mean division."

A more piquant reaction to IRD came in a 1998 column from the Rev. Wayne Findley, who directed the Kansas West Annual Conference Council on Ministries. "I and quite a few other people across Kansas have recently received a newsletter and a letter from 'UM*Action*,'" he wrote. "Mr. Tooley comes across as very angry. It almost seems like he would like to bring the whole church down with a big crash. His words don't say that, but that's the tone of his writing."

According to Findley, my writing implied that United Methodist officials "want every United Methodist worshiping Satan!" and that the "UM powers want to confuse the laity and destroy their faith." He bemoaned that the "sad part is that some folks will believe what he's saying." And the consequence of UM*Action's* work will be the "Bishop and Cabinet spending considerable time on damage control, time they could better spend doing something else." Findley predicted that some United Methodists will stop giving money, and "deserving ministries will go unfunded." He concluded, "I hope people will . . . take what my UM*Action* brother says with a good-sized grain of salt."

Even less than Bishop Blake did Findley address any of the details of UM*Action's* critique of church agencies. And while admitting that some United Methodists will agree with UM*Action*, Findley assumed it is because they are uninformed and feckless, not because church agencies are engaged in genuine controversies. It would be a predictable pattern for most IRD critics.

The reaction by Church and Society, Bishop Blake and the Kansas cleric to IRD/UM*Action* came after four years of UM*Action's* active ministry of publication and exposé. But hardly one year of UM*Action* had transpired before the head of United Methodist Communications began vociferously to target our work. General Secretary Judy Weidman frontpaged her attack on IRD in the October 1995 issue of *HeadsUp*, a newsletter from United Methodist Communications.

"Founded in 1981, the IRD has been a constant critic of the National and World Council of Churches," Weidman observed ominously. "But in recent years, the United Methodist Church has come in for renewed notice." She added, "The IRD hired a United Methodist specialist, Mark Tooley, who turns out to be a former CIA employee. Tooley has reinvented himself as a journalist, often quoting himself in his own news releases." Weidman cited a litany of UM*Action's* supposed sins: our critique of Jeanne Audrey Powers' publicly declared lesbianism; the exposure of Phil Wogaman's liberalism and the Doles' resulting departure from Foundry Church; and our report on United Methodist-supported youth conference that featured radical speakers. She even attacked the logo on UM*Action* literature.

"Recently Tooley has taken to using our denomination's symbol, the cross and the flame, on his material," she archly observed. "As it happens, monitoring the proper use of that symbol is assigned to United Methodist Communications. Tooley has been told to cease and desist." Well, she made it sound as though I were being arrested. But it took only one note of explanation for UM*Action* to stop using the official denominational symbol. The homosexual caucus groups that continued to employ the logo must not have gotten the same letter from UMCom.

Weidman pointed at IRD's funding sources. "Should someone not begin to question the authority of self-appointed critics of our church whose paychecks are written by foundation executives who have a certain political agenda?" she wondered. "Do these people care about the United Methodist Church? I doubt it. We have become a pawn in someone else's chess game."

The UMCom chief continued: "The United Methodist Church has taken it on the chin now for a quarter of a century from the IRD. It's time to take stock." Weidman warned that she would ask UMCom's directors to target IRD in a special General Conference resolution. "We shall be guided by an ancient mandate: 'Thou shalt not bear false witness.'" Clearly Weidman felt very strongly about us.

In fact, Weidman had earlier contacted IRD President Diane Knippers with very sharp complaints about IRD's coverage of Jeanne Audrey Powers' coming out. "Was Re-Imagining such a fund-raising bonanza that you must play loose and free with yet one more life?" Weidman wrote on July 25, 1995. "I have to wonder how long you are going to earn a living by manufacturing trouble for the mainline denominations. Will you be satisfied when the last member and the last dollar have gone? You are into the destruction of my spiritual home, and I write to register my dismay that you would waste your life in such a venue."

In her gracious manner, Diane responded on August 24, 1995: "I have not been involved in the church reform movement for over 20 years because it's simply a place to earn a living. It's a call God has laid on my life, Judy. I don't claim that I always do it wisely or well. My vocation is not to destroy your spiritual home, but to call it to repentance and renewal." Diane suggested they meet for lunch.

Weidman, writing back on August 29, 1995, said she would be "delighted" to meet for lunch when next she visited Washington. But irritably, she added: "I'm sad that under your leadership, IRD has become mean and hysterical." She warned: "Under my leadership I intend UMCom not just to report the news but to be a herald for professionalism in church journalism and a critic of those who use it falsely for their own ends. I intend to press the issue of where you get your funding and what right you think you have to set the agenda for the United Methodist Church."

Even more unpleasantly, Weidman concluded: "I don't defend everything that happens at the national level, but there is enormous good being done worldwide that is in mortal danger because of the decades of persistent sniping by the likes of you."

Earlier that year, in April, Weidman had convened a special task force at UMCom to develop media strategies for responding to conservative media criticism of events like the 1993 "Re-Imagining" Conference. That ecumenical women's event, endorsed by United Methodist Women, had ignited huge controversy by inviting worship of ancient feminine deities and exalting lesbianism. In a March 7, 1995, memo, Weidman noted that Tom McAnally, head of United Methodist News Service, had "been monitoring Mark Tooley, who seems to have been anointed to continue the controversy by attending events seen to be of the same kind." She also noted that McAnally would brief them about the Rev. Don Wildmon of the American Family Association, "who's been at it a long time."

McAnally had written a special story on February 28, 1995 headlined "Who is Mark Tooley?" It observed that "increasingly, the name of Mark Tooley is showing up in the public news media and in conservative religious magazines as he writes and comments about United Methodism." The three-page report, which mostly quoted from an IRD fundraising letter and several recently published articles by me, was sure to include that I had worked for eight years for the CIA before joining the IRD.

Doubtless, this was all very juicy for Weidman and her monitoring task force. "By the end of the day we want to have developed some strategies whereby we can be more pro-active and also how we mop up when an event catches us unawares," Weidman told the task force, which included Bishop Sharon Rader, then of Wisconsin.

In her report to the directors of the United Methodist General Commission on Communication on October 20, 1995, Weidman admitted that some believe IRD speaks for an "under-represented conservative voice" in the church. But she contended that such people would not want IRD's representation if they knew how IRD "routinely ignores professional ethics."

"I've been forced to conclude that it is the responsibility of this agency to expose the lies, the half-truths, the innuendos, which are common fare in these circles," Weidman declared, asking the directors to endorse anti-IRD legislation for General Conference. "I say 'enough' to those who rip and tear at the very fabric of our institution on a daily basis."

Weidman, in her zeal, overplayed her hand. In a special closed session, the directors questioned whether she was imposing her personal agenda upon the agency. Weidman, who presided over a $13 million agency with 125 employees, was reportedly asked to receive professional counseling in conflict management. And she was asked personally to meet with IRD. References to IRD were removed from Weidman's resolution, which originally was aimed at the "misuse of the media by the Religious Right." The directors changed it to "A Call for Truth, Fairness and Accuracy." The final language cited unnamed "groups from within and outside the church" whose goals seemed more "political than spiritual." But it also recognized the "right of any group to inform those who have common interests" and honored free speech.

As the *United Methodist Reporter* afterwards reported, "The General Commission on Communications recently showed that they understand the risk of angry words by avoiding some public name-calling involving an organization outside the church." The newspaper also offered to host "mediation" between United Methodist Communications and IRD. We readily agreed but asked that our meeting be "open" and not off the record. Evidently, Weidman refused altogether. Inaccurately, the *Reporter* claimed on December 15 that both IRD and Weidman had declined, without any "willingness to compromise or reconsider."

Early in 1996 Weidman came to the IRD office in Washington, D.C., and had a very cordial lunch with Diane Knippers, fulfilling the reported request of her directors. At the General Conference in Denver a short time later, Weidman warmly introduced herself to me. She never again spoke in print about IRD. Tragically, she later contracted cancer, retired from UMCom in 1999 and died the next year. Diane Knippers also died of cancer six years later. Knowing Diane, she will have sought Weidman out in heaven for a good conversation.

Almost as passionately as Weidman, United Methodist ethicist and abortion rights advocate John Swomley of St. Paul Seminary in Kansas City targeted UM*Action* in 1996, in a special letter that he sent to the General Conference delegates of that year. He repeated the same information in his regular "Watch on the Right" column for *Humanist* magazine in its July/August 1996 issue. His creative headline was: "Covert Ops, Christian-style - Former CIA Operative Mark Tooley Now Works for the Religious Right."

According to Swomley, IRD had hired me to "attack the United Methodist Church's social agenda." Conspiratorially, he recounted that I had been fresh from my CIA background when I "set up office" across the street from Foundry United Methodist Church to monitor the Rev. Phil Wogaman and the Clintons. Having "learned his trade of dirty tricks in the CIA," Swomley recounted how I had allegedly manipulated the Doles out of Foundry Church through media exposure. When the Doles had departed Foundry, "Tooley had won his first big battle for 'reform,'" Swomley sarcastically noted.

It would become a familiar refrain from IRD's critics. Rather than address our theological objections to liberal theology and its ambivalence about scriptural authority, the critics simplistically derided IRD as politically motivated conservatives assailing United Methodism's "prophetic" social justice ministries. These critics rarely admitted that the church had lost three million members, thanks partly to liberal theology's indifference to soul-saving evangelism. They preferred to lambaste IRD as a sinister and almost extra-terrestrial "outside" force.

West Virginia Bishop Clifton Ives condemned this "outside force" as president of the Board of Church and Society. He was addressing the Spring 2001 gathering of the Board's directors, who were joined by Church and Society activists from all the annual conferences for a special briefing session at an Arlington, Virginia, hotel.

"The IRD has been relentless in its attacks on the social justice ministries [of our church]," Ives complained. "The IRD program of reforming the church is targeting the United Methodist Board of Church and Society."

It was nearly the same script of three years earlier. Ives quoted an IRD fundraising proposal pledging to support the Board's few conservative directors. "Most of us have recognized that activity going on here," he observed. He alleged that UMAction would spend nearly half a million dollars a year to "undo the social justice ministries of our church."

"Do not allow those forces outside our church to divide us from each other," Ives pleaded. He recalled that 30 percent of the delegates at the 2000 General Conference had voted to support a UMAction resolution calling for the Board's closure. "UMAction wants to destroy the United Methodist Board of Church and Society."

"Mr. Tooley is in our midst," Ives acknowledged. "I thank the board's members for offering him hospitality. I believe you want reconciliation with him and his movement. But Mark, your tactics make it difficult."

Ives did not detail what IRD "tactics" he found objectionable. During his speech, several friendly directors looked back at me and smiled. Why had nearly one third of the General Conference voted to abolish the church's Washington lobby office? Ives preferred to credit only UM*Action's* supposed manipulation. But he had to know that his board was deeply controversial and divisive within the church.

Similar to Ives's denunciation, Bishop Melvin Talbert blasted away at IRD and the United Methodist renewal movement in June 2003 while addressing the Methodist Federation for Social Action (MFSA) of the West Ohio Conference. I journeyed to scenic Lakeside, Ohio, to listen in, my presence in the audience seemingly unnoticed by any in the MFSA crowd. Talbert had been one of the "Denver 15" bishops who opposed the church's teachings about homosexuality in 1996. Infamously, he had declined to discipline dozens of his California-Nevada clergy who jointly presided over a lesbian union ceremony for the conference lay leader and her companion in 1999. In reaction, nearly two dozen evangelical pastors in Talbert's conference quit United Methodism, most taking their congregations with them. After retirement, remarkably Talbert became the ecumenical officer for the Council of Bishops, despite his divisive record within his own annual conference.

Not holding back in his MFSA speech, Talbert denounced IRD and other church reform groups as "conservative segregationists" who promote "white supremacy" and "white male domination." He alleged they "are the same persons who fought against the civil rights movement" and "against women." Naturally, Talbert offered no evidence for his sensational allegation of racism.

Focusing on the IRD, Talbert called its board a "who's who of the political right-wing." He specifically cited IRD board members Richard John Neuhaus, Fred Barnes, Michael Novak, George Weigel, Tom Oden, David Stanley and Helen Rhea Stumbo, among others.

Talbert lamented that prominent IRD supporter John Stumbo, an attorney who has served on the boards of national church agencies, was once devoted to "justice and inclusiveness" but now is a "neo-conservative." Talbert inaccurately referred to me as a "former FBI agent." And he warned: "They are wolves in sheep's clothing" and "fronts for political right-wing groups."

Not sparing in his Manichaean rhetoric, Talbert claimed: "We face the destructive violence of bad people," who employ "evil tactics." He lamented the church's move to the right as "bad news," and complained that conservatives are now even in the seminaries and the Council of Bishops.

Talbert was understandably distressed by his church's increasingly moving away from his brand of 20th century liberal theology. So why not blame IRD rather than fault liberalism's own failures?

The following year, another radical retired bishop, similarly disgruntled by liberalism's implosion within United Methodism, devoted a whole speech to denouncing the church's reform groups, including IRD.

Bishop Dale White, another of the "Denver 15," attacked the reform groups' "polarizing style," and "intimidating tactics" that are "calculated to spread fear" and "impugn the motives of others," accompanied by "dirty tricks politics" and "right-wing ideology." White was speaking at First United Methodist Church in Schenectady, New York, on October 26, 2004, as part of its Carl Lecture Series.

Naturally, Bishop White targeted the IRD, which depends on "money from right-wing corporate foundations" and promotes "conservative policy goals." He charged: "Their goal is not a spiritual quest but a political take-over by the extreme right."

The bishop claimed that IRD is raising money to bring lawsuits and file charges against clergy who fail to uphold doctrines like Christ's Virgin Birth, the bodily Resurrection, and a "particular understanding" of Christ's atonement. "If IRD didn't have all that money, they would simply be dismissed as dysfunctional people who don't have any manners," he quipped.

White complained about famed United Methodist theologian and IRD board member Tom Oden. "Something happened to him over the years," he surmised about Oden, who once was on the leftist "cutting edge" of theology, but later turned toward renewing the church's orthodox tradition. "He's associating with groups that are damaging our church. He's saying what they want to hear."

"Many honest church members" are being deceived by "dysfunctional organizations that are impacting from the outside," White wailed. Afterwards, I had a pleasant exchange with the bishop, offering to share my article about his speech with a request for his comment. He readily agreed, and I afterwards did this. But the bishop never replied.

In 2003, White was part of a special task force called the "Information Project for United Methodists," which published *United Methodism at Risk*, an expose of the church reform groups, including IRD. The author was Leon Howell, editor of the now defunct and far-left *Christianity and Crisis* magazine, that for years United Methodist Board of Global Ministries subsidized. Howell's book alleged that the renewal groups are "spreading misleading and inflammatory charges" as part of their campaign to "control" United Methodism. It defended the church bureaucracy's "social-justice advocacy based on biblical mandates." And it insisted that Methodism had historically supported "openness and inquiry," while the renewal groups support a "new, rigid direction." By "rigid," Howell's book referred to classical Christian doctrine. By "openness," it meant theological fluidity, accompanied by dogmatic politics of the left.

Andrew Weaver celebrated Howell's book in a review for the Martin Marty Center at the University of Chicago in July 2003. A clinical psychologist and ordained minister, Weaver flamboyantly wrote: "The political right-wing, operating in the guise of a gaggle of so-called 'renewal groups,' one named the Institute on Religion and Democracy, has acquired the money and power to target three mainline American denominations." Weaver's hyperbolic rhetoric and bizarre techniques would degenerate after this first blast.

Typically rehashing quarter-century-old complaints that IRD is funded by "right-wing" foundations, Weaver has become a prolific attack writer and activist. When he absurdly emailed the mother of one young IRD staffer to complain of the IRD staffer's "disgraceful" behavior, the mother predictably sided with her son against Weaver. Even more outrageously, Weaver had copied the email to the mother's professional colleagues, having harvested their names off the internet. The mother had her employer's attorney ask Weaver to end his email campaign targeting her office.

I met Weaver in the press room of the 2004 General Conference in Pittsburgh. Glowering, he refused to shake my hand. "People think you're a nice guy, but I know better," he intoned, claiming that I had "hurt good people." Obviously uninterested in civil conversation, Weaver continued to berate me. A young radio reporter charitably rushed to my defense, but I knew it was useless with Weaver. I walked away laughing. "It's not funny!" Weaver growled, wanting to finish his tirade.

Ironically, Weaver and his allies have accused IRD of playing *Hardball on Holy Ground*, which was the name of a 2005 book edited by Stephen Swecker, editor of *Zion's Herald*. In it, Weaver and other writers chronicled how the "Religious Right" is trying to subvert the soul of the mainline churches. Weaver called the subversion an attempted "coup d'etat" and excoriated IRD's "unethical propaganda methods."

In an attempt at cleverness, former Church and Society General Secretary Thom White Wolf Fassett wrote in *Hardball* of IRD as "Purveyors of False Memory." According to Fassett, IRD functions like "recovered memory" therapists who tell vulnerable United Methodists that their church has taken "ridiculous and abhorrent positions on the most critical issues facing humankind today." These clueless church members, as Fassett described them, learn they suffer from "false memory syndrome" and sign on to IRD's agenda of attack against the church's "prophetic" ministries. According to Fassett, "IRD has expressed no interest in converting people to Christ."

More creditably than Fassett's psycho-metaphors, Swecker included in *Hardball* several extensive interviews with IRD President Diane Knippers and me. Readers were at least permitted some glimpse directly into our own thinking. In her interview Diane told of her struggle with cancer, which would take her life in 2005.

Hardball was high brow compared to *Renewal and Ruin*, an attack video aimed at IRD and produced by an East Tennessee minister. Introduced by theme music reminiscent of 1970s era horror movies about the Antichrist, the video includes the inevitable Andrew Weaver, along with Board of Church and Society Chief Jim Winkler and Bishops Beverly Shamana of Sacramento and Ken Carder, retired from Mississippi.

"Clearly their mission is to dismantle our church," insisted Shamana, who is now president of the Board of Church and Society. More colorfully, Winkler called IRD "a snake that has sunk its fangs into the dog. It's lame. It's poison." Weaver implausibly suggested that IRD is controlled by Roman Catholics. The video claimed IRD is funded by $70 million in Catholic donations.

Comparing IRD to the Ku Klux Klan (after all, both disapprove of homosexual practice), the video's producer, Steve Martin insisted: "By producing this video I hope to draw us into a new, civil discussion about our branch of Christ's church, its past, and its future." He continued: "The debate will no doubt be passionate, but let us, as the Church for whom Christ died, love each other in the midst of it."

Regrettably, almost none of IRD's critics has offered an intelligent critique of our work. And almost none has engaged in substantive debate about the real issues before our church. Is the Bible authoritative? Is Jesus Christ the only Savior of the world? Shall the church be faithful to traditional Christian sexual ethics?

Should the institutional church's primary goal be evangelism and discipleship, or shall it be political and social reform? Are church elites accountable to the church's members?

IRD is still waiting for serious answers to these questions from most of our major critics.

CHAPTER   SIX

A METHODIST IN THE WHITE HOUSE

George W. Bush was the first Methodist elected to the White House since William McKinley. (Hillary Clinton is United Methodist but Bill Clinton remained Southern Baptist). I was determined to find the new president a good United Methodist church to attend in Washington, D.C.! And I was partly successful. He accepted my suggestion to attend a black United Methodist congregation on Capitol Hill the first Sunday after his January 2001 inauguration. But he never found a United Methodist Church to attend regularly. Probably for the sake of convenience, he has mostly attended St. John's Episcopal Church, the "church of the presidents" located across Lafayette Park from the White House. How sad that a Methodist should have to attend an Episcopal church!

The lack of United Methodist options in the nation's capital illustrates what plagues our denomination. Many United Methodists, including IRD staff, who come to work in Washington would like to attend a United Methodist church that is not liberal and at least moderate. But nearly all the predominantly white United Methodist congregations have liberal clergy, and many of them have become "Reconciling," i.e., pro-homosexuality. Most famously, Foundry United Methodist Church, which the Clintons attended during their time in Washington, is outspokenly Reconciling.

Here's a sad illustration. A Korean-American woman, friend of mine several years ago, wonderfully became a Christian while attending a prayer meeting back in Korea during a visit with her devout mother. Enthusiastic about her new faith, she began attending a United Methodist church right across the street from her Washington, D.C., apartment. The church was typical of many urban mainline congregations. There was a beautiful building, no doubt with a congregation once many hundreds in size decades ago, but now attended by only a few dozen. An endowment sustained the church's finances. The pastor was liberal and the church was Reconciling. I ran into my friend many months later and remarked about having read in the *Washington Post* about defrocked lesbian pastor Beth Stroud having spoken at her church. "Oh, yes," my friend replied, "We believe in inclusion for all people," repeating the mantra of pro-homosexuality activists in the church.

United Methodists who are more traditional and live in Washington, D.C., either switch to another denomination or, more rarely, journey into the suburbs to find a non-liberal United Methodist church. More should attend the black congregations, but often the services at those churches are two or three hours long, which can be difficult for white bread United Methodists accustomed to services ending promptly at noon! My young assistant, a United Methodist from St. Louis who lives on Capitol Hill, searched for a United Methodist congregation for many months before settling on a medium-size church in Arlington, Virginia. His journey there requires a 30-minute subway ride. Most young United Methodists with less denominational loyalty pick one of several very popular and growing evangelical congregations in the city.

From the start, I believed that President Bush should attend a black United Methodist congregation where the gospel is preached. His worship at a black church would also be a wonderful example for others in a city where the white minority often has little social interaction with the black majority. The church that came to mind was Lincoln Park United Methodist Church on Capitol Hill. It is pastored by the very dynamic Harold Lewis, who several years earlier had readily agreed to host a gathering for Lifewatch, the caucus for pro-life United Methodists. But first, I needed to attend Lincoln Park to experience the worship for myself.

The Lincoln Park United Methodist Church marquee promised that services began at 10 a.m. It was 9:45 and the church doors were locked, the windows were dark and nobody was in sight! I stood bewildered in the January cold until a nicely dressed older lady invited me to sit in her nearby heated car. A church member, she effusively greeted me and promised that the church would open soon. With her was a very friendly young man who was new to the church. He was recently released from many years in prison, had been addicted to crack cocaine and enthusiastically told of his finding God's grace at Lincoln Park.

Eventually the church doors opened, and the worship began, lasting three hours. The only white person in a crowd of about two hundred, I was greeted by at least a dozen handshakes, a kiss and several hugs. Even well into the third hour, the service was never boring. The choir filled the sanctuary with its spirituals, accompanied by a trombonist, a trumpet player and a drummer. Rev. Lewis preached for nearly an hour about Jesus as the "Good Shepherd," sometimes shouting, sometimes waving his arms. He briefly played a rap song on a CD player, challenging the several hundred listeners: "How can you hear the voice of the Good Shepherd in that?" A chorus of "amens" responded.

While most Methodists are used to a 60-minute worship service, a recent service at Mr. Lewis's church concluded after three hours of singing and preaching. Yet it was never boring.

Lewis is a military veteran and Mississippi native who had transferred into the Baltimore-Washington Conference several years previously. Exuding charism and snappily dressed, he also does Christian comedy performances under the stage name of "Ice." His preaching was revivalistic and richly theological, accompanied by a four-page sermon outline. Not entirely averse to controversy, Lewis' church had gained attention the previous year when its outdoor sign advertised a sermon called "Was It Adam and Eve or Adam and Steve?" The city government tore it down, claiming that "historic preservation" standards were violated. The culture clash was not uncommon. The growing and predominantly white homosexual population of D.C. often resents the social conservatism of black churches, not to mention the inconvenience of crowds and double parking during lengthy services on Sunday mornings.

The service was both exuberant and wonderfully traditional. Men wore dark suits and the women were in dresses and hats. A laminated sheet in every pew explained the church's expectations for good behavior during worship, which included proper attire and not getting up during the sermon. The collection was taken up by a crew of ladies wearing white gloves and headgear similar to nurses' hats. Fans were passed out, with Jesus on one side, and an advertisement for Jordan Funeral Service on the other. Enthusiastically, I was going to recommend Lincoln Park to the incoming president.

But how would I transmit my great idea to the President-elect? Several years before I had coincidentally spoken in Midland, Texas, to a Sunday school that Bush's mother-in-law, Laura Welch, attended. She listened politely, with two dozen others, while I talked about the need for church reform. My hosts, Pat and Martha McNair, kindly agreed to transmit my letter to Mrs. Welch. First United Methodist Church is where Laura Bush had grown up, where she had married her husband and where he had joined after their marriage. Thanks partly to a Bible study there that George W. Bush attended with Dan Evans, who would later become his Secretary of Commerce, Bush vigorously renewed his Christian faith in mid-life.

Bush had been reared Episcopalian and Presbyterian, but he seems to have taken to United Methodism naturally, with its legacy of revivalism and historic emphasis on God's grace empowering changed lives. The churches that Bush has attended during his 20 years as a United Methodist have been moderate by Texas standards but probably right of center by national United Methodist standards. In Dallas, Bush joined the huge 12,000 member Highland Park United Methodist Church, where he officially remains a member. While governor, he attended the Tarrytown United Methodist Church. Both churches have both conservatives and liberals, with pastors who are largely orthodox but not especially doctrinaire.

In my January 11, 2001, letter to President-elect and Laura Bush, I described the difficulty of finding a vibrant United Methodist Church in the predominantly white, affluent neighborhoods of Washington's Northwest section. And I recounted the experience of the Doles at Foundry United Methodist Church. "My recommendation is that you consider attending an African-American congregation in the Northeast section of the city," I wrote. Rev. Lewis is a "social conservative" who serves on the board of United Methodism's pro-life caucus and defends the sanctity of marriage. Of him I said, "He preaches the Gospel and is not a political pastor."

"Your attendance at a socially conservative, African-American church in the city would send an important message to the nation," I wrote Bush. "I also believe you would find more vitality and spiritual growth there than in most of the predominantly white and liberal United Methodist churches in this city." Helpfully, the *Wall Street Journal* contacted me to write a column speculating about where Bush may attend church. I included in it my recommendation of Lincoln Park United Methodist. The column was published January 12, 2001, with the headline: "In God He Trusts."

PBS' *Religions and News Ethics Weekly* also interviewed me

on January 19, 2001, about possible churches that the Bushes could attend. I suggested that Bush might attend the upscale and once prestigious but now liberal Metropolitan United Methodist Church, which was the closest that Methodism had to a cathedral in Washington. But I urged that he take a look at Lincoln Park. "It has a pastor and a theology that is very traditional, even conservative. It's focused on personal transformation and changing lives and not on making political statements. And I think that would appeal to George W. Bush who has talked very openly and very freely about his own personal transformation because of his personal faith."

During Bush's January 20 inaugural ceremony, the Rev. Kirbyjon Coldwell, a hugely successful black minister and old friend of the President's who pastors 18,000-member Windsor Park United Methodist Church in Houston, gave the benediction. Coldwell boldly prayed in the name of Jesus Christ, which upset some secularists, but probably not many others. Before Bush's departure from Texas, Coldwell had joined Bush's two other United Methodist pastors, Jim Mayfield of Austin and Mark Craig of Dallas, in leading a special prayer service for the president-elect. In his memoir, "A Charge to Keep," Bush had cited an inspirational sermon by Craig as helping to persuade him to run for president.

Meanwhile, my Midland, Texas, friend Pat McNair reported that Mrs. Welch had carried my letter to her son-in-law, and that the new President planned to attend Lincoln Park. On Sunday, January 28, I attended my grandmother's church, Arlington Forest United Methodist Church in Arlington, Virginia, to hear a sermon by the Rev. Kathleene Card. The wife of Andrew Card, soon-to-be Bush's White House chief of staff, Kathleene was entering the ministry later in life. She had attended Wesley Theological Seminary in Washington and was being ordained in the Virginia Annual Conference. Now serving at Trinity United Methodist Church in McLean, Virginia, she had returned to Arlington Forest to thank her previous home congregation for their support.

Kathleene and I, thanks to mutual friends in her church, had recently corresponded. When I introduced myself to her, she enthusiastically told me that Bush had asked if she knew me after reading my *Wall Street Journal* piece. She told me that Bush was attending Lincoln Park United Methodist Church that morning. Kathleene also introduced me to Commerce Secretary designate Dan Evans, who was at Arlington Forest to hear her sermon.

In fact, the new President and his wife also brought along the former President Bush and former First Lady Barbara Bush for worship at Lincoln Park. The congregation gave the two presidents and their wives two standing ovations, while the pianist played "Hail to the Chief." Rev. Lewis preached on "The Church that Jesus Built." The effusive congregation shouted "Hallelujah," "Amen," and "Yes, Lord!"

"The church is not only an organization, it is an organism!" Lewis preached. "The first purpose of the church is to magnify the Lord!" A 25-member youth choir sang "This Is the Day" as they processed down the aisle, with Bush bobbing his head somewhat to the music. The service lasted one hour and 45 minutes, short by Lincoln Park standards. The Bush family stood and swayed to a refrain that went: "I've got a feeling everything's going to be all right." The church worship leader Norma Belt, in opening prayers, had asked God to bless the new President and to "put your hand around him and his family."

"He got right into it," Lewis told the *Washington Post*. "Our intention was just to provide an environment in which he could be spiritually fed. He seemed to fit right in." Lewis also told the newspaper that he had voted for Al Gore but Bush "is our president. . . . My team lost. But I'm a team player." During one point in the service, Lewis referred to Bush as the "president-elect." Some on the congregation shouted a correction. "Did I miss something?" the pastor jokingly asked. "I did that on purpose, because I've heard a lot of jargon about the 'president-select,'" Lewis later explained to the *Post*.

Old President George H. W. Bush told reporters, "Beautiful, beautiful," and gave a thumbs up when asked about the service as he was leaving. Less than a week before the Bushes' visit to Lincoln Park, Rev. Lewis had preached at Lifewatch's annual pro-life service in the chapel of the United Methodist Building on Capitol Hill, commemorating the 28th anniversary of the *Roe vs. Wade* Supreme Court ruling legalizing abortion-on-demand. "Brothers and sisters, one of the greatest indictments against the human race is the atrocious act of abortion," Lewis preached, once again providing a wonderful four-page outline of his sermon. "According to God the baby is divinely designed and cosmically created long before it is in the womb," Lewis said. "The womb is just the area where God announces his creation."

The day after the Bushes had attended Lewis' church, I opened my mail and found a hand-written note from the office of the President-elect, dated January 18, 2001. "Dear Mark: Thank you for your thoughtful letter. I appreciate your insights. I do not want to worship at a 'liberal' church. Lincoln Park sounds very interesting. I may just surprise Rev. Lewis and worship with his church. With best wishes, George Bush."

Afterwards, I wrote for *National Review Online* about all the United Methodists rising to prominence in Washington. The President and Vice President were United Methodists, as were other senior Administration officials, plus newly elected Senator Hillary Clinton. At least 60 members of the U.S. Congress belonged to the denomination.

"Perhaps Washington is experiencing a Methodist moment," I wrote. "After decades of dominance by refined Episcopalians, rambunctious Baptists, politically active Evangelicals and socially ascendant Roman Catholics, the nation's capital is now in the hands of United Methodists. And that means what, exactly? How can the same church produce both George W. Bush and Hillary Clinton?"

I explained that the church's leadership broadly reflected the beliefs of America's liberal cultural elites. But the church's membership mostly reflected the ethos of the suburbs and small towns of the South and Midwest, where United Methodism is strongest.

Like the church's hierarchy, Sen. Clinton was shaped by the 1960s, when Methodist activists eagerly joined the civil-rights and anti-war movements. She, like they, equated the church with social action. Thirty-five years later, she still credits her Methodist youth group for transforming her from a Goldwater supporter to a liberal activist. Her political life has often closely paralleled the official policy positions of her denomination, if not of most church members.

In contrast, Bush came to Methodism later in life. He married his wife, Laura, a lifelong Methodist. But he recalls he became a committed believer only after counseling from Billy Graham, a Baptist, and a non-denominational Bible study that also involved long-time friend Don Evans. Bush now says Jesus Christ has "changed his heart." This kind of talk discomfits some Methodist intellectual elites. But it fits easily with historical Methodism, which was founded after 18th-century English evangelist John Wesley also felt his "heart strangely warmed."

Bush was comparable in some ways with other Methodist presidents. Like Ulysses Grant, Bush overcame a weakness for strong drink. Like Rutherford Hayes, Bush won a bitterly contested election that centered on the electoral votes of Florida. And maybe, as William McKinley supposedly did, Bush could sum up his political philosophy with the words: I am simply a Methodist.

Unfortunately, the years of the Bush Administration did not fully become a Methodist Moment in American politics. Bush never returned to Lincoln Park Church, although Rev. Lewis did get invited to a White House Christmas party. Like the Doles five years before, Bush visited Clarendon United Methodist Church in Arlington, Virginia once. And he also visited the Rev.

Kathleene Card's Trinity United Methodist Church in McLean, Virginia.

Ultimately, Bush settled on the relatively short, early morning services at conveniently placed St. John's Episcopal Church, the "church of the presidents," where his father had attended while in office. The priest is somewhat left of center but largely non-controversial. When at Camp David, Bush attends worship at the U.S. Navy chapel there, whose chaplain during Bush's first term was a United Methodist pastor from the Virginia Conference.

Surely known to Bush, typical political statements from United Methodist agencies and officials were well to Bush's left, and almost certainly would be critical of his administration. The United Methodist Council of Bishops anxiously hoped for a meeting with the most prominent member of the Methodist flock to share their views about the nation. No such meeting occurred during Bush's first term.

Perhaps one reason was White House Liaison Officer Tim Goeglein's less than warm reception at a March 2001 briefing for the Board of Church and Society's directors and representatives from the annual conferences. Representing the President, Goeglein was pelted with hostile questions by the liberal activists. And he left the session at an Arlington hotel with the strong impression that many of these church officer holders hoped Bush would leave United Methodism.

After the September 11, 2001, attacks, Goeglein phoned IRD to ask for suggestions of mainline church officials who could attend a special prayer meeting with the President at the White House with other religious leaders. Coincidentally, Goeglein was breakfasting with IRD President Diane Knippers on the morning of 9/11. After pondering Goeglein's request, I suggested to him Virginia Bishop Joe Pennel.

Originally from Tennessee and elected bishop of Virginia in 2000, Pennel had movingly visited the Pentagon a few days after the attack. Impressed by this, I phoned his office and thanked him for his Christian witness at a dire time for the nation. Pennel seemed like a centrist, orthodox in theology but not outspoken. Not knowing him well, I wanted to be sure he was not the sort of Methodist bishop who might politically exploit a White House visit and create embarrassment.

A district superintendent friend back in Pennel's home state was reassuring. "Don't worry, he's from Tennessee!" With that strong recommendation, Goeglein invited Pennel to be the only senior mainline Protestant official among 26 religious figures who prayed with Bush on September 18. Other participants included the Roman Catholic cardinals of New York and Boston, the president of the Southern Baptist Convention, the presiding bishop of the Lutheran Church-Missouri Synod, evangelists Franklin Graham and Luis Palau, mega-church pastor Bill Hybels, the primate of the Greek Orthodox Church in America, the president of the Mormon Church, and Muslim, Hindu and Buddhist leaders.

All the religious leaders endorsed a statement that assured President Bush of their prayers for him and for "all who bear the responsibility of government." They declared that the September 11 attacks were not just against the U.S. but "against all humanity." It continued: "The common good has been threatened by these attacks, and we have both a moral right and a grave obligation as a nation to protect the sanctity of life and the common good."

"We should respond not in the spirit of aggression, but as victims of aggression who must act to prevent further atrocities of terrorism," the statement went on. It urged that any response must be "guided by sound moral principles" with a "grave obligation to protect innocent human life." It also thanked President Bush for seeking a "coordinated, international response" and for his condemning bigotry against Muslims or Arabs.

That evening Bishop Pennel joined just a few other religious leaders invited to be with First Lady Laura Bush in the balcony of the House Chamber to hear President Bush's address to the Congress and nation. Afterwards, the bishop wrote me a gracious letter and called his visit to the White house a "signature day in my life and I hope it was helpful to our President and ultimately to the cause of peace."

The Council of Bishops would repeatedly condemn the Bush Administration's war policies in the coming years. Still, in keeping with 200 years of tradition, the Council of Bishops congratulated Bush on his re-election in November 2004 and dispatched to him the gift of a Bible, just as early Methodist Bishop Francis Asbury had once presented the Scriptures to George Washington.

"We are grateful that President and Mrs. Bush are committed disciples of Jesus Christ, and we pray that they continue to grow in their discipleship," said Council President Bishop Peter Weaver of Boston. Perhaps alluding to the lack of any past contact between the council and the President, Weaver said: "I am looking forward to whatever is in the past being in the past," he said later. "We have four more years ahead of us, and I know that it will be four more productive years for the president and his cabinet as well as the people of the church to work together to bring about the kinds of changes that he [Bush] would like to see."

The Council of Bishops' statement pledged that they would "continue to keep our brother in Christ and fellow United Methodist, President Bush, in our prayers. We look forward to building a constructive relationship with him as we shape a world where we do justice, love mercy and walk humbly with God."

Finally, on May 3, five United Methodist bishops got into the White House to meet with President Bush for ten minutes. Bishop Weaver, several days later, was asked to say the closing prayer at the White House's annual National Day of Prayer Breakfast. "Laura and I are proud Methodists," Bush told the breakfast crowd.

Weaver hopefully speculated, "I think there is a new openness in the relationship." Bishop Schol, who helped to organize the get-together, warned against large expectations about United Methodist clerics dispensing advice to Bush: "The president is very clear and forthright about what his agenda and commitments are. If any particular denomination thinks it is going to sit down and influence this president on domestic and international policy, it doesn't know how [he] operates." Schol said of Bush, "He affirms that he has been influenced by the United Methodist Church," but on a personal level.

Careful not to seek policy advice from the bishops, Bush may have remembered an April 3, 2005, full-page magazine ad from numerous United Methodist officials, including several bishops, who denounced the President for contributing to "spiritual forces of wickedness." Signers included seven retired bishops and Board of Church and Society chief Jim Winkler.

Titled "A Prophetic Epistle from United Methodists Calling Our Brother George W. Bush to Repent," the ad called for Bush to "repent from domestic and foreign policies that are incompatible with the teaching and example of Christ." Specifically, Bush was accused of "threaten[ing] the very earth and all its inhabitants with open discussion of the use of nuclear weapons," promoting "redemptive violence" in his policy towards the "sovereign nation of Iraq" and of domestic policies that are "incongruent with Jesus' teaching."

By 2007, the Bush Administration had settled on Southern Methodist University as the likely site for the Bush presidential library. The possibility of proximity to Bush's papers and records excited angry anguish from 28 mostly retired bishops, who declared in a public anti-Bush library petition that: "As United Methodists, we believe that the linking of his presidency with a university bearing the Methodist name is utterly inappropriate."

Several dozen SMU professors also signed on, led by a Perkins School of Theology alumnus and retired professor. "What moral justification supports SMU's providing a haven for a legacy of environmental depredation and denial of global warming, shameful exploitation of gay rights and the most critical erosion of *habeas corpus* in memory?" asked the Rev. William McElvaney.

Bush's pastor, the Rev. Mark Craig of Highland Park Church in Dallas, vigorously defended the library as an SMU board member. Of the library opponents, he said, "I think it's a fringe group, a marginal group without any standing other than the fact they happen to be one of eight million United Methodists." The minister told the *Dallas Morning News* that Bush is "a good Methodist and anyone who says other than that is being grossly judgmental."

In contrast, United Methodist gadfly Andrew Weaver asserted that, "George Bush has been, in his presidency, so inconsistent with fundamental Christianity that he should not be associated with a Methodist university." The New York psychologist and IRD critic told the Dallas paper, "Methodist means decency, and this man has not been decent."

Bishop Scott Jones, himself an SMU trustee, wrote his fellow bishops defending the Bush library. "The Library with its documents, exhibits and other research materials will provide an excellent forum for debate, discussion and research about the accomplishments, mistakes, political philosophy and missed opportunities of this presidency." Citing both Bush and Hillary Clinton as United Methodists, Jones said, "At times I disagree with both, and at times I agree with both. But they are my sister and brother in Christ, and I claim them as part of my United Methodist family."

But many United Methodist elites preferred to slam the Bush Administration as uniquely sinister.

Speaking on behalf of United Methodism's Washington lobby office, Jim Winkler urged the impeachment of President Bush and Vice President Cheney at a March 2006 ecumenical legislative briefing. He cited Bush's "illegal war of aggression" that was "sold on lies."

"These are actions far more serious than a failed land deal on the White River or a sexual indiscretion with a White House intern," Winkler said, comparing Bush to Bill Clinton, whose impeachment was never urged by Winkler's agency.

United Methodism's first president in 100 years had less than cordial relations with his denomination's officials. If Hillary Clinton becomes president, she almost certainly can expect considerably more support from these same officials.

CHAPTER SEVEN

A METHODIST TRUST BETRAYED ON CAPITOL HILL

Ninety years ago, Methodism's Old Temperance Board built the majestic Methodist Building on Capitol Hill, across the street from the U.S. Capitol and what shortly afterwards would become the U.S. Supreme Court. The edifice was to model and advocate on behalf of Christian virtues, temperance above all.

Of course, the building is still very much there, and it is now owned by the successor agency to the Methodist Temperance group, which is the General Board of Church and Society (GBCS). GBCS's agenda, which depends on the considerable income that the Methodist Building generates, is dramatically different from the causes of the venerable Old Temperance Board.

One vignette in September 2007 colorfully illustrated the gap.

GBCS General Secretary Jim Winkler joined with other church officials in a press conference on the lawn of the Methodist Building to announce one more of a series of protests against the Iraq War. This time, it was an interfaith "fast" to coincide with Islam's Ramadan season.

There were representatives from mainline Protestant groups such as the National Council of Churches, along with Buddhists and other religionists. Among them was an official from the Islamic Society of North America. This ostensibly "moderate" Muslim group was named as an un-indicted co-conspirator in an ongoing terrorism trial involving the Holy Land Foundation for Relief.

In keeping with the intended interfaith theme of the anti-war press conference, a Jewish rabbi sounded a shofar, or ram's horn, that Jews have used for three millennia as an instrument of worship. Introducing the blower of the shofar was Rabbi Debra Kolodny, self-professed sexual liberationist and editor of *Blessed Bi-Spirit: Bisexual People of Faith*. Rabbi Kolodny is a noted advocate of "polyamory" and the ostensible holiness of multiple sexual partners. She is not your typical rabbi.

But how sublime that Rabbi Kolodny should stand on the lawn of the Methodist Building, taking a break from her crusade for polyamory, to introduce the blowing of a shofar against the Iraq War, with her Muslim and Methodist co-belligerents. And how often is an official from the Islamic Society of North America likely to spend a late summer morning in public solidarity with a bisexual Jewish rabbi? Only GBCS could facilitate such a cosmic event!

Back in 1923 did Methodism's Old Board of Temperance have this kind of event in mind when it dedicated the Methodist Building as a shrine to chaste and temperate living? Worried primarily about the destructive wages of intoxication, but also about "salacious" literature," racy Hollywood films and the vices of the race track, the Old Temperance Board raised dimes and quarters from Sunday school classes and Methodist women's groups across the nation. The old temperance crusaders likely never foresaw that the fruits of their labors would include the author of *Blessed Bi-Spirit*, or the Islamic Society of North America.

The wonderful old Methodist Building has been a direct eye-witness not only to nearly a century of presidential inaugurations, but also to the full circle of Methodist preeminence, decline and renewal. Its builders represented America's largest Protestant church. They had prospered from nearly 120 years of continuous growth and triumph. Methodists in the early 20th century were among the pillars of American civilization. Having already converted America to Jesus Christ, they were confident of supposedly purging the chosen nation of its worst iniquities, through spiritual and political warfare. It was perfectly appropriate that the Methodist Building would sit across from the U.S. Capitol and the future site of the U.S. Supreme Court. As the Congress legislated America's laws and the justices interpreted those laws, so the Methodists and their fellow mainline Protestants expected they would govern the souls and consciences of Americans.

Even as the Methodist Building triumphantly proclaimed Wesleyan holiness on Capitol Hill in the 1920s, the church's seminaries were already falling prey to liberal theology, whose fruits would eventually de-emphasize and then eradicate altogether the legacy of the Old Temperance Board. In future decades, the Methodist Building would no longer represent traditional social holiness or even mainstream Methodism. Instead, the agencies within it would espouse an endless array of utopian and radical causes.

During the final years of the Cold War, the apologists for communism's worst tyrannies would find a welcome home in the Methodist Building. The zealots of population control, convinced that the earth was soon to be overrun by a surplus of people, were also housed in the Methodist Building, helping to hatch the eventual regime of unrestricted abortion, which dehumanized all of human life. Reportedly, the justice who penned the *Roe versus Wade* decision, Harry Blackmun, himself a Methodist, used the Methodist Building as a refuge in which he wrote the landmark ruling.

The interest groups who came to dominate the Methodist Building were not interested in the old Methodist vision of social holiness. Their aim was social, political and sexual revolution. The patriarchs of the Old Temperance Board had seen a nation that was bound for Zion. But their ecclesial successors saw only a corrupt and oppressive America, whose innate racism, greed and imperialism could be overthrown only through the most radical action.

Nearly a century ago, the Old Temperance Board had cheerfully collected support from tens of thousands of Methodists. Its cause was popular and wide-based. But the eventual occupants of the Methodist Building would not be populists. Their support, such as it was, sprang not from Sunday school classes but from the faculty and alumni of radicalized seminaries, who believed themselves unaccountable to the wider church. Unable to garner their own support, these new church lobbyists instead had to disguise their purposes and finagle funds that were originally devoted to temperance.

The Old Temperance Board was born out of revival and hopefulness, however misplaced its optimism. The eventual rulers of the Methodist Building were, in contrast, distrustful and resentful over the movement and nation that had endowed them. None of this cynicism was evident at the beginning. "In order to make effectual the efforts of the church to create the public sentiment and crystallize the same into successful opposition to the organized traffic in intoxicating liquors, the General Conference hereby authorizes the organization of a Board of Temperance, Prohibition, and Public Morals," declared the 1916 General Conference of the Methodist Episcopal Church. This new agency, whose antecedent agency dated even before 1912, would be based in Washington, D.C.

First headquartered in an ancient structure that had housed the U.S. Supreme Court after the U.S. Capitol was burned in 1814, the Temperance Board's first general secretary, Oregon pastor and tireless temperance activist Clarence True Wilson, was walking about Washington when he noticed three vacant lots across from the Capitol's Senate wing. "I believe that God kept those lots for us and we are going to buy them," he confidently surmised. As the 1928 General Conference observed, "Today there stands on that location a white building which is . . . a visible indication, not of Methodism's purpose to interfere with government but of its watchful and patriotic interest in the attitude of its country towards the great moral questions of the day."

Wilson's primary zeal was reserved for fighting the liquor traffic. But he was steadfast in his orthodox theology. He told the 1920 General Conference of the Methodist Episcopal Church that liberal theology had defeated Germany in World War I. Germany had been "the bulwark of Protestant Christianity," Wilson recounted, but the nation became "backslidden" in the 19th century through a "process it called 'higher criticism' to undermine the faith of the people in the integrity of their own Book."

As Wilson warned his fellow Methodists, Germany's theological liberalism "sought to explain away every sacred thing in her own religion, the inspiration of the prophets and the miracles of Jesus; the virgin birth and the resurrection, the ascension and the Pentecost." This "materialistic philosophy dismissed God and annihilated the souls of men in leaving the Spirit a nonentity, and thought but the result of physical forces at play. When religion had evaporated there was nothing for morals to stand on. You cannot have a moral system without a religious basis."

Clearly Wilson hoped that the General Conference would heed Germany's sad example. In contrast to Germany's theological liberalism, he insisted that that the "whole Bible" had given America its "national ideals, our moral standards" and should be returned "back into the public schools." He continued: "The Book that Washington kissed and Lincoln loved ought to come back that educated Americans may have some knowledge of the book that has made our type of civilization and that our children may have an intellectual foundation of American morality."

Wilson, hoping to institutionalize such biblical ideals in Washington, D.C., in 1920 had successfully encouraged "erecting a suitable building in the nation's capital." He enthused: "We believe there is no cause for which Methodists are asked to give their money which will result in larger dividends for the Kingdom in the establishment of civic righteousness, in the furnishing of a medium for activities of Methodism in the nation's capital, in signalizing the influence which God calls us to exert upon the greatest representatives of democracy among the nations of the earth, than the erection of this temperance, prohibition and public morals center of world activities just fronting the doors of the Capitol of the United States." He reported that $25,000 already had been pledged by the Woman's Christian Temperance Union of the $300,000 that was needed for the building. "We have this building site clear," he earnestly related. "We have the plans perfected. We have marble in keeping with the capital buildings." Wilson was clearly a Methodist man of action.

Although devoted mostly to alcohol issues, the Temperance Board was also concerned about Sabbath "desecration," narcotics and cigarettes, the "beastliness" of prize fighting, the "immoral influence" of the motion picture industry and prostitution. In its report to the 1920 General Conference, the Board emphasized the importance of "obedience to the laws of God, the sanctity of marriage, the evil of unscriptural divorce, and the single standards of morality for both sexes."

The Methodist Building was dedicated on January 16, 1924. President Calvin Coolidge wrote in a letter to the Temperance Board's presiding bishop: "This structure will stand as a temple dedicated to the purposes of inculcating obedience to law, respect for the righteous fundamentals of society, and law enforcement as a basis of absolute impartiality as between individuals or classes. It will visualize to all here in the nation's capital the definite and concrete aim to maintain our institutions on the firm moral basis which the founders intended them to stand."

A close friend of Wilson's, though not himself a Methodist, famed orator William Jennings Bryan keynoted the building's dedication. Himself an outspoken champion of Christian orthodoxy, Bryan declared in his ode to the new Methodist Building: "Back of those who contributed to this building is the intangible spirit of the Methodist Episcopal Church. It is the sentiment back of this building that built it and now stands behind it. He presciently warned: "If that sentiment should ever depart, someone else would take possession of this structure and what we are now consecrating might be desecrated." The original Methodist Building of the 1920s housed the Old Board of Temperance, the district superintendent of the Washington District and the resident bishop of the Washington Area, plus the legislative headquarters of the Women's Christian Temperance Union (WCTU). The rest of the building comprised residential apartments, whose rent generated $30,000 annually for the Temperance Board.

Even at difficult financial times, the Temperance Board seemed relatively prosperous, thanks to the widespread support of thousands of Methodists. At the 1936 General Conference, the Board reported the Methodist Building's value at $1,100,000 even at deflated Depression prices. And the Board's equity was $600,000. The Board, ever zealous in its cause, intoned to the 1944 General Conference that "when the prosecution of war calls for sober men and women to serve for victory, when sobriety is none too small a sacrifice to lay on the altar of patriotism, when strength in life alone is enough for times of national crisis, the church calls its people to take the lead in a movement for temperance." In 1956, the Board reported total assets of just under $1.1 million, including $700,000 in real estate and almost $300,000 in investments.

As of 1960, the *Discipline* still specified that the Old Board of Temperance's duty was to "promote . . . voluntary total abstinence from all intoxicants and narcotics . . . and to seek the suppression of salacious and corrupting literature and degrading amusements, lotteries and other forms of gambling." But interest in suppressing "vice" was waning among the liberal elites that by now governed most of Methodism. These new elites were far more interested in the church's addressing more provocative issues of social justice. They successfully urged the merger of the Temperance Board into a larger Board of Christian Social Concerns, which was the predecessor agency of the current Board of

Church and Society.

The Old Temperance Board would briefly be known as the Division of Alcohol Problems within this new broader agency. In 1965, no doubt fearing further inroads on its autonomy and foreseeing the dwindling interest in alcohol concerns by the new regime, the Old Temperance Board drew up a "Declaration of Trust" for "The Methodist Building Endowment Fund." Recalling that "in the early days in the years following 1912, large sums were collected on a nationwide basis to further the work in the area of temperance and alcohol problems," the Declaration sought to guarantee that these assets would remain devoted to "purposes for which the funds were originally given, that is to say, work in the areas of temperance and alcohol problems."

Seeking to avoid any ambiguity, the Declaration cited the phrase "temperance and alcohol problems" 13 times across five pages in describing the exclusive focus of the Methodist Building Endowment Fund. Both the principle and accumulated income of the Trust were to be devoted permanently to temperance and alcohol problems. The Methodist Building, a second Washington, D.C., property, and more than $500,000 in stocks were defined as the corpus of the Trust. The value of the Methodist Building was estimated at $1.5 million. The second property's value was pegged at $400,000. "It is the purpose and intent that the Trust Fund be invested and reinvested so as to produce an income to be applied and used for the Trust purposes," the Declaration stated. The trustees of the Trust were declared to be the executive committee of the Division of Alcohol Problems or its successor agency, i.e., the General Board of Church and Society (GBCS).

In 1960, the General Conference added words affecting the Trust that largely remain intact in today's *Discipline*: "Funds vested in any of the predecessor boards shall be conserved for the exclusive use of the appropriate division and for the specific purposes for which such funds have been given." But by the 1970s, the Declaration was already being reinterpreted to justify expenditures outside of "temperance and alcohol problems" by the new and increasingly radicalized GBCS.

Now functioning as the denomination's political lobby office in Washington, GBCS gained legal advice during the 1970s that asserted the Trust could fund activities relating not just to temperance and alcohol but also "public morals, drugs, gambling and general welfare type problems of individuals." But then and later, legal advisors warned against over expanding the meaning of the Declaration of Trust. A legal opinion for the Board sought in 2002 warned, "The language of the Declaration of Trust is quite specific. We doubt that it could realistically be interpreted to stretch any further." The lawyer suggested that for an "expansion" of the Fund's permitted uses the Board could bring suit before the Superior Court of Washington, D.C. That court could release the Trust's restriction if it's "obsolete, inappropriate or impracticable."

GBCS was shopping for legal opinions in 2002 because of a challenge to its very wide interpretation of the Trust Declaration. A retired insurance adjustor in Richardson, Texas who heads a small group called the Independent Group on Alcohol and Drugs for United Methodists, Howard Lydick was an old temperance activist who was challenging GBCS through a letter-writing campaign to bishops and other church officials. He persistently charged that the Trust was improperly funding general operating expenses rather than temperance work, and his campaign was sufficiently plausible to arouse worries within Church and Society.

Lydick's concern also eventually aroused the Review and Audit Committee of the United Methodist General Council on Finance and Administration. "It is unconscionable for GBCS management to convey and assert to legal counsel that temperance and alcohol work is no longer an emphasis of the UMC in order to justify using trust income for other purposes," wrote committee member Joe Whittemore of Hartwell, Georgia, on January 21,

2004, to committee chairman R. Stanley Sutton of Worthington, Ohio. "What GBCS has done over the years is, in effect ignore the Trust document," Whittemore disclaimed. "They have looked for ways around the trust provisions and have done what they pleased with the assets and income from the assets placed in trust. They have not strictly accounted for the assets or income from the assets. I believe these type actions and this type attitude places at risk the integrity of our church and our credibility to be trusted in future fiduciary capacities."

I submitted legislation to the 2004 General Conference calling for GBCS' compliance with the 1965 Declaration of Trust. In the Church and Society legislative committee, Oklahoma delegate Jessica Moffatt, a GBCS director, stepped down from her position as committee chair to defend GBCS's public claim that it is in full compliance with the Trust. The committee voted against my proposal. On the floor of General Conference, Judge Ron Enns was prepared to give a minority report. But Bishop Ernest Lyght of New York who was presiding, ruled Enns's proposal to be out of order. Lyght ruled out of order all six delegates on the floor who attempted to address the issue. Bill Smallwood of Mississippi asked that copies of the Trust document be distributed to delegates. "We've been told that it's been complied with, and I simply do not believe that's the truth," he said. Lyght referred Smallwood to GBCS for further information.

Howard Lydick had proposed to General Conference the creation of a new Commission on Alcohol and Drugs, whose income would come from the Methodist Building Endowment Fund. Delegate Jared Thomas, a college student from East Ohio, asked, "If our United Methodist universities condone underage drinking in their own freshman dorms, how much more does our world need to hear and be ministered to in light of the terrible evils of addiction?" Thomas reported that in 1960, 70 denominations were using materials produced by Methodism's Temperance Board. But now GBCS does not even have a specific budget line item for alcohol concerns. "If it is argued out that they [GBCS] will be losing money for other projects, it will only be because they were not following their moral obligation to follow the Trust in the first place," he said. General Conference delegates voted 66% to 34% to refer the proposal for study by GBCS!

Although General Conference failed to act, the Review and Audit Committee remained attentive to GBCS non-compliance with the Trust. In September 2005 the committee refused to approve GBCS's audit because of the Trust issue, declaring: "We cannot state with assurance that there have been no illegal acts; and cannot accept the 2004 Financial Disclosures regarding the Building Trust, as they are presently written." A mini-crisis arose between the two church agencies, prompting GBCS to begin litigation. Bishop James Swanson of the Holston Conference, chairman of the building's trustees, urged GBCS's directors at their October 2005 meeting in Washington, D.C. not to fret. "The trustees are not anxious about this," he insisted, announcing that they were going to the Superior Court of Washington, D.C., to seek judicial relief from the Trust's unwelcome constraints. "We would seek the declaratory judgment so that we can put this to rest one way or another," the bishop said. "Don't be fighting and fussing. Behave like persons who have been transformed by the blood of Jesus Christ." He also pledged to abide by the court's ruling, without appealing the decision.

GBCS General Secretary Jim Winkler still did some fussing: "There is a campaign of deliberate disinformation, distortion and misrepresentation taking place about the so-called misuse of the United Methodist Building Endowment Fund." He insisted, "The claim that the income is being misspent is the great urban legend of the United Methodist Church."

The financial stakes were high for GBCS. It derives about one third of its five-million-dollar annual income from the Methodist Building's gross rental income. About 10 percent of its income comes from $12 million in stock assets. And often about 15 percent of its income has come from released assets. Only about 40 percent of GBCS income comes from World Service giving by local churches. Since much if not most of GBCS stock assets probably date to the Old Temperance Board (although no public accounting has been presented in recent years), a majority of GBCS's annual income depends on the Methodist Building Endowment Fund, including both rental income and stock assets.

Despite the controversy and high stakes, most GBCS directors were remarkably passive and incurious at meetings. But the Rev. Robert Renfroe of Houston, Texas, pressed for details, asking if directors could have copies of the Declaration of Trust at the October 2005 meeting. Bishop Swanson reluctantly said yes but warned: "Reading it by itself would be prejudicial. It's only partial truth." The bishop claimed that the Trust needed to be "interpreted" through a series of historical documents dating back to 1917.

Reluctantly at that meeting GBCS staff placed on a back table a few copies of the 1965 Declaration of Trust, along with several legal opinions from the early and mid-1970's. But only a few directors picked them up. Dissatisfied by GBCS' inability to justify its policies towards the Trust, Renfroe soon after resigned from the Board. Meanwhile, Winkler complained to the directors that there "has not been a day, including weekends, that I haven't had to spend on this issue" of the Trust. And outspoken liberal director Jo Ann Fukumoto of Hawaii expressed indignation that the General Council on Finance and Administration would "accuse" the directors of possible "illegalities."

"I have found not a single shred of evidence to indicate any abuse of funds," Winkler further insisted. He asserted that the money given early in the 20th century to the Old Temperance Board for construction of the Methodist Building was "given to address a broad range of social concerns" beyond just alcohol. He also claimed that the "fight against the abuse of alcohol" remains a "historic concern" for his agency, even though there is no specific budget line item for GBCS regarding alcohol concerns. On February 7, 2007, GBCS asked the D.C. Superior Court to declare that GBCS may "expend income from these assets. . . for purposes other than the problems associated with alcohol issues."

At GBCS's March 2007 directors meeting, Bishop Swanson explained that the court ruling that GBCS sought would not only allow continued usage of the trust funds for broader political purposes, but would also retroactively validate past spending. "We have filed this [legal motion] to make sure we are doing what is proper," the bishop said, noting that "this [trust fund issue] has continued to consume a lot of time and energy of our staff." At GBCS's September 2007 directors meeting, it was announced that five "interveners" had been accepted into the litigation by the D.C. Superior Court to argue for compliance with the Trust. But no directors expressed any outward concern.

The Methodist Building's story illustrates the larger epic of liberal Protestantism, which, after decades of implosion, is fast drawing to a close. The constituency and the money for its aberrant theologies and corrosive politics are drying up. A bisexual rabbi who headlines a press conference on the Methodist Building's lawn is a near perfect book-end for the radical era that is soon to conclude. That an Islamic official from a dubious group should quote the Koran at the same event is also highly appropriate. Unlike many of the current residents of the Methodist Building, the Muslim cleric actually believed in the authority of his scripture, and in the transcendent power of his doctrines.

Nearly a century ago, the Old Temperance Board's intentions were magnificent. But their optimism about the institutional church's power to guide the nation's conscience was probably overstated. A more realistic appreciation of human nature could have potentially predicted that the Temperance Board's successors would end up in court, striving to overturn the legal restrictions that were to guard the original dimes and nickels of temperance's early supporters.

Through the court GBCS wants litigating to protect its unfettered access to the Methodist Building Endowment Fund. But whether it wins or loses, GBCS will continue to decline. Its radicalized social gospel protest theologies of the 1960s are dated and unpopular. But what will replace GBCS' current failed policies? And will there always be a Methodist Building on Capitol Hill in Washington, D.C.?

CHAPTER   EIGHT

UNITED METHODIST SUPPORT FOR TERRORISTS AND FIDEL CASTRO?

In 1999 President Clinton granted clemency for 16 imprisoned Puerto Rican terrorists, briefly igniting a political brouhaha. Both houses of Congress overwhelmingly denounced any early release for the Puerto Rican separatists, who robbed banks and set off bombs killing several people. A U.S. Department of Justice report later acknowledged that their release would hamper deterrence against domestic terrorism.

The inmates had for some time been a cause célèbre for the Religious Left, including the United Methodist General Board of Church and Society (GBCS). And I was there when GBCS first unveiled its support for the terrorists, likening them to the Apostles Peter and Paul! It was one more cause emanating from the Methodist Building that would have mightily surprised its Old Temperance Board founders.

During the final minutes of GBCS's October 1995 directors meeting, the board unanimously called for the immediate release of 16 Puerto Rican "political prisoners." The resolution unabashedly likened the prisoners to Nelson Mandela, America's Founding Fathers, the Apostles Peter and Paul and even Jesus.

"We see in Scripture how some of our greatest spiritual heroes spent time in jail for political reasons," the GBCS resolution intoned, as it noted that "colonialism" (which the United States supposedly practiced in Puerto Rico) is a "crime," as defined by the United Nations.

The 16 inmates were Puerto Rican separatists whose groups had plotted and perpetrated several years of murderous bombings, robbery, kidnapping and other mayhem during the late 1970s and early 1980s. Most had served with the Armed Forces for National Liberation (Spanish acronym: FALN), while several were affiliated with the Macheteros (the Machete Wielders). One of the prisoners had been on the FBI's "10 most wanted" list during the 1970s. They received sentences of up to 90 years for their crimes.

GBCS claimed that the terrorists had "taken up arms against the colonizer," and GBCS lamented that their "resistance" had been "criminalized." According to GBCS, the "actions of the Puerto Rican political prisoners are comparable to those of American patriots. Our patriots denounced the tyranny of British control over their colonies. They fought for the principle of democracy, and gained independence." It incredibly continued: "The Puerto Rican political prisoners are conscientious activists for freedom and justice, not criminals."

The GBCS resolution claimed that the Puerto Rican terrorists had received harsh prison sentences compared to "preferential treatment given to people linked to right-wing, anti-communist, or anti-abortion groups accused of violent crimes." In comparing the inmates to Jesus, St. Peter and St. Paul, all of whom were persecuted, GBCS declared: "All were seen as subversives to the colonizing powers." GBCS resolved to send its appeal for the terrorists' release to President Clinton, asking him to grant pardons. Remarkably, there was little discussion among the directors about what most United Methodists would regard as highly controversial. The few conservatives on the board had already left for the airport at this time.

Afterwards, I sought comment from these conservative directors, several of whom gladly—and strongly—replied. One of them was the Rev. Joseph Harris, then a district superintendent in Oklahoma and later the general secretary of United Methodist Men. He regretted that GBCS had ignored the "left-wing history" of the Puerto Rican prisoners and added, "whatever the cause, nothing can justify the use of terrorism."

Former Virginia District Superintendent Eugene Wooldridge Jr. blamed the resolution on the "self-serving agenda" of GBCS staff. He observed that GBCS had pushed United Methodism into a "liberalized corner," where the church shall "ultimately perish" unless the "mainstream" rejects GBCS's politics. San Antonio attorney Donald Hand called the GBCS resolution "perverse" and "radical." He observed that the statement had failed to describe the "cowardly bombings" committed by the "convicts."

IRD disseminated a news release about GBCS's support for the Puerto Rican inmates, quoting from the conservative directors. And I later wrote an op-ed about it for the *Washington Times*. I described one of the terrorists who had worked by day for the Episcopal Church translating hymnals into Spanish, while by night he utilized his apartment as a bomb factory. The FBI suspected he was using the church to disguise his terrorism. "Sadly," I concluded, "even after he has been in prison for 16 years, he and the other Puerto Rican inmates still are [using the church to disguise terrorism]." Commentator Cal Thomas did a national radio commentary based on our news release. "The board [GBCS] is the largest church lobby in Washington," Thomas opined. "Remember that the next time you hear an attack on right wing religious extremists!" He wondered, "Now that we see liberal groups formed to oppose the so-called Religious Right, who is going to oppose the United Methodist Board of Church and Society? Thank goodness the Institute on Religion and Democracy is."

The amnesty call for the Puerto Rican terrorists had been written by GBCS staff Eliezer Valentín-Castañón, a clergy from New Jersey who was of Puerto Rican background. A Spanish-speaking missionary friend of mine who then worked in the Washington,

D.C., area arranged for me to have lunch with him and Valentín-Castañón. We pleasantly lunched at a Chinese restaurant on Capitol Hill, where Eliezer talked about his education at Drew Theological Seminary and his work for GBCS. He was very personable, and we avoided any direct debate, keeping our conversation personal. Twelve years later, Valentín-Castañón remains on the GBCS staff and is unfailingly friendly to me. Sometimes the familiarity of constant acquaintance over the years transcends, at least partly, intense political disagreements.

By no means did Valentín-Castañón step away from his advocacy on behalf of the Puerto Rican terrorists. In January 1997 he invited all United Methodist pastors in the Washington D.C., area to attend a prayer rally for the "political prisoners"at a Unitarian church. Valentín-Castañón asserted that "the pardon campaign is based on principles of social justice which have inspired and propelled many of us." The prayer vigil was urging the inmates' release based on "humanitarian grounds," he said. Valentín-Castañón was able to tell the pastors that the 1996 General Conference had approved a GBCS-initiated resolution that advocated for "justice and freedom for the Puerto Rican political prisoners."

Neither Valentín-Castañón nor GBCS ever openly admitted to the details of the inmates' crimes and goals. The prisoners claimed they are prisoners of war incarcerated for advocating a "free and socialist" Puerto Rico that is independent of the United States. The FALN, of which most of the prisoners were a part, was involved in 130 bomb attacks from 1974 to 1983 that killed six people, including a six-year-old, and injured 130 others, mostly in Chicago and New York. The Machete Wielders, to which the remainder of the prisoners belonged, masterminded a $7.1-million Wells Fargo robbery in Connecticut in 1983.

Most of the prisoners showed no remorse for their years of terrorism. "I have no regrets for serving a noble cause," Oscar Lopez Rivera announced from his federal prison cell in Marion, Illinois.

He was one of the two inmates who had refused clemency, which required the prisoners to reject future acts of violence. "Would we be willing to renounce the struggle for Puerto Rico's independence to get out of jail? I will never do that."

Although supporters of the prisoners complained of U.S. "colonialism," no plebiscite in Puerto Rico has ever shown more than a tiny fraction of the electorate favoring independence from the U.S. The Puerto Rican Independence Party typically gets five percent of the vote, and direct plebiscites on separatism have garnered even fewer votes.

Neither GBCS nor any of the other religious groups insisting on release for the terrorists ever demanded any repentance or remorse from the prisoners as a precondition of their release. When Clinton pardoned the Puerto Ricans on August 11, 1999, he at least required that they renounce violence, which not even GBCS had required as a condition for its support.

In the midst of GBCS and other church groups calling for the Puerto Rican terrorists' release, a young man from New York City phoned me, distressed about the religious pardon campaign. On January 24, 1975, his father had been one of four people killed by the FALN bombing of the historic Fraunces Tavern, which also injured 50 others. The young man, who was too young to have remembered his father well, was perplexed and angry by any prospective release of his father's murderers. I assured him that GBCS did not represent most United Methodists but could offer him little other consolation. His questions made me embarrassed for my church.

As the U.S. Congress prepared to vote its disapproval of Clinton's pardons for the Puerto Rican terrorists in late 2000, GBCS sternly warned "certain members of Congress to support the President and cease partisan campaigns of misinformation which have been so grievously supported by the media and some law enforcement agencies." The news release, which came from Valentín-Castañón, insisted that the pardoning of the "political prisoners" was a "right and just act." The U.S. Senate voted 95-2 to disapprove of the pardons, and the U.S. House of Representatives voted likewise 311-41.

Again during the Clinton Administration GBCS advocated for a dubious pardon, this time for convicted murderer Leonard Peltier, who was convicted in 1977 for killing two FBI agents in 1975 at the Pine Ridge Indian Reservation in South Dakota. Some radical groups claimed that Peltier was framed because he was supposedly a leader in the American Indian Movement (AIM). Peltier was sentenced to two consecutive life terms and has been repeatedly denied parole.

At their April 1999 meeting, GBCS directors voted unanimously to ask President Clinton to grant Peltier an "executive clemency." The GBCS statement asserted that he had been "falsely accused and falsely convicted," according to his parole hearings. GBCS General Secretary Thom White Wolf Fassett reported to the directors that he already personally urged clemency for Peltier to President Clinton and to U.S. Attorney General Janet Reno.

"Leonard Peltier did not commit those murders," Fassett assured the directors. Fassett claimed that another person, "known to the Native American community," had confessed to the killings. Meanwhile, he warned that Peltier is "dying" in a federal prison, and the prison was denying him medical care. In fact, Peltier remains alive today, 8 years later. "I used to talk to Leonard," Fassett confided. "He used to call me from Leavenworth." Fassett described Peltier as "the only Native American political prisoner from the activist era of the 1970s."

An April 27, 1999 United Methodist News Service (UMNS) report about the GBCS endorsement of Peltier uncritically accepted GBCS's claims. UMNS called Peltier an "internationally recognized Native American activist" who has been "recognized as a human rights defender." According to UMNS, Peltier had nobly been at Pine Ridge to "support the Oglala Sioux, whose land was under threat of government mining." As UMNS told it, "tensions were high" and a "gunfight ensued," as though the ambush by Peltier and his cohorts of two isolated FBI agents were little more than a gang brawl. UMNS claimed that "Human rights activists charge that Peltier was framed and convicted with no supporting evidence." And it quoted a federal judge alleging "misconduct" by the FBI, while passing over the fact that all of Peltier's appeals had been rejected.

Actually, the legal case against Peltier was considerably stronger than Fassett, GBCS or UMNS admitted. Peltier initially confessed to killing the two FBI agents. Later, he changed his story that he had only shot at them but that somebody else delivered the final coup de grâce to the wounded officers. They were shot execution-style while lying prostrate on the ground after a shoot-out with possibly dozens of American Indian Movement (AIM) militants. The wife of an AIM leader would later testify that she had personally overheard Peltier boast: "The mother f--ker was begging for his life, but I shot him anyway."

In 1975 the two murdered FBI agents, 28-year-old Jack Coler and 27-year-old Ronald Williams, followed a van carrying several men with rifles onto a ranch where Peltier was residing. The van stopped and its passengers came out shooting. The agents were trapped by their car in an open field. Armed only with service revolvers and one shotgun, they got off only five shots and were nearly defenseless against long-range rifles. Their car was shot at least 125 times.

After shooting only once, Coler's arm was nearly severed by return fire. Williams, already shot in his side, attempted to apply a tourniquet to his colleague. Coler was unconscious and Williams, realizing that further resistance was futile, apparently attempted to surrender. They both were executed instead. Williams held up his hand in front of his executioner's gun before the bullet smashed into his face. Coler was then shot in the head and throat.

Dozens of Peltier's militant colleagues may have been present at the ranch and participated in the gunfight. An FBI rescue party killed one and captured another, but Peltier and the rest escaped. Later, an Oregon state trooper stopped a vehicle that Peltier was driving. Peltier responded with gunfire and escaped into the woods. He left behind in his vehicle Agent Coler's revolver with Peltier's thumbprint on it, along with eight other guns, a collection of hand grenades and 350 pounds of dynamite.

Peltier later escaped to Canada, where he was captured by the Royal Canadian Mounted Police in 1976. After a lengthy appeals process, he was extradited to the United States to face trial. He admitted to Canadian police that he thought the FBI had been pursuing him to serve a warrant for his arrest in the 1972 attempted shooting of a Milwaukee police officer.

During Peltier's 1977 trial, the prosecution produced three witnesses who said they saw Peltier walk toward the wounded FBI agents with an AR-15 rifle moments before the fatal shots. A jury in Fargo, North Dakota, took ten hours to convict Peltier on two counts of murder, for which he would be legally guilty even if he had not shot the actual bullets that killed the FBI agents. He was given two consecutive life sentences.

In November 1999, the Free Leonard Peltier Committee rallied in the nation's capital. Using the United Methodist Building on Capitol Hill as their headquarters, they demonstrated in front of the White House and lobbied congressional officers on behalf of their imprisoned hero. Religious groups like the National Council of Churches and the United Methodist Board of Church and Society have joined the campaign. These crusaders see Peltier as one of the most recent victims of U.S. misdeeds against Native Americans.

"He was a scapegoat used by a system seeking to 'settle up' or even the score against vocal Native Americans," Fassett said. "Since he was a well-known Native American figure, he was specifically targeted as a suspect."

Defenders of Peltier, such as Fassett and GBCS, portrayed him as a significant American Indian Movement (AIM) leader. But Peltier was only a "bodyguard" for AIM. He performed "security" for AIM when its leaders ransacked the Bureau of Indian Affairs in 1972. The defenders also ignored Peltier's long history of violence. He was implicated, but not convicted, in the attempted murder of a Milwaukee policeman in 1972, for which he jumped bail. And in 1973 he was linked to shootings of two policemen at the Pine Ridge Reservation in South Dakota. He also jumped bail on an illegal weapons charge in Washington State.

Peltier himself has never expressed any regrets. "I was there that day," he has said of the murders for which he was convicted. "I've never denied that. But we were attacked, and we had a right to defend ourselves, and so I fired back." He sees himself as a martyr and gladly accepts the mythology that has grown up around him. His signature includes "In the Spirit of Crazy Horse."

During the 1999-2000 campaign for a Peltier clemency, the FBI Agents Association suggested that Peltier's victims and their families are the rightful recipients of sympathy, rather than Peltier. This suggestion was unheeded by GBCS. Two retired FBI agents who belonged to United Methodist churches in the Dallas area publicly challenged GBCS to repudiate its support of Peltier. The April 21, 2000, *United Methodist Reporter* more factually described the details of the Peltier murder case.

"What's at issue here is the accountability of the church," former FBI agent Herbert Hoxie told the *Reporter*. "We pay for this board to exist, and yet they publish blatant untruths such as this!" In response, Thom Fassett did not back down: "We stand behind the resolution passed by our Board of Directors and the press release announcing that resolution."

As his presidential term was ending, rumors circulated that Bill Clinton might pardon Peltier as he had pardoned the Puerto Rican prisoners. Five hundred FBI agents and their families protested on December 15, 2000, outside the White House against Peltier's release, while FBI Director Louis Freeh wrote Clinton opposing any clemency, advice that Clinton accepted. Peltier today remains in prison.

The cases of Leonard Peltier and the Puerto Rican prisoners were both tangentially related to the Cold War. They committed their crimes in the 1970s, and they became heroes of the international left because they portrayed themselves as heroic resisters to U.S. oppression. Both Soviet front groups and non-Marxist left-wing groups around the world spotlighted Peltier and the Puerto Rican inmates as their poster children across years of propaganda and publicity.

Under Thom White Wolf Fassett during the Cold War's final years and the immediate aftermath, GBCS stayed closely aligned with the international left on Cold War issues. One even more direct example was GBCS's consistently uncritical attitude toward Fidel Castro's communist dictatorship in Cuba. Fassett met with Castro several times and strongly lobbied against U.S. sanctions against the Castro regime. Revealingly, Fassett did not argue that lifting U.S. sanctions would undermine Castro's dictatorship, whose repression never seemed a major issue with Fassett. Instead, GBCS under Fassett and under his successor have faulted Cuba's communist-created poverty almost exclusively upon U.S. policies.

GBCS under Fassett worked closely with Pastors for Peace under the Rev. Lucius Walker, an unabashed fan of Castro. "I would be honored to have a person like Fidel as president of my own country," Walker enthused in a 1999 interview. "He's a person of great integrity." Walker commended Cuba's wisdom for not rushing to multi-party democracy, which would allow the U.S. to buy elections as he believes it has elsewhere in the Third World. "I think democracy is expressed in [Cuba's] current system," he said. "Arguably it's among the most democratic in the world."

A former executive with the National Council of Churches (NCC), Walker organized "Pastors for Peace" in 1988 from his hospital bed, while recovering from wounds inflicted by the anti-

Marxist Contras in Nicaragua. Walker's new group wanted to support the "victims" of "low-intensity warfare" waged by the United States and its proxies against oppressed Third World peoples.

Starting in 1992, Pastors for Peace began challenging U.S. trade sanctions against Castro by organizing seven "Friendship Caravans" of material aid for Cuba and refusing to apply for licenses from the U.S. Treasury Department. "To send simple aid to our Cuban brothers and sisters we shouldn't have to ask the permission of their enemy," Walker explained.

For his efforts, Walker and his colleagues received medals from Castro personally in 1996. Upon receipt of his reward, the Baptist pastor from Brooklyn hailed Cuba's communist system as exemplifying the social values preached by Jesus. Castro responded: "I do not have words to express the highest appreciation for what they have done." He called Walker's work "one of the most beautiful stories of solidarity ever written."

In 1994 Pastors for Peace organized an historic meeting in New York between Castro and 100 U.S. church leaders, including Fassett. "We did not want the revolution to be anti-church or anti-clergy," Castro patiently explained to an appreciative audience. "We fought within the Party to establish that even those with religious beliefs should be able to join the Party and participate in government."

"Sometimes the church has issued strong pastoral letters against the revolution," Castro was also careful to include. "We do our best to be tolerant." He effusively thanked Pastors for Peace. "Like the early Christians, they have been willing to stand up for their beliefs, even against those who would crucify them." Castro told the assembled church leaders representing 20 Protestant, Roman Catholic and ecumenical groups: "We love you very specially and always welcome you to our country."

The most hair-raising caravan adventure of Pastors for Peace's was in 1996, when the U.S. Customs Service decided not to ignore Walker's open violation of U.S. trade policy toward Cuba.

A 30-vehicle caravan carrying 200 activists and 300 computers was blocked at the Mexican border south of San Diego by U.S. Customs officers. To back them up, around 100 San Diego police officers and California Highway Patrolmen in riot gear lined up at the border, in case the caravaneers should attempt to cross the border on foot.

As expected, Pastors for Peace activists dismounted from their vehicles and began running their computers towards the border, trying to ram through U.S. Customs officials and police officers. Ten members of the caravan were arrested, and seven others were detained after resisting attempts to seize the computers. The melee injured one protester and four Customs inspectors, three of whom required hospital treatment. According to Pastors for Peace, their activists had been trained in "non-violent techniques." Walker later said he had never seen law enforcement behave so brutally.

To protest the U.S. confiscation of the computers, Walker and three colleagues began a hunger strike on February 21, 1996, near the Mexican border crossing. In April, they moved their fast to the United Methodist Building in Washington, D.C. "I'm 65," Walker melodramatically pronounced, "I simply don't want to live any longer in a country that continues to hurt people the way my country does." He professed to be living on a diet of water, lemon juice and maple syrup.

"Our government has pursued a policy of death toward Cuba for half of my life time," said Walker, "Working with [U.S. policy] is to be in complicity with killing our neighbors 90 miles south of Florida. I'd rather lose my life than lose my soul." He contrasted himself with "right-wing groups" that are sending computers to "dissident" groups in Cuba.

Walker rarely if ever acknowledged that the food, clothing and medicine for humanitarian purposes could be shipped legally to Cuba if licensed under the Trading with Enemies Act. Nor did they explain why the computers could not have been shipped quietly through Mexico or Canada without the fanfare of caravans and civil disobedience. In a joint press conference with Walker, Fassett called the U.S. an "outlaw nation" because of its sanctions against Cuba.

During Walker's hunger strike in the Methodist Building, Freedom House, a Washington-based human rights monitor, sent Walker a list of 1,000 political prisoners, including Christian clergy, who were detained in Cuban prisons. Walker did not respond. Instead, Walker contrasted "Cuba's example of good will to its own people" with the "outpouring of hatred, abuse and violence by our own government against us." He claimed the "U.S. is committed not to democracy but to the destruction of democracy." And he blasted "right-wing Cubans" who left their homeland to live in Cuba's enemy. Unlike exiled Cubans, Walker said he would remain in his native land, despite the "hegemony and abuse of power" by the U.S. government.

Walker's hunger strike was politically successful. In late May 1996, the U.S. Treasury Department finally acquiesced, turning the computers over to GBCS, in whose building Walker was still encamped. The computers were finally shipped to Cuba in September 1996 for use in several hospitals. In solidarity with Pastors for Peace, GBCS officials insisted they never asked for a license. But the U.S. Treasury Department still granted one to GBCS so as to close the issue.

Even more controversially, and gaining far more nationwide publicity, was GBCS' support for sending six year-old Elián Gonzalez back to Fidel Castro's Cuba. In 1999, Elián was escaping from Castro's Cuba in a small boat with his mother and several other refugees when the boat sank, and his mother drowned. Elián reached Florida and was living with his relatives there when the Cuban government pressured Elián's father to demand Elián's return to Cuba. Washington super lawyer Greg Craig, who had also represented Bill Clinton during his impeachment, represented Elián's father.

At GBCS, Fassett created a "Humanitarian Advocacy Fund" to help fund legal expenses for Elián's return to Cuba. Although there was no public appeals for the fund, it quickly raised tens of thousands of dollars, from sources that Fassett declined to reveal. It was speculated that Dwayne Andreas of agri-business giant Archers Daniels Midland was a source. Andreas was anxious to expand his already considerable business dealings with the Castro regime, publicly opposed the U.S. sanctions and had already contributed $1.3 million to the National Council of Churches, which was also active in the campaign to return Elián to Cuba.

On April 12, 2000, Fox News' Brit Hume pressed Fassett for details about his fundraising for Greg Craig. Fassett explained that he had approached Craig about representing Elián's father, and that Craig was "being paid through a voluntary contributions fund set up by the executive committee" of GBCS. Hume asked Fassett how the fund was created, and Fassett explained: "We initially set it up at the request of persons who wanted to contribute funds in order to help in this effort."

Hume asked Fassett, "Is it troubling to you, as a man of faith, that in the country from which [Elián's father] Juan Miguel Gonzalez comes, to which this little boy will return, that freedom of religion is not practiced?" Fassett responded: "I have spent several hours negotiating with Fidel Castro myself," going on to say that he had "negotiated with Fidel Castro around principles of religious practice in Cuba." The Fox interview did not provide time for Fassett to explain what if any results came of his negotiation with Castro.

On April 10, 2000, I also was interviewed by Brit Hume on Fox News about Fassett's involvement in the Elián issue. Hume asked if the anonymous funds channeled through GBCS to Greg Craig were a "church version of soft money." I agreed that was accurate. I also explained that much of the media had described GBCS as an "impartial mediator" in the Elián case, when actually it is "almost reflexively left of center to far left on a whole range of political issues, domestic and foreign, Cuba being one issue that they've been outspoken on."

Hume asked if there were not "very powerful arguments that one can imagine a person of deep Christian faith making that say this young child should be with his father." I readily agreed but responded, "If it were just a matter of restoring the son to a father, I would say maybe the Roman Catholic Church, another denomination that hasn't been so outspokenly supportive or apologetic about the Castro government, would be a more appropriate mediator for the situation." I continued: "The Methodist Board of Church and Society has been so close with the Cuban government, I would think [that] should rule it out as being an appropriate player in this situation."

Not surprisingly, Florida United Methodists, who live among many anti-Castro Cuban exiles, were distressed by GBCS's involvement in the Elián case. Florida United Methodist Bishop Cornelius Henderson told *World* magazine that the GBCS action "took place in a presumptuous manner with no prior consultation with United Methodist leadership in Florida." The church's beliefs emphasize both the importance of family and political freedom, he said, and "It is painful to see one's church appear to lend support to a government whose record on human rights is not acceptable by Christian standards or the principles of the United Methodist Church."

Two weeks before the May 2000 General Conference in Cleveland, the United Methodist General Council on Finance and Administration told GBCS that its legal fund for Greg Craig violated church rules and must be closed. GBCS turned the $50,000 balance of the fund over to the National Council of Churches on April 19, 2004. At the General Conference a delegate asked Fassett to explain the fund to the Church and Society legislative committee.

Fassett complained about that "floating pieces of flotsam and jetsam, the disinformation and the misinformation" that had been circulating about the fund without specifying what those inaccuracies were. Although no church funds went directly to Greg Craig, Fassett admitted that GBCS staff time and travel expenses were incurred in the fund's administration. But he insisted that this money was "infinitesimal compared to larger issues." And he said the GBCS fund was being audited.

"This is about a child and a little boy," Fassett said. "We believe in family values." He argued that his board had not advocated Elián's return to Cuba, just his return to his father, although he did not explain the distinction. Fassett explained that he had organized the fund in response to pleas from the Cuban Council of Churches to "ensure equal representation before the law" for Elián's father, Juan Miguel Gonzalez.

Later, at a special GBCS banquet organized for delegates, Fassett boasted, "We broke the stalemate involving Elián." In an indirect criticism of Elián's mother, who drowned during their sea escape from Cuba, Fassett pointed out that little Elián "didn't choose to board an unsafe boat or live with distant relatives whom he had never met." Fassett's last point was incorrect, as Elián's great uncle and cousin, with whom he had stayed in Florida, had visited Elián in Cuba in 1998.

Fassett said that Elián's father never "chose to have his child taken from him." Elián's Florida relatives claimed that Elián's father had phoned them when his son and ex-wife left Cuba to alert them to their impending arrival in Florida. And Fassett also oddly blamed the U.S. embargo for preventing an earlier reunion between father and son. In fact, the U.S. Government, which had largely sided with Elián's father, never blocked his entry into the U.S. The timing of Elián's father's arrival instead seems to have been decided by the Cuban government. Fassett declined to acknowledge that it is Cuban government restrictions that prevent its citizens from leaving Cuba freely.

"Jesus doesn't let us withhold our mercy," Fassett implored as a justification for his Cuba policy. "We respond to cries for help even when unpopular." In an apparent reference to the United Methodist General Council of Finance and Administration, which compelled Fassett to abandon the fund, he said, "Coals [were brought] upon our heads by the bureaucracies of the church."

"It's not right that those who condemn Castro would abuse the rights of [Elián's father] Juan Miguel, abusing Juan Miguel for political reasons," Fassett said. "God will be our judge." Fassett also reported that he and his daughter had visited little Elián and his father at the Maryland estate where they were staying prior to departing for Cuba, along with Cuban government officials. "It was like coming into an American family," Fassett insisted.

The uproar over GBCS's legal fund to return Elián to Castro's Cuba was Fassett's last hurrah in Washington, D.C. His 12 years as GBCS general secretary ended in 2000, and he returned to Western New York to become a district superintendent. But his years as United Methodism's chief political spokesman in the nation's capital had crystallized perceptions of GBCS as radical and detached from mainstream church opinion. Would GBCS ever change?

CHAPTER NINE

REJECTING EVANGELISM AT THE MISSIONS BOARD?

During the 1980s, the United Methodist General Board of Global Ministries (GBGM) lacked interest in evangelism in favor of politicized "liberation theology." That had fueled the creation of the alternative Mission Society for United Methodists, now called the Mission Society. The 23-year-old Atlanta-based society, hoping to fill the void left by GBGM, now sends 223 missionaries around the world, most of them United Methodists.

GBGM's political and theological radicalism had also fueled my own personal vocation toward church reform, starting with my 1988 report to the administrative board of my local church in Arlington, Virginia about GBGM's spending priorities.

By 1998 I had spent four years attending GBGM's biannual directors' meetings as a reporter. GBGM usually met at a hotel in Stamford, Connecticut, about 30 miles outside New York City. After 1992, in response to criticism over the expenses of New York City, where each directors' meeting cost several hundred thousand dollars, GBGM moved its gatherings to the suburbs. By act of the 1996 General Conference, GBGM's board was also reduced from 180 directors to 90.

The meetings were still enormously expensive, of course. Directors were flown in from all over the world. Each gathering includes four days of plenary meetings, often preceded by additional days of committee meetings, not to mention the previous week's gathering of the Women's Division, whose riches help to ensure its influence over the rest of GBGM.

In October 1998, GBGM hosted Dr. Wesley Ariarajah, a former official of the World Council of Churches, who openly questioned the need for evangelism and personal conversion. Ariarajah, who teaches at United Methodism's Drew Seminary in New Jersey, was warmly received by GBGM's applauding directors and staff.

But a few directors privately expressed "consternation" over Ariarajah's dismissal of missions evangelism. At least one director noted that Ariarajah's speech contradicted what was then GBGM first priority in its missions statement, which was to "witness to Jesus Christ" to gain "an initial decision" for Christ.

In his speech, Ariarajah commended a "new understanding" of missions that included four shifts away from the traditional "Protestant party line" that once cited "Jesus as the only way to salvation." The first shift was a move from exclusion, which emphasizes Christ's centrality, to inclusion, which acknowledges truth in other religions.

Ariarajah's second shift was from the concept of "conversion" to the "process of healing." Instead of converting adherents of other faiths, he suggested showing how God can heal people wherever they are. The third shift involved moving from a majority to a minority mentality. Our goal, as the church, should not necessarily be to convert most people to Christ.

And Ariarajah's fourth shift de-emphasized doctrine in favor of "spirituality." Young people, he claimed, do not want to confine their religiosity to the church's ostensibly rigid beliefs. Ariarajah approvingly noted that Hindus see salvation as a lifelong process that moves toward total union with God.

"Other people [non-Christians] pray and have spirituality," Ariarajah said. "God is a god of all nations. All life is within God. This is a firm, clear biblical view." He regretted that the classical missionary movement had "a fear of . . . universalism [the belief that all people are saved] and syncretism [the belief that all religions are true]." He described Christians in his native Sri Lanka as believing that all Sri Lankans should accept Christ. But the church there comprises less than seven percent of the population, and converting the whole nation is not realistic. Instead, the church must realize that "Buddhists and Hindus are part of God's work of reconciliation."

Ariarajah claimed the early church did not seek to convert the world. "Jesus talked about healing and wholeness," not conversion, he said. "There's not one place where Paul demands that the church go out to world mission. He wanted communities that witness to truth." Ariarajah complained that the traditional missionary movement, although sincere, came to misinterpret its global role. Even the liberal idea of mission was once to "bring the whole world to Christ," he recalled. Missionaries once thought that the religions of the world must be "displaced by Christianity."

But Ariarajah insisted that the "whole creation will participate in the glory of God." The church's role is to witness to God's presence by not "worshiping mammon." We must show that God can heal, he said, rather than "dragging people" from one faith to another. "The whole world should not perhaps become Christian," Ariarajah concluded. "We should [instead] witness to the saving love of God that will bring all the world to perfection."

Ariarajah's speech was unusual in explicitly rejecting evangelism, even by GBGM's standards. GBGM's critics had long alleged that GBGM had denied the need for personal salvation in favor of social justice ministries. Typically, GBGM's defenders had denied the allegation. But Ariarajah's exposition drew public praise and little open criticism from the assembled directors and staff. GBGM's Evangelization and Church Growth Program committee hailed Ariarajah for having "enriched our understanding of expectations and objectives for engaging in the mission of evangelization in the new century."

Revealingly, in contrast to Ariarjah, another speaker was openly criticized for her remarks to GBGM. Episcopal priest Minka Sprague led the Bible study for GBGM's meeting. She seemingly was in sync with GBGM's liberalism, likening the recent murder of Matthew Shepherd, the young homosexual man in Wyoming, to the killings of civil rights activists in the South during the 1960s.

Speaking about leadership in history, Sprague then expressed admiration for George Washington's having freed his slaves in his will. Some directors afterwards expressed anger over her praise of the slave-owning president. The Committee for the Elimination of Institutional Racism condemned Sprague's "racist statements." For GBGM, rejecting evangelism was less controversial than commending George Washington! Another speaker at the GBGM meeting was an activist New York pastor who condemned "police brutality" under then Mayor Rudy Giuliani and called for drug legalization. No directors openly criticized his remarks.

Yet GBGM seemed perplexed that it remained highly controversial. Louisiana Bishop Dan Solomon, GBGM's president, criticized United Methodist groups that "denigrate the work of the board" in mass-produced fundraising letters, clearly referring to IRD. "There is a better story to hear than some people are hearing," said Solomon, who lamented that some laity base all their knowledge about GBGM upon such letters. "Stories whose appeal is alarm are fraught with harm," he warned.

At that time in 1998, GBGM had close to $400 million in assets. Its budget for 1999 was over $142 million, of which $16.4 million, or 11 percent, went toward missionaries. GBGM had 282 full-time career missionaries.

IRD's *UMAction Briefing* reported about Ariarajah's rejection of evangelism, and GBGM's evident approval, in an issue that went to more than 100,000 United Methodist homes. This reporting provoked a discussion at GBGM's April 1999 meet-

ing, where Bishop Solomon distributed an April 13, 1999 letter from Ariarajah, responding to UM*Action's* report. "The idea
that we should call and listen only to those who would repeat
and reconfirm what some of us already believe in, to me, looks
like a betrayal of the traditions of this country and our beloved
church," Ariarajah wrote, without specifically defending his missions theology. "It is not my intention to defend the contents of
my speech, for I am well aware that there are several other ways to
understand the evangelistic mission of the church, and I respect
those positions."

Ariarajah insisted there was "no truth" that the GBGM had "uncritically accepted or applauded my ideas." He said he had heard
both affirmation and disagreement in the "personal responses"
after his speech. GBGM director Robin Mitchell, a minister
from Hackensack, New Jersey, asked his fellow directors to affirm Ariarajah's "thought-provoking" presentation in response to
UM*Action's* "unfair and hostile characterizations." But Director
Joe Whittemore from Hartwell, Georgia, responded that he did
not "share the enthusiasm" for Ariarajah's comments. He said that
he had been troubled by the speech and thought GBGM should
not endorse Ariarajah's approach to missions. Whittemore noted
that GBGM had not featured speakers who offered "the other
side" in favor of evangelism and the Great Commission.

Bishop Solomon then summarized GBGM's statement as one
of appreciation for the "spirit" of Ariarajah's "gracious" April 13th
letter. But the resolution, as Solomon described it, fell short of
actually affirming Ariarajah's controversial speech or criticizing
IRD's coverage. Seemingly, GBGM preferred not to follow the
Board of Church and Society's earlier example of denouncing
IRD.

Although not so explicit as Ariarajah in rejecting the Great
Commission, the Bible study leader for GBGM's spring meet-
ing did hint in that direction. Cuban Presbyterian Minister Dora
Arce-Valentín of the Women's Department of the Christian

Peace Conference in Cuba described missions as a "dialogue" and a "dialectic" process rather than a conversion effort.

"I would be contradicting myself if I [as a missionary] said I was bringing the truth," said Arce-Valentín. Missionaries should instead speak of the "journey together" between themselves and the missioned. "Both have something to receive." Arce-Valentín lamented that missionaries have "treated people as if they have not much brains," and treated the Word of God as if it were a "vaccination." She said, "It is [in] the other where we find Jesus."

Arce-Valentín continued: "It doesn't matter how you worship God but how you live your worship." She affirmed the church should proclaim Jesus Christ and evangelize. But she was vague as to whether evangelism should win individuals to faith in Jesus Christ, or simply transform societies toward social justice. She warned against the "great transnationals of the global economy" that have expelled minorities to the periphery. And she recommended an interpretation of scripture that illustrated Jesus' rejection of the "centers of power" through geography. (An example: Jerusalem was a center of power, but Samaria was a land of the dispossessed.)

Behind the scenes of Ariarajah's and Arce-Valentín's speeches were debates over evangelism within GBGM's Mission Development Committee. Officially, GBGM's first priority was to "Witness to the Gospel for an Initial Decision to Follow Jesus Christ." The second goal was to renew Christian congregations, the third was to alleviate human suffering and the fourth was to "seek justice, freedom and peace," i.e., GBGM's political work. GBGM staff urged changing the first goal away from working for "initial decision to follow Jesus Christ" to more generically "making disciples of Jesus Christ." A director from upstate New York agreed, suggesting, "If we are not doing goal #1, maybe we should change the goal." But another director defended the "initial decision" language.

"We have no lack of enthusiasm for pushing our social agenda in many areas where our ideas are not welcome," he noted. "Why the reluctance to proclaim the Gospel with the same aggressiveness and proactive insistence as we proclaim our ideologies?" This director ended up voting for the wording change anyway, observing that it more closely reflected GBGM's reality, but he still called it a "significant mistake."

Another director on the committee, defending the language change, noted that the "concept of personal salvation is troublesome to me." He asked. "Can I be saved without the group to which I belong being saved? I don't think so! I do not see salvation as individualistic." At an earlier gathering of the committee, GBGM General Secretary Randy Nugent had urged that we can "reclaim evangelism as a priority for GBGM." But in the end, the Missions Development Committee moved GBGM in the opposite direction.

GBGM's theological difficulties were even more vividly evident at its April 1997 "Global Gathering" in Kansas City, where Brazilian Methodist theologian Nancy Pereira mocked the idea that Jesus Christ had died for the sins of the world. "We have to stop praising Abraham's knife, she implored. "We have to stop praising Solomon's sword. We have to stop praising Jesus' cross." Pereira affirmed that these "traditions" from the Bible portrayed a God who welcomes "child sacrifice." More than 4,000 United Methodists attended the quadrennial gathering, whose theme was "Whose Child is This?"

"We have to find other expressions of salvation and liberation," Pereria insisted. "We have developed a Christology with a tradition of the cross. That is a sacrificial Christology. It's a mechanism of salvation that heeds guilt, pain, whipping and death. We have to look at Jesus' cross as tragedy, a human episode without any sense of meaning." Although 10 United Methodist bishops spoke at the Global Gathering, none expressed any open disagreement there with Pereira's denial of Jesus Christ's atonement for the sins of the world.

Pereira asserted, "We cannot say that the cross was God's will. We have to change our point of view." As a replacement, she urged taking Jesus' birth and infancy as a "christology tradition" without sacrifice. "That child is a savior just because it's a child. Just because it's a poor child." But Pereira underscored that even the baby Jesus was not unique. "Jesus is not the messiah of himself. He is appointing the child as a criteria, as a mediation for taking part of the Kingdom of God. The messiah must always be a child. We have to learn how to look at those kids and say even again Immanuel. God with us."

This redefinition of the Incarnation as not uniquely in Jesus Christ but rather in every child was a bracing challenge to Christian orthodoxy. But few at the Global Gathering seemed to notice as thousands stood to applaud Pereira. Afterwards I wrote all the bishops who were at "Global Gathering III" to ask their views about Pereria's denial of the Atonement and of Jesus' uniqueness.

In response, GBGM chief Randy Nugent sent me a May 13, 1997 joint statement with GBGM President Bishop Solomon, which declared that Pereira had been invited because of her "commendable" ministry with street children in Brazil. "The theological views which she expressed were her own," it said. "Rev. Pereira was not invited to speak to the Global Gathering about nor because of her theological views." They insisted that GBGM "neither subscribes to her theological views nor agrees with the theological perspectives which she expressed." The statement declared that "when the views of speakers or leaders may have been in conflict with the doctrinal position" of United Methodism, GBGM "clearly and forthrightly affirms its strong adherence to United Methodist doctrine" as found in the church's *Discipline*.

None of the other bishops responded except for Bishop Jonathan Keaton of East Ohio, who had introduced Pereira at the Global Gathering. In his first letter to me he asked why I wanted his comment about Pereira. In his second letter, he simply affirmed the statement from Nugent and Solomon. An earlier article that Keaton had written about the Global Gathering enthused: "Time and space won't permit the sharing of all the wonderful sights and sounds which spoke to me." He recounted: "During the Global Gathering United Methodists dwelled together in a spirit of unity."

Although gratified that GBGM leaders at least felt obliged to separate themselves from Pereira's rejection of Christian orthodoxy when challenged, the disavowal of her comments seemed overly careful. Only four years earlier, GBGM's Women's Division had been embroiled in controversy because of its role in the 1993 "Re-Imagining Conference," where a feminist theologian had denounced Christ's atonement as "divine child abuse." Understandably, GBGM wanted to avoid more of such controversy. But speakers like Pereira kept getting invitations to GBGM events.

Early in his 12-year tenure as GBGM chief, Randy Nugent had excited evangelical hopes by reporting a personal "conversion" experience. But as his term as general secretary neared expiration, there was little evidence that GBGM had recovered very much from its radical theologies of the 1970s and 1980s. GBGM's budget in 2000 reached more than $170 million, thanks mostly to huge gains in its stock assets. But only about 11 percent was direct support of missionaries, of whom there were now fewer than 300 full-time. This compared to more than 400 when I first began taking a look at GBGM in the late 1980s. GBGM's total assets approached nearly $400 million. About one-third of its budget supported headquarters and its staff of more than 400.

In a 16-page, rambling address at the October 1999 directors meeting, Nugent spoke at length about U.S. elections, campaign financing and the cult of celebrity in the United States. He quoted from a speech by actor Warren Beatty about global poverty. The secular media in the U.S. often focuses on the "trivial" versus the substantive, Nugent complained. This was true even of coverage about GBGM, with Nugent clearly referring to IRD's reporting. GBGM's "mission story is conspicuously absent from those publications so quick to feature controversies and disputes within the church," he complained. "Divisiveness, it would seem, is deemed more newsworthy than reconciliation and unity, community and sharing, harmony and shalom. How else can the absence of emphasis upon the mission story" of GBGM be explained, he wondered. "One would think that such publications might at least sometimes report on changed lives, conversions and commitments to God in Christ Jesus which have come about because of mission-conversions and commitments" by GBGM, he insisted.

"If the true mission story were told and publicized, the church as a whole would be better equipped to respond to the divisive criticism designed to denigrate the mission outreach" of GBGM, Nugent asserted, seemingly oblivious to why GBGM's policies were controversial. He repeated the common liberal mantras about the gospel of "inclusion." New life in Christ means separation from the "old life" that is "based on exclusion, a conscious separation of people based on race, birthplace, ethnic identity, gender or sexual orientation." Nugent's understanding of Christian transformation, like GBGM's as a whole, seemed to be primarily a celebration of multiculturalism and diversity.

It was little wonder that near the end of Nugent's tenure, GBGM suffered major financial setbacks. A sharp drop in the stock market, without commensurate additional support of GBGM from local churches, prompted a slashing of headquarters staff from more than 400 to about 300 in 2001. The full-time career missionary force continued to decline, and today stands at fewer than 180. GBGM's expenditures in 2006 were $170 million, while receipts were $161 million. Total assets stood at just under $398 million. In 2006, just over $16 million, or 11 percent, went toward direct support of missions personnel.

Struggling against the declining GBGM support, the Rev. Bill Hinson became a director on GBGM in 2000. Recently retired from United Methodism's largest congregation, First United Methodist Church in Houston, Texas, Hinson was a leader in United Methodist evangelical renewal. Like other evangelical directors on GBGM, he preferred not to meet with me openly at GBGM meetings. We often met in his hotel room after meetings, where he described to me his plans to steer GBGM at least partially in more evangelistic directions. He successfully championed and raised funds for direct grants through GBGM to new United Methodist church plants overseas. At GBGM's October 2003 meeting, Hinson described his recent visit with Cambodian Methodists, in particular a Cambodian mission worker named "Paul." As a teenager, Paul had survived the communist holocaust in the 1970s under Pol Pot by hiding in a small hole beneath a floor. Unable to move, eat, drink or properly relieve himself for days at a time, he nearly went insane.

In desperation, Paul cried out, "If there is a God, please help me." Though he had never heard of the Bible or Jesus, he recalled that a great light filled his cramped space and a small voice whispered, "Don't be afraid. I will never leave you or forsake you." After later converting to Methodism, Paul realized that the voice had been Jesus Christ's. "How can you defeat a God like that?" Hinson asked his fellow GBGM directors. "If He can do that for a Buddhist who has never heard His name, what can He do for us if we cry out?" Hinson continued: "If one of our bishops who doesn't believe in the Resurrection were to tell this to Cambodians who are having visions of the risen Christ and hearing Scripture that they've never read before, they would have him arrested for indecent mental exposure."

The directors heard Hinson in silence. But Hinson's prestige as a mega-church pastor and fundraiser gave him credibility not typical for the few evangelicals among GBGM's directors. Hinson also played a role in discouraging or moderating some of GBGM's political pronouncements. At the October 2000 meeting, GBGM prepared to condemn Israel for its actions against Palestinian rioters on the West Bank. The resolution called the "popular protest" of the Palestinians an "expression of deep frustration" that resulted from "ongoing disrespect, dehumanization and denial of their basic human and national rights by an unjust political system."

There was no discussion about the resolution's substance. But Hinson asked why there was no resolution criticizing the recent terrorist attack against a U.S. Navy destroyer in Yemen that killed several U.S. sailors. Some directors and GBGM staff expressed reluctance to address that issue. But the Rev. James Mooneyham, a director from Snellville, Georgia, added his support to Hinson's proposal. "Those people gave their lives so we could have the freedom to have this discussion," Mooneyham said of the dead U.S. Navy personnel.

Other directors added their support for Hinson's proposal. In the end, a short resolution from GBGM "deplored the recent act of violence against the U.S.S. Cole and extends our deepest sympathy to the families and friends of those sailors who were killed or injured." It also called upon "all parties in the Middle East to cease hostilities immediately."

The Middle East has long been an area of sharp political interest for GBGM. During the final years of the Cold War in the 1980s, when the influence of liberation theology was peaking, GBGM funded missionaries in Nicaragua whose nearly sole purpose was to support the Marxist Sandinista regime. There were no Methodist churches in Nicaragua, so the "missionaries" mostly "interpreted" the Sandinista's revolution for visiting U.S. church groups. Similarly, there are no Methodist churches in the Middle East, but GBGM maintains several missionaries in "Palestine" to support politically the Palestinian perspective against Israel.

As of late 2007, GBGM had five missionaries in "Palestine." Their role is mostly chronicling Israeli transgressions and advocating for a Palestinian state. The missionaries oppose Palestinian suicide bombings and other Palestinian terrorism, but they do not dwell on these points. One typical GBGM missionary, Janet Lahr Lewis, serves as a "liaison between ecumenical groups and Israel and Palestine," according to her GBGM biography. She focuses on "advocacy and activism," which includes circulating "updates," suggesting "courses of action," developing "media campaigns" and hosting delegations.

"After taking a typical Holy Land tour and seeing the devastating consequences of the ongoing illegal occupation of the West Bank and Gaza, I experienced not only a 'call,' but rather an undeniable 'push' to go back to that not-so-holy land and do whatever I could to help bring about 'freedom for the oppressed,'" Lewis recalled in her GBGM bio. She lives on the West Bank "with my neighbors under the heavy hand of injustice and military occupation." Formerly she worked for the Sabeel Ecumenical Liberation Theology Center in Jerusalem, which is a religious thinktank that advocates pro-Palestinians perspectives.

Lewis, with the other GBGM missionaries in the region, is influenced by a Middle East brand of liberation theology, which portrays Israel as the Western colonizer and the Palestinians as the oppressed Third World victims. Evangelism is not the focus of their public statements, and their chief mission is simply to tell church audiences and international media about Palestinian suffering, in hopes of stimulating political support for one side in the conflict.

Do all or even most GBGM missionaries share Lewis' brand of liberation theology? Undoubtedly many do. At GBGM's October 2006 directors meeting, one director called on GBGM "[t]o spend more time and resources on spreading the Word and words of our Lord and less on political issues." But retiring missionary Ron Ray instead condemned the Bush administration for the Iraq War, the War on Terror and "welfare for the rich." Ray criticized attempts to "propagandize" voters into believing that

President Bush "represents Christian values." He portrayed the U.S. administration as illustrating "how totalitarian government operates."

A "Statement of Concern" was distributed to directors from the United Methodist Missionary Association, a group of active and retired missionaries. It decried "the arrogance we see manifested" in U.S. government policies that "do not show reverence and support for God's children which the gospel expects of us." The statement condemned the U.S. for "the allocation of many times more money for war" than for addressing worldwide "suffering, hunger and lack of health care and education." It blasted the U.S. for its "failure to take strong leadership" against global warming and its laws that allegedly "legalize torture." The missionaries asked God to "forgive our perceived silence" about such issues.

Meanwhile, GBGM continues to approve grants to left-wing political groups. In 2006, it approved $2,500 grants to the pro-Fidel Castro Inter-religious Foundation for Community Organizing, the pro-Palestinian Middle East Research and Information Project and to the U.S. Campaign to End Israel Occupation. Other political groups receiving smaller grants were the Washington Office on Africa, the Center for Constitutional Rights and the Washington Office on Latin America, all of which were active in the Cold War in defending Marxist libration movements.

Prior to the October 2007 GBGM meeting, my assistant John Lomperis emailed the directors about the proposed grants to controversial political groups that they would be considering. GBGM staff sent a four-page rebuttal to the directors, asserting that IRD has "no links" to United Methodism and "often attacks Protestant denominations and their agencies from a right wing political perspective." It claimed that "IRD's language often assumes that American patriotism and the Gospel are identical," without citing examples. And it asserted that IRD writers "seem not to have noticed" that the church's allegiance to God means its social positions will not be "always in harmony with the policies of a particular nation or of all nations." It insisted that the grants to secular political groups are consistent with "the Wesleyan theological heritage and biblical faith" and "reflect an allegiance to God and love of neighbor."

Inaccurately, GBGM staff denied John's report that MAR-CHA, a Hispanic caucus that received $60,000 from GBGM, had "endorsed a statement strongly opposing United Methodist teaching on homosexuality." In fact, MARCHA had specifically backed a statement criticizing the United Methodist Social Prin-ciples stance on homosexuality. Similarly, GBGM defended its grant to Progressive Christians Uniting (PCU) by equivocating on whether or not PCU had endorsed same-sex unions, when in fact PCU's website had advertised that cause by a PCU chapter.

Even so, compared to 20 years ago, when my call to reform GBGM first began, GBGM is less formidable, less intimidating and less radical. GBGM seems trapped in a transitional gray area. Its staff is still overwhelmingly composed of theological liber-als who do not share evangelical beliefs about evangelism and discipleship. But influenced somewhat by United Methodism's increasingly conservative direction, and deprived of provocative Cold War issues about nuclear weapons and U.S. "colonialism," the staff has lost its radical edge of 20 years ago.

In 2003, GBGM staffer Randy Day replaced Randy Nugent as general secretary. Although undoubtedly liberal, Day rarely ex-pressed controversial opinions in public. In October 2007 he was abruptly fired by GBGM's directors because of administrative problems within GBGM. Evangelicals among GBGM's directors supported the dismissal. But will Day's successor represent a no-ticeably different philosophic direction?

CHAPTER   TEN

POLITICS AMONG THE BISHOPS

It was less than two months since the 9-11 attacks had killed 3,000 Americans. The United Methodist Council of Bishops was meeting at Lake Junaluska, North Carolina, in the crisp mountain air of early November. What would the bishops say?

Rejecting an early draft that quoted official United Methodist teaching about "just war,"* the bishops decided on neutrality about the U.S. military action against Osama bin Laden's terrorist network and his Taliban protectors in Afghanistan. They were opposing all "violence" and praying for all who were in harm's way.

The bishops had debated among themselves whether to be "pastoral" or "prophetic." Arguing for the "prophetic," the more liberal bishops wanted a specific denunciation of the U.S.-led war against terror. The more centrist bishops wished to avoid an anti-war statement and argued for a "pastoral" one that offered sympathy and prayer.

No bishop openly suggested that being "prophetic" might entail criticizing radical Islam or upholding the scriptural responsibility of governments to defend their citizens from assault. Instead, "pro

---

*Christianity's traditional "just war" teaching, often dated to St. Augustine, describes the circumstances when armed force is morally legitimate.

phetic" meant condemnation of the United States and its policies.

"Violence in all of its forms and expressions is contrary to God's purpose for the world," the bishops declared, making no distinction between "violence" by lawless terrorist or criminal groups and "violence" by legitimate governments in defense against them. The letter's final draft was considerably different from the first draft, written by Bishop Joe Pennel of Virginia. Pennel was one of two dozen religious leaders who were invited to meet with President Bush at the White House in the aftermath of the September 11 atrocities. He also visited the Pentagon the day after the terrorist strike there.

Pennel's draft specifically condemned terrorism, instead of just "violence" in general, declaring that "terrorism in all of its forms and expressions is contrary to God's dream for the world." His draft also quoted from the 2000 United Methodist Social Principles, which said "we regretfully realize that when peaceful alternatives have failed, the force of arms may be preferable to unchecked aggression, tyranny and genocide." Pennel called the events of 9-11 a "shattering evil." But the revised draft approved by the bishops avoided any mention of "evil" and omitted the United Methodist official stance, approved at the 2000 General Conference, that war is sometimes justified.

The first to respond to Pennel's draft was Bishop Joe Sprague of North Illinois, who is a pacifist. He suggested changing the letter's focus from terrorism to "violence," suggested mentioning the "root causes" of terrorism and wanted to include that "monstrous acts are conceived in monstrous circumstances." In essence, Sprague wanted to fault U.S. policies for provoking al Qaeda.

Sprague complained that Pennel's draft "presupposed that this military action comes from just-war theory," which is Christianity's traditional justification for war in some circumstances.

Although Sprague said he disagreed with just-war theory, he thought the U.S. war in Afghanistan failed to abide by even its standards.

In defending his draft, Pennel said he wrote it "out of personal emotional involvement with people who have suffered great loss." He mentioned his visit to the Pentagon and also a neighbor who had lost a daughter on 9-11. Tending to the "hurt and need" of the victims should be the pastoral letter's primary responsibility, Pennel said. If there is to be a "prophetic" letter, you might need somebody else to write it, he advised. "There's no one I respect more than Joe [Sprague]. At the same time, the need for pastoral care is greater than the need for prophetic words."

Bishops Robert Fannin of North Alabama, Ernest Lyght of New York and Marion Edwards of North Carolina spoke in favor of a pastoral letter. Bishop Ann Shearer of Missouri favored being more prophetic, especially acknowledging "our complicity in creating some of the chaos there [in the Middle East] and the Palestinian situation." Bishop Ken Carder of Mississippi spoke for a balance between the prophetic and the pastoral, expressing alarm about the "idolatrous" form of patriotism that was affecting the church.

"I would never understand that you could divorce the pastoral from the prophetic," Bishop Sprague responded. "We feel deep pain about Afghan and Iraqi civilians being killed [by the U.S.]. We can't sit quietly. That's not who I am. That's not the Gospel."

Retired bishops Calvin McConnell and Robert Grove asked that prayers for the U.S. military be included. But the final statement declined to do so, instead simply praying for "people who have been placed in harm's way and their loved ones."

Bishop Tim Whitaker of Florida took issue with a reference to the "root causes" of terrorism. "I am bothered by the implication of moral justification for terrorism," he said, suggesting it be changed to "conditions exploited by terrorists." The final draft refers to "alleviating the root causes of poverty and the other social conditions that are exploited by terrorists."

Thanks to pressure from their most liberal colleagues, the Council of Bishops was unable even to quote from the United Methodist Social Principles about war. They preferred instead to pretend that United Methodism is a pacifist tradition and in essence took a neutral stance between al Qaeda and the military and police forces that were attempting to eradicate the terrorists.

It's an ongoing problem for the Council of Bishops. In their public statements, they are unable to defend the church's teachings about marriage and sexual ethics, much less traditional Christian teachings about the family or the sanctity of all human life, including the unborn. The bishops do not even make statements about the ills related to gambling or pornography, to which presumably even most liberals could agree. Instead, the bishops in their often stale and repetitious political statements are largely confined to condemnations of U.S. military and foreign policies. Rather than relying on centuries of Christian social thought, they typically resort instead to repeating the slogans and clichés of 1960s protest activism, which had shaped many of the bishops in their youth.

Senator Jeff Sessions of Alabama, a United Methodist, gave the bishops a gentle warning about their politicking at their November 2003 meeting in Washington, D.C. When retired Bishop Don Ott asked if the bishops should not make political pronouncements, Sessions responded: "You've got every right to do that. But I'm not sure bishops know much more about Afghanistan than lay leaders in your churches."

"We can't be a political organization," Sessions told the bishops. "The liberal churches—politics has hurt them. Conservative churches will be hurt too if they get too close to that flame. We have to be careful."

"I believe in this church," Sessions said. "I want us to be a prophetic voice in the world. But I don't want to see it [United Methodism] in decline and failing to reach its potential." Sessions, who called himself a "conservative Methodist Christian," is a member of Ashland United Methodist Church in Mobile, Alabama. He is a frequent lay member of the Alabama/West Florida Annual Conference, and he attended the 1996 General Conference as a delegate.

Sessions said President Bush, also United Methodist, has probably been disappointed by the criticism of his policies by his church. "I'm sure it was hurtful for him for his church to question his faith," he said. "President Bush has a high degree of moral commitment," Sessions pointed out. "His belief is that the U.S. has a leadership responsibility to liberate people from oppressions. It's a deep moral belief coming out of his faith."

When retired Bishop Melvin Talbert asked Sessions why President Bush had declined to meet with United Methodist bishops as a group, Sessions said, "Presidents are people too. They get hurt. He's usually pretty open to meeting with people." The senator also said he was disappointed and "hurt" by his church echoing secular groups with some of the same criticisms aimed at presidential judicial nominees who have traditional religious beliefs.

After Sessions finished speaking, he was surrounded by several of the more conservative bishops. Perhaps he had said a little of what they knew they should say? When *Good News* published my article about Session's remarks, the senator wrote me a nice thank you letter, noting that his wife wished he had been "tougher" with the bishops. But I think he had gotten his message across.

Earlier that year, in April 2003, the bishops were meeting outside Dallas, and the April 26 *Dallas Morning News* quoted me as saying: "My hope is that some day at least some of the bishops will feel an obligation to more represent their own local people

rather than be preoccupied with conforming with the expectations of the Council and the national church bureaucracy." The
article mentioned that Bishop Melvin Talbert would address the
Council about opposing the Iraq War, and many bishops had
signed a recent *Christian Century* magazine ad demanding that
President Bush "repent from domestic and foreign policies that
are incompatible with the teaching and example of Christ."

Stephen Drachler of United Methodist Communications was
helping the bishops with their public relations and kindly asked
me to lunch during the bishops' meeting outside Dallas. Having
read the *Dallas Morning News*, he asked if I really believed the
bishops are beholden to the church bureaucracy. I responded,
"YES!" In their political statements, the bishops never diverge
from the agenda of the Board of Church and Society or of the
Board of Global Ministries. They could show occasional leadership by articulating United Methodist positions that the church
bureaucracy prefers to ignore, if not undermine. But almost
without fail, the bishops in their collective statements will accommodate the lowest common denominator demanded by the
most liberal bishops.

Occasionally, some courageous bishops will dissent from the
conformity. At the council's October 1998 meeting in Lincoln,
Nebraska, Bishop Richard Looney of South Georgia thoughtfully opposed a resolution condemning the U.S. Army's School
of the Americas at Ft. Benning, Georgia, where Latin American
military officers are trained. The resolution admitted "positive
changes" at the school, but intoned that the school is "perceived
by the marginalized to be a source of oppression and a symbol of
violence." Left-wing activists have condemned what they call the
"school of the assassins." A few dozen of the school's more than
50,000 graduates have been implicated in human rights abuses
over the decades. The school's opponents opposed U.S. policies
in the 1980s that helped defeat Marxist insurgencies in Latin

America, and they fault the school for successfully professionalizing some Latin militaries.

The proposed bishops' statement urged closing the school as an "act of solidarity with our Latin brothers and sisters" and self-importantly called the bishops "the voice of the voiceless." But Bishop Looney pointed out that the "accused have a right to be represented," and he thoughtfully defended the school with a prepared speech. "I've read reams of material from opponents of the School of Americas," he said. "It was incomprehensible that the military and the President could support such activities."

Looney had personally visited the school. And like the Episcopal Diocese of Atlanta, which also investigated the school, he "found no evidence" justifying closure. The school "provides more human rights training than any other U.S. Army program, he said, and "includes anti-narcotics training." Every Latin American country except Cuba is now democratic, Looney pointed out, and the school "takes some credit for that." There had been 13 human rights violations by school graduates since 1984 out of 15,000 graduates, the bishop reported. "We've had 13 cases of sexual misconduct in South Georgia," he added. "That doesn't mean we train sexual predators in South Georgia."

Bishop Sprague responded that he was in "constant activity with Latino immigrants," among whom there is a "perception that the School of the Americas is a participant in violence to block the indigenous ones [so as] to advance our economic interests." He said the "worst side of U.S. policy is exemplified by the school," although he provided no example of the school's alleged misdeeds.

Bishop Joel Martinez reiterated Sprague, calling the school a "breeding ground for the militarization of Latin America" that "trains and indoctrinates in the arts of war." He melodramatically insisted that he spoke for "the victims, for the jailed and the murdered." And he urged his fellow bishops to "stand with the victims of violence in Latin America."

In the end, only Bishop Lindsey Davis of North Georgia voted with Looney in opposing the resolution. Although Looney had crafted a careful, fact-filled speech, the generalities and "perceptions" offered by Sprague and Martinez prevailed. Afterwards, I thanked Looney for making the effort. Since then, no conservative bishop has similarly attempted to resist a liberal political resolution. One conservative bishop, after the vote, explained that he and other bishops voted for the resolution as an act of "solidarity" with Bishop Martinez, who was then enmeshed in controversy over his handling of a pastor who had conducted same-sex unions. The School of the Americas, now called the Western Hemisphere Institute for Security Cooperation, remains open, although thousands of demonstrators gather there every year in November for their annual angry protest, with dozens routinely getting arrested.

The Council of Bishops often speaks as a reunion of former hippies of the 1960s and 1970s, constantly rehashing the old protest themes of American imperialism, militarism and economic exploitation. Their statements imply that the world would be entirely prosperous and peaceful were it not for the insidious influence of the U.S. In recent decades, they have never collectively expressed concern about totalitarian Marxism or about radical Islam, both of which have murdered millions over the last century, and both of which see Christianity as a special enemy.

Even moderate bishops are often embarrassed by American patriotism and quick to judge it as idolatrous, neglecting to acknowledge that all Christians are called to love their country, subordinating that love to their love of God. Bishop Carder seemed to embody this discomfort in a post 9-11 commentary in United Methodist News Service that expressed reservations about the revived popularity of the patriotic hymn "God Bless America."

"Prayer for God's blessing is presumptuous when we expect

God to bestow blessings in accordance with national boundaries and preconceived notions," Carder wrote. "To seek God's blessings for America and not for the world fails to recognize the wideness in God's mercy and the expanse of God's love." The headline of Carder's article was: "God Bless America . . . and the World." I afterwards wrote a commentary for IRD's website, later published in *Touchstone* magazine, which cited Carder's article as an example of mainline church officials discomfort with American patriotism.

I affirmed that Christians should not be reluctant to love most passionately those with whom they have the most immediate contact: their family, their friends, their church, their community and nation. "As finite humans, we cannot abstractly love every one of the earth's creatures with absolute equality," I wrote. "Only a transcendent God can achieve such wideness. And even He forges special bonds of love, with His Son and with His church."

My critique of Carder led to several years of sometimes acrimonious exchanges with him. I shared an advance copy of my commentary with him, whom I quoted only briefly at the article's start, to seek his comment. He quickly responded that I was "unfair, inaccurate and misleading," without explaining how. And he asked that I reprint his essay in its entirety "rather than selectively excerpting and providing your own interpretation." When I responded right away to the bishop that my article was on our website and would include a direct link to his original essay, he immediately complained that I had posted his article before awaiting his comment. "It seems apparent that you were not interested in truth or fairness but in furthering your ideological, political and perhaps economic agendas," he surmised. He invited me to "talk personally, confidentially and in a spirit of mutual accountability" about my "methods and the resulting disservice to Jesus Christ, to other people, to the church and to the stated purpose of UM*Action*."

Immediately I phoned Carder to apologize for the misunderstanding, explaining that the website version was only an early draft that easily could have been amended with his comments if he had offered any, and that the final version would appear in a future *Touchstone* magazine. Our conversation was civil but not satisfactory to either of us. Four years later, a now retired Bishop Carder wrote me again, referencing my "perverted use" of his essay "God Bless America . . . And the World," and comparing my "propaganda" to the tactics of the KKK. He continued: "From my observation, your behavior continues to jeopardize your own soul."

Surprised that Carder was still angry, I emailed the bishop that his comparison of me to the KKK was a "cheap shot," but that I would be glad to hear from him further if he was interested in exchanging "reasoned arguments." We had a sometimes civil email exchange discussing our differences, though Carder seemed more interested in condemnation than persuasion when I pressed for details as to how I had been specifically unfair or inaccurate. At the 2004 General Conference in Pittsburgh, Carder smilingly greeted me in the street and asked if all was well with my soul. I assured him that I hoped it was!

A few months later, in August 2004, IRD critic Andrew Weaver wrote about my earlier exchange with Carder over his patriotism essay as evidence that "IRD lacks journalistic ethics." Weaver quoted Carder: "I challenged Mark Tooley's tactics as a violation of basic Christian discipleship and invited him to enter a confidential mutual covenant to hold one another accountable for our discipleship and faithfulness to the Wesleyan tradition. I shared with him that his article and the tactics used violated the stated purpose of the IRD as 'protecting faith and freedom.' He refused to enter such a covenant."

In fact, I never refused to enter this "covenant" with Carder and have quickly responded to all his communications, however frustrating their vague charges have seemed. Carder repeated his allegation in an interview for the anti-IRD video produced in 2007 called *Renewal or Ruin?* I suspect that Carder's irritation with IRD was not ignited originally by our exchange over his "God Bless America . . . And the World" essay. IRD critiqued his episcopal address to the 2004 General Conference, which was long on liberal social gospel themes and short on Christian doctrine. Carder had condemned the "widening gap between the rich and the poor, the pervasiveness of market forces dominated by the wealthiest of nations, and the prevalence of personal and corporate greed [that] threaten the every existence of vast populations and the ecosystem itself."

The episcopal address, which is approved by the whole Council of Bishops, denounced the "reliance on violence and military solutions to conflicts destroys life and compounds terror in the name of resisting terror" and the "current mood of political imperialism." Carder insisted that the church's witness to the gospel is seen in "those who support social and economic policies that make the earth's resources accessible to all of God's beloved children." It was boilerplate verbiage, repeating the usual bugaboos of the secular left, confusing lofty goals with questionable policies, and offering little that was creative or rooted deeply in Christian teaching prior to the 1960s.

Echoing similar themes, Carder had likened cruel political conservatives to King Herod when he addressed the General Board of Global Ministries' Global Gathering II in April 1997. "The slaughter of the innocents continues," he declared, citing welfare reform, immigration laws and monetary policies as his evidence. "The preservation of the powerful wreaks havoc on children." He asked, "Who will shelter the suffering ones" from "Herod's violent descendants?" Carder further inquired:. "Where are the prophets waiting in the halls of government? Are we so obsessed with pleasing the powerful?" Once again, the welfare state was equated with Christian compassion, and skeptics of statism were compared to the king who sought to kill baby Jesus.

Closer similarities to King Herod might be found among the defenders of unrestricted abortion, about which the Council of Bishops has long been silent. Although the 2000 General Conference formally declared the church's opposition to partial-birth abortion, the council has said nothing. One heroic exception to the silence is Bishop Timothy Whitaker, who denounced abortion as a "moral horror" when speaking to United Methodism's pro-life caucus, Lifewatch, in January 2005.

"What I feel is revulsion at the moral horror that is abortion," Whitaker said in Washington, D.C. "This revulsion is magnified when I reflect upon the fact, as [Lutheran theologian] Carl Braaten has said, 'ninety-nine percent of all murders in the United States are abortions.'"

The United Methodist Board of Church and Society, which owns the Capitol Hill United Methodist Building in which Bishop Whitaker spoke, is a founding member of the Religious Coalition for Reproductive Choice (RCRC) and lobbies against restrictions on abortion. The United Methodist Women's Division is also a member of RCRC.

Besides regretting United Methodist support for RCRC, Whitaker lamented that the United Methodist Bishops' Initiative on Children in Poverty, which focused on ministries for children, included "not even scant mention [about] the deaths of unborn children because of abortion."

Whitaker regretted that United Methodism has succumbed to American culture's preoccupation with "private rights." Christianity believes in both rights and responsibilities, he said. "Therefore, we cannot endorse a woman's right to abort an unborn child as a morally neutral decision because we understand that the child also has a right to live and the community has a responsibility to care for this child if the mother is unable to rear it."

Surmising that many United Methodists do not oppose abortion because that would align them with the Republican Party, Whitaker insisted that Christians cannot let ideology "constrain our witness to the living God" and must "view abortion as a concern that transcends ideological or partisan loyalties." Noting that many United Methodists are outspoken against war and capital punishment, Whitaker asserted that opposition to violence requires as much "vigilance" against abortion as against war as a "normal political tool" and against state executions. He listed these things, along with opposition to euthanasia, as a witness to God in a world "under the evil spell of violence."

"I think our silence and passivity about abortion comes from the difficulty of being a Christian in America," Whitaker observed. Unlike nations where the culture is overtly hostile to Christianity, the "seductions of American life" are more subtle, with their emphasis on "autonomous individuals." Christians, he said, have a "different anthropology" that emphasizes people as part of a community with responsibilities towards each other.

The United Methodist *Book of Discipline* illustrates this tension between Christianity and American culture, Whitaker said. On the one hand, *The Discipline* declares, "Our belief in the sanctity of unborn human life makes us reluctant to approve abortion." On the other hand, it continues: "But we are equally bound to respect the sacredness of the life and the well-being of the mother, for whom devastating damage may result from an unacceptable pregnancy."

What does this "but" mean?" Whitaker asked. If it means saving the life of the mother in "extreme medical conditions," then "well and good," he said. He wondered if this "but" clause really was "an escape from moral responsibility in the name of one's individual right to choose as an American."

Admitting the lack of "clear prescription" against abortion in the Bible, Whitaker explained this was because "such a horror" was "unthinkable" to Israel and to the church. "Do no harm," was the first of John Wesley's General Rules for Methodists, Whitaker recalled. Being faithful to this rule means, "Do no harm to the unborn! Do no harm to the witness of the Church as a peaceable people! Do no harm to the Gospel of peace!"

No less boldly, Whitaker later in 2005 defended the right to life of Terry Schiavo, the Florida woman in a vegetative state whose estranged husband wished to deprive her of food and water. A person in a "persistent vegetative state" is not a vegetable to her loved ones, Whitaker observed. The love that Mrs. Schiavo's parents and siblings showed her was of "immense value" and no expert could judge that love's effect upon even the severely disabled woman, he said. For Christians, this kind of love is a witness to God's love in Jesus Christ.

"Moral reflection should include consideration of the value of the love of caregivers as well as the condition of the one receiving care," Whitaker wrote. "I believe it would be better to let her live because she is the beneficiary of abundant love." He questioned the wisdom of a law that would allow a spouse, especially one "compromised by conflict of interest" like Mr. Schiavo, to be the sole witness to her intentions, without considering the moral claims of other family members.

Whitaker criticized the "individualistic perspective" that believes a person may decide whether to live or die without considering the ability of others to love and care. Such "absolute individual autonomy" could lead to physician-assisted suicide and active euthanasia," he warned. "The church's mission is not to be the chaplain to a culture of death," Whitaker concluded, "But to be a witness to the love of God in the world."

Bishops with Whitaker's mind, courage and comprehensive understanding of orthodox Christian faith are rare on the Council of Bishops. This was seen once again in the bishops' repeated denunciations of the Iraq War. At their November 2007 meeting at Lake Junaluska, the bishops issued their fourth official condemnation of the U.S., demanding an "immediate" withdrawal of U.S.-led forces from Iraq. The statement, which made no reference to al Qaeda and to sectarian terrorist groups in Iraq, was approved almost unanimously.

Almost alone in expressing concern was Bishop Joseph Humper of Sierre Leone in Africa. "Others are ready to step in," he warned if the U.S. left prematurely. "Iran is ready to step in. What will happen to the Iraqi people? Is the government strong enough? Are they strong enough to maintain order and decorum? I speak from a moral perspective." But none of the Council of Bishops' statements heeded the plight of Iraq's people after a quick U.S. exit. Instead, the bishops portrayed the U.S. as the only sinister force in Iraq.

The United Methodist Council of Bishops anti-Iraq War statements contrasted with statements from the U.S. Catholic Conference of Bishops. Like the United Methodists, the Catholic bishops opposed the U.S. ouster of Saddam Hussein, while also opposing an immediate U.S. retreat, citing the importance of establishing democracy, rule of law, religious liberty and economic reconstruction. The United Methodist bishops have never affirmed decent government for Iraq, with the need for security against terrorism and sectarian strife. And the bishops have adamantly refused to quote the United Methodist Social Principles' acknowledgment that war is sometimes regrettably justified, language that 2004 General Conference reinforced.

According to United Methodist Social Principles paragraph 164I, "We deplore war and urge the peaceful settlement of all disputes among nations." It goes on to say that "some of us believe that war, and other acts of violence, are never acceptable to Christians." Meanwhile, "many Christians believe that, when peaceful alternatives have failed, the force of arms may regretfully be preferable to unchecked aggression, tyranny and genocide."

Social Principles paragraph 165C says, "We believe war is incompatible with the teachings and example of Christ. We therefore reject war as an instrument of national foreign policy, to be employed only as a last resort in the prevention of such evils as genocide, brutal suppression of human rights and unprovoked international aggression."

The reference to war's potential permissibility in 164I was added at the 2000 General Conference. The reference in 165C was added at the 2004 General Conference. These references reflect United Methodist understanding of historic Christian teachings about just war. But the Council of Bishops, quoting only a fragment of the Social Principles, refers only to war as "incompatible" with Christ's teachings.

Again, one notable exception has been Bishop Whitaker, who opposed the Iraq War, but argued from a just-war perspective. He opposed the U.S. military effort in Iraq. But unlike the Council of Bishops and other church agencies, Whitaker's arguments are not pacifist, obsessively hostile to the United States or divorced from traditional church teachings. In his September 2002 statement on Iraq, prior to the U.S. led overthrow of Saddam, Whitaker wrote: "Nor am I a pacifist." He continued: "Neither do I criticize the administration of President Bush in its attempt to destroy the international network of terrorists who attacked the United States on Sept. 11, 2001."

Whitaker said: "As someone who believes the 'just war theory' is the best moral perspective we possess for deciding whether to wage war and how to wage war, I do not believe that a virtually unilateral decision by the United States to wage war has sufficient moral justification." Unlike nearly all other United Methodist officials, Whitaker affirmed that the U.S. military was protecting the Kurds of northern Iraq and Iraq's neighbors from potential aggression by Saddam's regime. He also admitted it may be "necessary to conduct air strikes on sites where weapons of mass destruction are manufactured or stored."

Whitaker even admitted that ultimately an invasion of Iraq might be necessary, but he insisted it should be "under the authority of the community of nations known as the United Nations." He cited Iraq's possibly having nuclear weapons in the future and/or intercontinental ballistic missiles, which could strike other nations in the region if not the United States.

Again in sharp contrast to the Council of Bishops, Whitaker in a December 8, 2005, commentary referred to Saddam's "clear record of cruelty and injustice towards his own people." Whitaker disavowed any "dreamy notion of internationalism" or "purity of the United Nations." But he said U.S. participation in regime change should have UN backing because the U.S. is committed by its treaty obligations to do so.

Whitaker argued that international weapons inspectors should have been given more time to search for weapons of mass destruction in Iraq. In the absence of those weapons, the United States should have worked through the UN to force Saddam into exile and authorize an "invasion, occupation and reconstruction" of Iraq. Whitaker went further, saying that if the UN refused to fulfill its responsibility, the United States and other nations could have "justly claimed a moral legitimacy to take action on their own for the sake of the Iraqi people."

With humility not in the Council of Bishops' statements, Whitaker wrote that, with Iraq now occupied, "It is not easy to judge what should be done now." He admitted that "such a judgment requires . . . information and expertise not possessed by ordinary citizens." He added, "We are not experts in strategy. . . ."

Unlike the Council of Bishops, Whitaker wrote, "Christians understand that in a world still under the power of sin, war may be necessary as the only way to restrain evil, enact justice and establish the conditions that make for peace." He argued that the U.S. military cannot prevail in what has become a civil war in Iraq. The U.S. had "accomplished its optimal goals," which were Saddam's removal and the creation of an elected government under a new constitution. But the bishop did not argue for an immediate U.S. military withdrawal but for a "plan for redeployment."

"It is not conscionable to consider letting terrorists succeed in their geopolitical aims that are a threat to all nations," Whitaker concluded. "But not letting the terrorists prevail in their long-term aims in what will be an indefinite conflict does not mean there should not be a change in strategy in the particular contest being fought in Iraq."

Unlike the Council of Bishops and other United Methodist officials, Whitaker did not cynically question the motivations of the United States, ignore the monstrousness of Saddam's regime, insist that Saddam had no connection to terrorism, or ascribe mystical authority to the United Nations. Nor do Whitaker's statements, unlike others, connect the Iraq War conspiratorially with a wider web of exploitation of the poor, fawning allegiance to Israel or depraved subservience to oil interests.

Instead, Whitaker argued that the U.S.-led removal of Saddam's regime was premature and lacked international backing. Such a U.S. led effort, even without UN backing, may have become morally desirable at some point, he admitted. Whitaker urged an eventual, orderly, U.S. military withdrawal from Iraq, which he hoped would de-escalate the conflict and empower Iraq's new government.

Whitaker's public policy statements about Iraq, as on abortion, reflect Christian realism and are rooted in Christian tradition. Will future United Methodist bishops follow his example, or will they follow the ineffective political witness of the Council of Bishops of recent decades?

The United Methodist Council of Bishops, during their November 2003 meeting outside Washington, D.C., heard from several members of the U.S. Congress, including Senator Sessions, who urged them to be more cautious in their political pronouncements.

Speaking about the important issue of homosexuality within United Methodism, Sessions approvingly recalled reading *A Moral Vision of the New Testament* by Richard Hayes, a Duke Divinity School professor who opposes homosexual practice. The senator read the book at the recommendation of his bishop, Larry Goodpaster.

Sessions also spoke about the Bush Administration's nomination of Alabama Attorney General William Pryor to a federal judgeship, a nomination fiercely opposed by liberal senators because of Pryor's opposition to abortion.

Referring to Pryor as "my good friend," Sessions lamented that Pryor's nomination has been blocked because Pryor is a devout Roman Catholic who supports his church's teaching about abortion.

"Will we disqualify a member of the greatest church?" Sessions asked, pointing out that Pryor's stance on abortion is the same as the Pope's. "He [Pryor] and his wife have guided their lives by it [the Roman Catholic faith]," the senator observed. "They deserve respect."

"We were founded by them." He wondered how a devout Orthodox Jew or Muslim could be confirmed to a federal position if devout Roman Catholics were to be excluded.

Sessions complained, "My church is using the same rhetoric," as has been employed against Pryor's nomination. "That hurt my feelings," he said.

Sessions cited some of his colleagues in the U.S. Senate who, in trying to model themselves after British evangelical statesman William Wilberforce, try to "improve the culture of America on abortion, pornography, honor and responsibility and commitment in marriage."

"Maybe we could work together," Sessions said. "Let's affirm rather than undermine marriage."

Sessions said, "It's a great blessing to have a United Methodist heritage."

Other members of the U.S. Congress who spoke to the Council of Bishops were Senator Richard Lugar (Republican of Indiana), Representative Barbara Lee (Democrat of California), Representative Elijah Cummings (Democrat of Maryland), Senator Craig Thomas (Republican of Wyoming) and Senator Paul Sarbanes (Democrat of Maryland), along with former Representative Lee Hamilton (Democrat of Indiana). Lugar, Thomas and Hamilton are United Methodists.

During a break, Bishop Joe Sprague of Chicago took the floor.

"I have promised to maintain my vow of silence but now must break it," Sprague said. He lamented the growth of U.S. military spending and complained that U.S. foreign aid was too low. Sprague also lamented that the U.S. comprises only four percent of the world's population but has 25 percent of the world's prison inmates.

"The greatest experience of my life took place here," Sprague recalled of his arrest earlier this year while performing civil disobedience outside the White House in a demonstration against the U.S. war in Iraq. "Seventy-seven of us were arrested [for being against] an immoral war," he observed. "It's been said that I'm an incompatible bishop, but on that occasion I was in good company."

Later, in their November meeting, the bishops decided to appoint an executive secretary for the Council of Bishops who will work in Washington, based in the Methodist Building on Capitol Hill. Retired Bishop Roy Sano will serve in this position.

The cost of this will be $240,451 for the quadrenium, including at least $15,600 for a residential apartment in the Methodist building, at least $5,000 a year for a one room office there, and salary for the executive secretary. This will be paid out of the Episcopal Fund.

CHAPTER ELEVEN

GENERAL CONFERENCE 2000 – TURNING POINT?

Still somewhat bloodied by the 1996 General Conference in Denver, when 15 bishops had led a full court press in advocating an overthrow of United Methodism's teachings on homosexuality, evangelicals looked to the 2000 General Conference in Cleveland, Ohio, with some foreboding.

Like all General Conferences, Cleveland was tense, acrimonious and exhausting. The liberal bishops and radical caucus groups performed even more street theater than usual. Bishop Joe Sprague got arrested twice at pro-homosexuality demonstrations!

The General Conference even had to adjourn briefly because angry, pro-homosexuality demonstrators, including a dozen bishops, were obstructing the stage. But after the smoke had cleared and the numbers were counted, Cleveland turned out to be a turning point for United Methodism.

If Denver was the high tide of liberalism in our church, then Cleveland seemed to mark a new beginning for renewed theological orthodoxy within United Methodism. As always, the votes over homosexuality marked the main battle lines, and they were the prime yardsticks to measure conservative versus liberal strength.

In the end, with support from two-thirds or more of the delegates, the Cleveland General Conference decisively rejected all efforts to repeal or weaken United Methodism's disapproval of homosexual practice, same-sex unions and actively homosexual clergy.

As always, pro-homosexuality lobby groups aggressively pressured the nearly 1,000 delegates who met May 2-12, 2000. The demonstrators even resorted to disruptive acts that twice forced the General Conference to recess. Two bishops were arrested for their illegal actions, while 12 other bishops openly demonstrated for accepting homosexual practice as normative.

But the delegates were not intimidated. They voted by two to one on the next-to-last day of the conference, to uphold the church's opposition to homosexual behavior, the prohibition against practicing homosexual ministers, the ban on same-sex unions and the restriction against church funding for pro-homosexuality groups. They also reaffirmed the church's expectation of fidelity in marriage and celibacy in singleness.

The margins of the votes were at least five percentage points greater than in the 1996 General Conference, strongly rebutting pro-homosexuality advocates who argue that the church's acceptance of same-sex behavior is inevitable.

Sixty-five percent of the delegates voted to reaffirm the church's stand that "the practice of homosexuality is incompatible with Christian teaching." Sixty-seven percent voted to retain the rule that "self-avowed practicing homosexuals" cannot be ordained ministers. Sixty-nine percent voted to reaffirm the prohibition against same-sex unions in our churches or by our clergy. Seventy-four percent voted to continue the prohibition against church funding "to promote the acceptance of homosexuality." And 79 percent voted to continue the expectation of celibacy in singleness and faithfulness in marriage.

The delegates followed the recommendations of the Faith and Order Legislative Committee, whose Chairman, the Rev. Robert Hayes of Houston, affirmed that the church's current opposition to homosexual behavior "conforms to the clear and true teaching of Scripture." Hayes would be elected bishop of Oklahoma in 2004.

Giving the "minority report" was the Rev. J. Philip Wogaman, then pastor of the Washington, D.C. church that President Clinton attended. "Will we one day have to hold a service of repentance for our gay and lesbian sisters and brothers'?" he querulously asked.

But Hayes reminded the delegates that there is indeed a "discipline that is higher and greater than the one that is made for United Methodists [referring to *The Book of Discipline*]. It is the Word of God as printed in the Holy Scriptures and it is to that discipline that we must be faithful."

Tension and emotion permeated the debates and voting. On the day before the votes on homosexuality, 300 demonstrators gathered outside the convention hall. About 180 of them were arrested for blocking the convention center driveway in carefully planned acts of civil disobedience. Among the arrested was the inevitable Joe Sprague of Chicago. For the benefit of photographers, he even locked his wrists together, so as to appear handcuffed!

On the day of the votes, about 200 pro-homosexuality demonstrators silently marched up and down the convention center's audience gallery. Many of them were not United Methodists and had been organized by Soulforce, founded by former Jerry Falwell speech writer and later homosexual activist Mel White, who pastors a large, predominantly homosexual congregation in Dallas. After the delegates had voted to affirm the church's stand against homosexual practice, nearly 30 demonstrators walked onto the convention floor, where only delegates were permitted. Many delegates and audience members rose in support. Among the intruding demonstrators was Mark Miller, professor of music at United Methodist Drew Seminary in New Jersey, and co-worship leader for the upcoming 2008 General Conference. The presiding Bishop Dan Solomon of Louisiana called a recess. During the recess, 14 pro-homosexuality Bishops took to the stage to applaud and sing.

They were Judith Craig of West Ohio, William Dew of Phoenix, Susan Morrison of Albany, Fritz Mutti of Kansas, Don Ott of Michigan, Roy Sano of Los Angeles, Mary Ann Swenson of Denver and Melvin Talbert of Sacramento, along with retired Bishops Jesse Dewitt, Leontine Kelly, Cal McConnell, Jack Tuell, and Joe Yaekel, plus of course, Sprague. (Craig, Ott, Sano and Talbert retired later in 2000. Sprague retired in 2004.)

Presiding Bishop Solomon proposed, in an unprecedented action, that the demonstrators be allowed to remain on the convention floor near the podium as long as they were not disruptive. A majority of delegates agreed. The demonstrators asked the General Conference to declare a moratorium on enforcement of all church laws regarding homosexuality. But delegates decisively voted against that proposal by 637 to 320.

After a strong majority also voted to reaffirm the current church law explicitly prohibiting same-sex unions, pro-homosexuality demonstrators on the convention floor began singing. Bishop Solomon asked them to uphold their "covenant" not to be disruptive. But Miller, as spokesman for the demonstrators, asserted that because of the General Conference's vote, they would no longer abide by their promise.

Bishop Solomon responded that he was in "anguish" about the situation. He called a recess, and several Cleveland police officers escorted the demonstrators out of the convention center, including Bishops Morrison and Sprague (for his second arrest of the week). These demonstrators were quickly booked, fined, and released by Cleveland police.

When General Conference reconvened, delegates debated a proposal to water down the church's teaching on homosexuality by adding "some" to the Disciplinary statement that homosexual practice is incompatible with ["some"] Christian teaching.

Oregon delegate Stephen Frantz argued for the proposal, calling the stage "holy ground" because of the demonstrators' disruptive acts. When his proposal was defeated, Frantz ripped up his credentials in front of the microphone, angrily declaring, "You've made it clear that I don't belong in this church!" He then stomped away from the microphone.

Delegates overwhelmingly went on to reaffirm the church's expectation of "fidelity in marriage and celibacy in singleness."

Even more revealingly, the Cleveland General Conference did not just reaffirm United Methodism's teachings about marriage and sex by larger margins than previously. It went on to condemn partial-birth abortion, abandoned its pacifist stance in favor of just-war doctrine, supported voluntary school prayer and elected some solid evangelical Christians to the denomination's highest church court.

The delegates even voted to join with evangelicals and Catholics to pray for persecuted Christians around the world, despite claims by some church liberals that the "Day of Prayer for the Persecuted Church" was a "religious right" ploy.

The United Methodist Church, like most mainline denominations, has been losing membership for 35 years. But the fastest rate of decline has been in the church's most liberal regions. United Methodism on the West Coast and in the upper Northeast is imploding. In the South and lower Midwest, it is holding steady. Overseas, it is growing.

In recognition of these trends the General Conference voted to reapportion delegates for its next meeting in 2004, subtracting numbers from the declining West and Northeast and adding new delegates from the growing South and overseas. This would ensure that southern U.S. and overseas churches would together have a clear majority of delegates creating a potential evangelical governing majority.

This reapportionment meant that the homosexual lobby would likely fail by even greater margins at future General Conferences.

Church liberals, who traditionally champion the impoverished Third World, seemed unable to understand why delegates from Africa and Asia were the most adamant against accepting homosexual practice.

Church liberals also seemed unprepared for the decisive vote against partial-birth abortion by 70 percent of the delegates. Just four years before, during the 1996 General Conference, Board of Church and Society General Secretary Thom White Wolf Fassett signed on to an ecumenical letter of support for President Clinton's veto of legislation that would have banned the procedure.

Just as surprising was the relatively quick election of three evangelicals, Mary Daffin, Jim Holsinger and Keith Boyette, to fill vacancies on the Judicial Council. Daffin, a Houston lawyer, and Holsinger, the former Virginia Conference lay leader and later a Lexington, Kentucky, hospital executive, were both officers of the Confessing Movement. Boyette, a former lawyer and Virginia pastor, was a former Good News board member. Also pleasantly surprising was the election of the President of an independent evangelical seminary to the University Senate, which oversees the church's official seminaries and is traditionally the preserve of liberal academics. He was the Rev. Dr. Maxie Dunnam, who was president of Asbury Seminary in Wilmore, Kentucky.

A majority of the delegates were not yet willing to withdraw from the nearly comatose National and World Councils of Churches. But they did vote to seek observer status in the National Association of Evangelicals and the World Evangelical Fellowship, a move that few could have predicted only a few years ago.

Some traditionally liberal positions were adopted. Capital punishment was denounced. More gun control was endorsed. Without discussion, resolutions were passed that condemned the U.S. Navy presence in Puerto Rico, demanded an end to U.S. trade sanctions against Iraq and Cuba, called for a "Jubilee" global debt cancellation and urged closure of the U.S. Army's School of the Americas training school for Latin American military officers.

Conservatives saved their ammunition for battles over theology, sexual ethics and church governance.

Perhaps most important was the overwhelming passage of an addition to the UMC mission statement, affirming that "Jesus Christ is the Son of God, the Savior of the world, and the Lord of all." This strong statement implicitly ruled out theologies that declare all religions to be equally true.

A resolution advocating outright abolition of the General Board of Church and Society (GBCS) even got 30 percent of the vote! Treated unseriously in the Church and Society legislative committee, lay delegate Robert Ladd of Lebanon, Pennsylvania, took it to the floor of General Conference as a symbolic protest against GBCS. Ladd cited GBCS' involvement in the Elián Gonzalez case and GBCS's support for compelling the Boy Scouts to accept homosexual scout masters. "Every time this sort of thing happens . . . it has a negative public relations effect that will not be offset by the positive one of the Igniting Ministry campaign," Ladd told the delegates, referring to the church's media outreach campaign. As Ladd returned from the microphone, he noticed GBCS General Secretary Thom White Wolf Fassett casting a wary eye on him!

The conservative victories at Cleveland were shocking to liberals, long accustomed to decades of legislative dominance. And though they had never won on changing the church's stance on homosexuality, they had long assumed that triumph on this issue was inevitable. The set-backs in 2000 created rage and frustration among the liberal caucus groups.

At a rally sponsored by the Methodist Federation for Social Action (MFSA) during the conference in Cleveland, long-time liberal warhorse, the Rev. James Lawson, launched a bitter attack against "right-wing" United Methodist renewal organizations. He naturally faulted them for MFSA's own unaccustomed legislative defeats.

"The church is under assault by Good News, the IRD [the

Institute on Religion and Democracy], the Confessing Movement and the Mission Society [for United Methodists]," Lawson declared. "They are not interested in serving Jesus Christ. They are interested in the management and control of the United Methodist Church."

Lawson, a leader of the civil rights movement during the 1960s, had by 2000 retired from his Los Angeles pastorate. MFSA, with a 100-year history, is Methodism's oldest liberal caucus.

As Lawson loosed his thunderbolts against IRD and the other renewal groups, several colleagues and I sat in the balcony, carefully listening and surprised by Lawson's oratorical vehemence! The event was in an old downtown church in Cleveland, just blocks away from the convention center.

"They are more interested in preserving white supremacy and male domination," Lawson angrily and absurdly alleged about the renewal groups. "They are not voices of God but voices of white privilege, greed, capitalism, racism, wrong and American domination of the rest of the world," he shouted to hundreds of applauding supporters. So much for the liberal caucus groups pleas for tolerance and civility!

Lawson wove the UM renewal groups into a larger web of sinister conspiracy around the world. "Good News and the IRD, with backing from money they will never tell us is coming from [sic], don't want The United Methodist Church to become the voice of Iraq or Palestine or hungry children in this country." Lawson alleged that Good News and the IRD, with "their counterparts in other denominations and in the political world," are responsible for imprisoning two million Americans, in an apparent reference to the total prison population of the U.S. "It's our own version of the Holocaust. And it's not going to get any better."

My colleagues and I quietly smiled at each other as Lawson launched one fiery fusillade after another against us, apparently unaware, or at least indifferent, to our presence overlooking the pulpit.

Touting the benefits of disruptive demonstrations, Lawson warned: "We will make the church unmanageable until the church decides it will serve God and not America." He also asserted the greatest "enemy of truth and justice in the world today is the United States of America."

In a final jab at the renewal groups, Lawson insisted they "belong to the right-wing ideological junk of America. They have the money and the staff and the attention of the media." But Lawson insisted they cannot win and that their "assault on the church" is a sign of their weakness, not strength. Unfortunately, Lawson surmised, these groups will still cause "men and women and children and young people to suffer unnecessarily." He also warned, "We cannot win unless we see the enemy for who he is."

In a justification for planned upcoming acts of civil disobedience by pro-homosexuality caucus groups at the General Conference, Lawson surmised that "the church will not be persuaded by our conversation" because "the church is seduced by elements that are not of the church."

Lawson, a powerful pulpit presence, was predictably acclaimed by raucous applause by the several hundred frustrated MFSA activists. My colleagues and I declined to join in the applause. Instead we shook out heads and quietly filed out the back of the church into the Cleveland night.

A woman ran out of the church and down the street after us, handing us a handwritten note, and then running back to the church. It read: "Hey—I will be happy to tape any meetings for you and have them transcribed in order to keep you from bringing your negative energy into a group of loving people. You should be ashamed of your tactics. Stares, grimaces and negative presence only serve to cement your reputation. Shame." It was signed by Karen McCrocklin, who was a videographer for Reconciling Congregations.

Other than our occasional smiles and declining to join in the applause when Lawson denounced our renewal groups as racists, it's not clear what McCrocklin exactly meant by "negative energy." Rev. Lawson's speech had seemed very strong on the negative. It was very sad. Lawson had been a courageous figure in the civil rights movement decades ago. But the final years of his ministry were given over to a rejection of Christian orthodoxy to political radicalism and to ugly condemnations of traditional Christians who opposed the full liberal agenda for the church. It was an unfortunate closing chapter to a notable ministerial career.

Lawson's tirade was only a reflection of the despair on the liberal side. IRD/UM*Action* focused on the positive accomplishments at the Cleveland Conference, achieved while working closely with Good News, the Confessing Movement and the other renewal groups working for United Methodist reform.

UM*Action* had urged that United Methodists join with other Christians around the world in the International Day of Prayer for the Persecuted Church on behalf of suffering Christians under despotic Communist and Islamist regimes. United Methodist agencies, like the Board of Church and Society had not only refused to endorse this effort but had actually condemned it as a "religious right" ruse. But the delegates overwhelmingly endorsed the Day of Prayer.

UM*Action* had advocated that The United Methodist Church seek observer status in the National Association of Evangelicals and the World Evangelical Fellowship. We hoped this would expand our ecumenical cooperation beyond the reflexively liberal and declining National and World Councils of Churches. The delegates strongly agreed and voted to seek observer status in the NAE and WEA.

UM*Action* advocated changing United Methodism's official pacifist stance to one that acknowledged that most Christians understand war may be justified in extreme circumstances, including tyranny, genocide and unchecked aggression. Delegates agreed. Interestingly, one UM*Action* ally on this issue was the Rev. Philip Wogaman, pastor to the Clintons and chief advocate for the pro-homosexuality cause. He had also submitted legislation echoing my own submission. The Church and Society legislative committee ended up melding our two proposals. Seeing him in the hallway, I kidded him about the novelty of being allies on this one issue. Unsmilingly, he acknowledged having "heard something about that."

The church's stance on war would become highly relevant in a little over a year, after 9-11. Unfortunately, church agencies and the Council of Bishops refused to quote the new language, preferring to quote a Social Principles phrase about war's incompatibility with Jesus Christ.

UMAction had been troubled by the opposition of United Methodist agencies like the Board of Church and Society to any effort to allow voluntary prayer in public schools and other public situations. Delegates readily agreed with our proposal that we oppose any government restriction on voluntary prayer in the public schools or elsewhere.

Most importantly, delegates by a huge majority adopted a proposal from UMAction leaders that our denomination's mission statement should affirm Jesus Christ as "the Son of God, the Savior of the world and the Lord of all."

UMAction hosted two lunches in Cleveland that were well attended by delegates. The first featured David Coolidge of the Washington-based Marriage Project, who described why United Methodists should work for laws defining marriage as the union of one man and one woman and excluding legal recognition for same-sex couples. In 1996, President Clinton had signed the "Defense of Marriage Act." But liberal state courts were anxious to redefine marriage.

The second UMAction lunch featured Michael Horowitz of the Washington-based Religious Liberty Project. Horowitz implored the audience to speak out on behalf of persecuted Christians, especially in Communist China, who cannot speak for themselves. Horowitz was joined on the podium by Bishop S.K. Dass of

Hyderabad, Pakistan who recounted the persecutions that Christians commonly endure in his native land.

The *United Methodist Reporter* prominently reported about Horowitz's speech. "The thug regimes of the world can't use my people as scapegoats anymore because they've killed most of us," Horowitz declared, referring to his own Jewishness. "Now they're using your people, the Christians." Horowitz described a growing interfaith movement behind international religious freedom, from which mainline denominations like the United Methodists were noticeably absent. "Methodists can help right this wrong," he urged.

Rather than help persecuted Christians globally, the Board of Church and Society, along with several bishops, preferred to condemn the U.S. Navy's munitions testing facility at Vieques, Puerto Rico. They convened an anti-U.S. Navy press conference during General Conference to deplore the arrest of demonstrators who trespassed at the U.S. Navy base. Among the arrested was Methodist Bishop Juan Vera Mendez of Puerto Rico.

"We are disappointed that the U.S. government chose this course of action rather than continuing negotiations (with Vieques), and we stand in solidarity with the people arrested and the citizens of Vieques," said Bishop Charlene Kammerer of North Carolina.

"We ask that United Methodists and all people of conscience continue responding to God's call for justice until every single one of the 33,000 acres of the island now occupied by a hostile U.S. military presence is returned, bomb-free, to the people of Vieques," the Board of Global Ministries declared at the same press conference.

A majority of the delegates at General Conference almost seemed to operate in a parallel universe to the bishops and church agencies that were heavily present in Cleveland. While delegates had resoundingly defeated the pro-homosexuality initiatives, bishops seemed reluctant to defend the church's teachings.

At a press conference after pro-homosexuality demonstrators performed mass acts of civil disobedience outside the convention center, prompting nearly 200 arrests, several United Methodist bishops spoke only about their obligation to uphold church policy, not defend biblical beliefs.

Bishops Ken Carder of Tennessee, Woodie White of Indiana and Mary Ann Swenson of Colorado talked to reporters in the Cleveland Convention Center. Swenson had earlier attended the Soulforce demonstration outside the convention center, although she declined to be arrested along with Bishop Sprague.

"My own learning in [the ways of] non-violence to change our society is progressive," Swenson explained about her involvement. "I wanted to push for change." She defended Sprague's civil disobedience. "I do think it's appropriate that Bishop Sprague was arrested. He's being jailed on behalf of the Gospel."

Carder admitted that the conference delegates were "experiencing a gamut of emotions" in response to the demonstration and the debate over homosexuality. But he tried to minimize the controversy. "Our church continues to struggle. We are united in our commitment to Jesus Christ." Carder did admit the divisions within the Council of Bishops by acknowledging the "diversity" and "differences as to doctrine" among them.

Neither Carder nor White would describe their own views regarding the church's stance on homosexuality, saying to do so would be inappropriate during the General Conference. Although Swenson echoed their statements, her demonstrating with Soulforce had already answered the question. As if to remove any further doubt, she told the press conference that "her most moving moment" of the General Conference so far was serving Communion at an earlier demonstration by the pro-homosexuality Reconciling Congregations. She called it a "holy experience."

"I hope we're open to gifts from all God's people," Swenson further explained. "We shouldn't deny gifts because of someone's [sexual] orientation." When asked what her response would be if one of her pastors conducted a same-sex union, she said, "I don't know what I would do," adding, "I want pastors to have freedom of conscience." She grudgingly admitted her obligation to uphold church policies.

White responded to the same question, explaining he would have no alternative but to enforce the church's *Discipline*. Carder also said he was bound to abide by the decisions of General Conference and the judicial process within the church. He stressed that the bishops do not make church law, but play an "interpretative and prophetic role." He pointed out that "prophetic witness," which may include violations of church or civil law, have consequences.

Carder also remarked that "irresponsible heterosexual behavior" was doing great damage to the church. And he pointed to issues that he believes unite the church, such as ministries to children and confronting the "holocaust" among poor people. White tried to reinforce Carder's point by citing continued difficulties with racism.

White also pointed to "stands of a positive nature" that the church has adopted on homosexuality, which includes "civil rights" for homosexuals, the right to church membership, and a church policy that condemns the practice of homosexuality but not the "orientation."

Providing clarity where many U.S. bishops were not, Liberia's Bishop Arthur Kulah explicitly defended the church's teachings about homosexuality in a sermon to the General Conference.

Citing both the Old and New Testaments, Kulah preached: "It is against the background of such biblical imperatives that we, the global United Methodist Church, do not condone the practice of homosexuality and consider it incompatible with Christian teaching."

Warning against ordaining active homosexuals into the ministry, Kulah declared: "For to do so is to contravene the very faith we proclaim. For we cannot afford to ruin the hearts and lives of the church and hence the world by engaging in practices not even easily mentioned among believers."

Calling evangelism the church's "lifeblood," Kulah urged proclaiming Jesus Christ "crucified and resurrected," offering transformation to all people, including homosexuals. "We have the authority to proclaim Christ as the uniting force; as the bridge. In him, there is no East or West, no South or North, but one great fellowship divine throughout the whole wide world."

Speaking from a far different stance, retired Bishop Judith Craig spoke at the same MFSA rally where Rev. Lawson had excoriated the conservative renewal groups. She presented an award to Reconciling Congregations' chief, Mark Bowman. Craig sadly recalled that, years before, church law had forced her to refuse ordination to Bowman because he was openly homosexual. "You knew a lot more about faithfulness than I did," Craig said to Bowman. "This award is balm on a gaping wound that remains in the church. You are loved and honored."

Bowman celebrated that because he had been refused ordination by the United Methodist Church, he had been "liberated for the ministry that God had in store for me." But he and Craig indirectly acknowledged that they did not expect to win at this General Conference. They encouraged the crowd instead to expect victory at the next General Conference in Pittsburgh in 2004.

Summarizing the liberal defeatism later on, retired minister Harry Kiely of Silver Spring, Maryland, wrote for the November/December 2000 issue of the Board of Church and Society's magazine an article called: "The Conservative Shift in The United Methodist Church." Comparing the success of United Methodist renewal groups to the conservative take-over of the Southern Baptist Convention in the 1980s, Kiely cited the votes on homosexuality, the evangelicals elected to the Judicial Council, the reapportionment of delegates giving more representation to the

South and "increasing conservative representation" in the University Senate, which oversees the seminaries.

"The conservative coalition . . . has demonstrated a ruthless quality that is—more concerned with legalistic righteousness than with healing and recognition in the Body of Christ," Kiely alleged. "Rank-and-file United Methodists are now on the spot to resist the destructive tendencies of hatred and to reclaim the church's authentic ministry."

What Kiely and other liberal activists could not admit was that their liberal caucus groups, along with most of the church agencies, never represented most United Methodists. The votes in Cleveland indicated that the liberal elites were losing their once unquestioned control, and populist renewal groups were becoming better organized.

A religion reporter for the *Peoria Journal Star* summarized the Cleveland conference differently. "It's important to note that the gap in the votes indicates that many more than just the evangelical wing of the church thought it important to draw a line," Michael Miller wrote. "The lop-sided votes in essence said that while delegates understand homosexuals exist and are in need of ministry like everyone else, Christian teaching doesn't condone certain things."

Miller's point was simple and based on plain Christianity. But many bishops and church elites still did not understand it. The General Conference in Cleveland showed that despite the lack of leadership from them, most of the rank and file of the church knew which way the church should move.

CHAPTER TWELVE

TROUBLE IN THE SEMINARIES

In February 1998, Duke Divinity School's Center for Continuing Theological Education hosted a seminar that featured radical Jesus Seminar scholars. It was ominously called "Jesus in Context: Who Was He?" I drove down for the three-day event, and it turned out to be my introduction to the radicalism that has been on much of mainline Protestantism's seminary campuses for much of the last century. About 400 attended the conference, about half of them clergy from many denominations.

Only one of the seven scholars at the Duke event defended traditional beliefs about Jesus, his Virgin Birth, bodily Resurrection and miracles. The conference opened with each of the scholars being asked to cite gospel stories that were untrue. Former Catholic priest John Dominic Crossan of De Paul University declared that Jesus never said the Lord's Prayer, never instituted the Eucharist, never referred to himself as the "Son of Man" and did not have 12 disciples. These stories were developed by early Christians as part of their "crisis management" after Jesus' crucifixion, Crossan insisted.

United Methodist scholar E. P. Sanders of Duke University said that Jesus never claimed to save the world in a sacrificial death, which would be "too perfect to be Jesus' original idea." Paula Fredriksen of Boston University, a convert to orthodox Judaism, said that Jesus never walked on water and never predicted His own death and Resurrection. Jewish scholar Amy-Jill Levine of Vanderbilt University said Jesus was not born of a virgin, was not born in Bethlehem, never received gifts from wise men, did not return from the dead, never said the Sermon on the Mount and did not urge his disciples to carry out the Great Commission.

Episcopalian Marcus Borg of Oregon State University said that Jesus never walked on water, never multiplied loaves of bread, never proclaimed his divinity and was never tried before the high priests in Jerusalem. Kathleen Corley of the University of Wisconsin said that Jesus did not have 12 disciples and never convened a Last Supper. The Virgin Birth and resurrection stories were, she believed, created by the early church.

"I told you this would be fun," said Duke Professor Dale Martin amid laughter, as he moderated the discussion. Only panelist N. Thomas Wright, an Anglican cathedral dean from Britain, declined to dismiss any historical events in the canonical Gospels. Instead, he cleverly cited an inaccuracy in a Gnostic gospel! Wright was invited only after Jesus Seminar critic Luke Timothy Johnson of Candler School of Theology in Atlanta declined to attend.

"If Jesus did come back [from the dead], then good for him," Levine laughed. "I wish he would appear to me." Borg agreed. "I doubt anything happened to his corpse. The Resurrection has nothing to do with an empty tomb."

Corley speculated that the gospel stories of Jesus' post-resurrection appearances to various persons merely reflected debates over leadership in the early church. Crossan doubted that any early Christians believed that Jesus literally rose from the dead.

"How do appearances of Jesus differ from Elvis?" Levine joked. "They both ended being called king." She said the Gospels' claim that all saints will arise from the grave sounded like an unappealing "Night of the Living Dead"-style scenario.

Crossan said. "It doesn't matter where Jesus' bones are. It doesn't matter where Elvis' bones are either because Elvis is still around. The real question is: Why is Elvis important? Faith doesn't need superstition."

An audience member asked if any panelists believed in the Virgin Birth." "Yes," Wright replied. But Fredriksen countered, "I expect Mary's sexual history was the same as other mothers." Borg agreed. "The birth stories are spiritual imagery. They can be spiritually true but not factually true."

Alone among the panelists, Wright defended the Gospels' historicity. "I get anxious about contrasting real truth with fact, as in some detached Gnostic realm, which is distinct from the Jewish view." Crossan asked him if he also believed the Roman myth that the mother of Caesar Augustus was impregnated by the Greek god Apollo. "No," replied Wright, "Because the god in question is not a real god."

When the panelists were asked whether Jesus ever claimed to be divine, most said no. "The idea never crossed his mind that he was the second person of the Trinity," Sander said. "The Trinity wasn't developed for centuries. He had a very high opinion of himself. He was a spokesman for God in God's absence." Sanders believed that Jesus saw himself as the Messiah but not divine.

"I don't think Jesus was that arrogant," said Corley. "It's unlikely he thought himself divine." Borg agreed that Jesus' divine titles emerged only after his death. "I don't think people like Jesus spend time thinking about what they are really," said Borg. "He may have thought himself a prophet."

"If he actually said what is reported in John [about his divinity], He would have had no following," Fredriksen opined. "It's okay to think what you think without making Jesus think the same thing."

"I'm not sure he predicted his death or thought there was a purpose to his death," said Corley. Levine concurred. "He might have anticipated death. But he wasn't an atoning sacrifice. He was not a ransom for many." Borg likened Jesus to Gandhi and

Martin Luther King in anticipating his likely martyrdom, but "he didn't intend his death to have salvific purpose."

"Does God want atonement?" asked Crossan. "I find that incredibly obscene. Atonement is transcendental child abuse. I will not worship that God. I would rather stay in hell away from him."

But Wright defended the Christian understanding of God's Son dying upon a cross. "I take charges of divine child abuse very seriously. The church developed the Trinity to show it's not God doing it to somebody else, but to himself, as part of his self-giving love." But Borg countered, "The Atonement only works in the completed Christian myth. But it doesn't work for a Galilean peasant."

A disappointed audience member asked what the church's purpose was without the miracles, Virgin Birth and the resurrection of Jesus.

"I'm amazed by the question," Crossan responded. "The Virgin Birth is a parable. The people who made these stories knew exactly what they were doing. Luke didn't intend a literal meaning."

"Truthfulness and factuality don't go hand in hand," agreed Borg. "People didn't believe in Jesus because he did spectacular things." But Wright countered, "You can't explain the rise of the church unless you accept that the disciples believed something happened to his body."

Crossan concluded, "We need open heart surgery on Christianity and our culture."

The headline in the *Raleigh News and Observer* during the Duke conference was "Scholars Don't Take Beliefs about Jesus as Gospel." Based on the event, the article explained that "the most renowned group of Jesus experts" believe that Christianity's "most basic beliefs," such as the Virgin Birth, are mostly "myth." This seemed like a poor way for United Methodist affiliated Duke Divinity School to witness to the local community.

I shared my article about the Duke event, which quoted all

the speakers at length, with Carol Voisin, who had organized the conference as head of Duke's Center for Continuing Theological Education. She had few suggested changes but disputed that Wright believed in the Virgin Birth. So I contacted Wright, and he confirmed that he believed in the "physical factuality of the virginal conception" of Jesus. Affirming his role in the conference, Wright said it "is vital to engage in debate with any and all serious scholars (which they all are) who have something to say about Jesus." And he noted that "U.S. biblical scholars are trained in great detail on technical exegetical matters but not at all on theology or philosophy; then when they really are devout, thinking Christians, they have little to fall back on to work things out, so [they] tend to go with whatever flow seems most appealing."

Wright went on to become a bishop in the Church of England and an internationally celebrated biblical scholar and defender of Christian orthodoxy. Voisin soon left her job at Duke. And the incoming dean of the divinity school, Greg Jones, was theologically orthodox. Under Jones, the seminary at Duke was less inclined to host events like "Jesus in Context: Who Was He?" Later in 1998, Jones hosted the 21st annual Christmas Conference for A Foundation for Theological Education (AFTE), which IRD founder Ed Robb had also founded to fund orthodox scholars for United Methodism. Jones himself had been an AFTE scholar, as are six other professors now at Duke, including Richard Hays, whose *The Moral Vision of the New Testament: Community, Cross, New Creation* is a classic presentation of orthodox theology. Duke Divinity School is one of United Methodism's 13 official seminaries and is often cited as the closest to being theologically orthodox, though AFTE now has scholars on the faculty of eight United Methodist seminaries.

The radicalism of the "Jesus in Context" event was not reflective of the overall theological climate at Duke in recent years. But the event did helpfully showcase what has been for decades common fare in most liberalized mainline Protestant seminaries, where orthodox faculty are typically a small minority. Jesus Seminar fellows such as Crosson and Borg sometimes express astonishment that orthodox theology has any representation in academia. But the event at Duke was helpful in showcasing what many young United Methodist seminarians have heard for many decades.

Besides the seminaries, more than 100 universities and colleges are affiliated with The United Methodist Church, including Duke University. Unfortunately, few of these schools, which prominently include Emory in Atlanta, Southern Methodist in Dallas and American in Washington, D.C., have remained meaningfully Christian in their academics or campus atmosphere. This was amply illustrated in December 2000, when Duke's President Nanerly Keohane announced that the campus' magnificent gothic chapel would permit same-sex unions by clergy whose denominations allow them. In her December 5, 2000, letter, Keohane specifically cited Unitarians, the United Church of Christ and "some Baptists," who had been "experimenting with these unions for some time now."

Keohane cited Duke's "wonderful tradition of rich religious diversity," thanks to its "Methodist roots." Her letter said "any couple with a Duke relationship may ask to schedule a commitment ceremony for a same-sex union in the Chapel." She noted that United Methodism prohibits same-sex unions, but she assumed this policy had no authority over Duke. Unfortunately, the letter was co-signed by Duke's Dean of the Chapel, William Willimon, a celebrated United Methodist preacher who also taught at Duke Divinity School.

Bishop Charlene Kammerer of Western North Carolina observed that Duke's policy was in "conflict" with United Methodism's position but "reflects an open spirit of hospitality and pastoral care to the wider Duke University community." More stalwartly, Bishop Marion Edwards of eastern North Carolina accepted that Duke Chapel was not bound by church policies but said, "I uphold the teaching of the church that marriage is between one man and one woman. The clear affirmation of the Scripture calls us to that standard."

More strongly, Duke Divinity School theologian Geoffrey Wainwright noted that the university's founder, James Duke, had invoked "Jesus Christ, the Son of God," in the school's stated aims, that the ecumenical church "rejects homosexual practice, that it was a "mistake" to think that same-sex unions were the "wave of the future" in Christianity and that such rites in the chapel would "desecrate a space . . . hallowed by decades of prayer."

Wainwright was correct about the chapel's explicit Christian origins. When dedicated in 1935, Duke University President B. R. Lacy had declared: "The chapel says to the world that here God has the preeminence and that all life should be lived under His shadow, within the sound of his voice, and under the influence of His beauty and holiness." Lacy continued: "This chapel must speak of Christ;" "its simple ceremonies of our Protestant faith (must) center in the open Word of God;" and be filled with a "thousand voices" within its walls reciting the Apostles' Creed.

Believing that the new Duke policy was a betrayal of Duke's Methodist history, our March 2001 *UMAction Briefing* urged readers to ask Willimon to "renounce the new policy" at Duke Chapel and, "if the university persists in carrying it through, to resign his position as dean in protest." Evangelicals long considered Willimon to be a friend, and some hoped that he would disavow a decision clearly imposed by Duke University's liberal president. Apparently Willimon was deluged with emails. Some apparently were ugly, about which he complained to me. On April 9, 2001, I responded to him:

> I apologize for persons who have contacted you in a hateful or rude way. Every week for the last six or seven years I have been on the receiving end of such correspondence. I do not understand people professing to be Christians who cannot

express their opinions with grace, even when angry. Please also know that nowhere have I written that you personally support same-sex unions, have violated your ordination vows or that you should be silenced, much less that your ministry should be ended. It's not silence that we want from you, but a more forceful articulation of the views I know you have. As I wrote you last, you are respected as a man of God in our denomination, which is why expectations of you are high. We suggested that you consider resignation as dean of the chapel after the first same-sex union is celebrated there because it would powerfully convey your own opposition to same-sex unions. I firmly believe that God would bless such an act of conscience, and that the vast majority of United Methodists would honor you for the strength of your convictions. The growing acceptance of same-sex relationships on our university campuses, even including our church-affiliated schools, is bad for our churches, bad for our society, bad for the young people at those schools, bad for persons who are trapped in homosexual conduct, bad for the institution of marriage, and bad for any effort to teach that self-restraint, chastity and fidelity are virtues still worth upholding. I know that you believe these things, and my prayers are with you during this Holy Week and through future years, as you continue to contend for the faith in a difficult environment.

On May 2, 2001, Willimon penned a column about the episode in *Christian Century* magazine. He wrote that UM*Action* had "trashed" him and had "informed its constituency that the time had come to pull the plug on Willimon. The group demanded my immediate resignation, and printed my e-mail address on its website." He reported getting a hundred emails a day over two weeks as a result of UM*Action*, one third of which were supportive and two-thirds called him "cowardly for not resigning."

Willimon noted that for 20 years he had "been agitating for United Methodist renewal, and I have never met people like these UM*Action* people." After forwarding "some of the more salacious e-mails" to me, he characterized my response as: "If you can't take the heat, get out of the kitchen." He noted that he was "trapped between my unwillingness to invoke liberal canons of tolerance and diversity and my repugnance for the skewed biblical interpretation of Mark Tooley's cyberstorm troops." And he concluded: "Sorry, UM*Action*, you're going to have to push me out of here with a crowbar."

Of course, UM*Action* was NOT trying to push Willimon out but encourage him to SPEAK out against a policy that was being imposed by the ongoing secularization of once meaningfully United Methodist schools. Willimon was elected a bishop of North Alabama in 2004, and I met him for the first time right after the election at Lake Junaluska. He was very friendly and has remained so at all of our subsequent encounters. Creditably, he apparently declined an invitation to appear on the 2007 anti-IRD video *Steeplejacking*. And he has presided over his episcopal area admirably, largely avoiding controversy. In 2005, he criticized Lake Junaluska for hosting the "Hearts on Fire" rally by prohomosexual caucus groups. He chafed a little when UM*Action* publicly praised him. A quirky and independent spirit, Willimon does not like to be seen aligned too closely with anybody!

Both the "Jesus in Context" event and the chapel controversy sadly involved Duke, when many of United Methodism's schools are far more estranged from traditional Christian teaching. Iliff School of Theology in Denver is considered one of the most radical. Its annual "Week of Lectures" often provides a window into the latest liberal theological fads, and the February 1999 keynote speaker was Marcus Borg, a fellow of the controversial Jesus Seminar. Even more than at the Duke event, Borg dismissed New Testament stories of Jesus' miracles and divinity as myth and metaphor.

Bishop Mary Ann Swenson of Denver warmly introduced Borg at Iliff as a "man who has risked all in order to bridge the gap between academy and church pew." "He feeds us," the bishop said. "His presence with us is blessing to us. His personal way of being is blessing to us. He helped me to recall my first memory of Jesus."

In his address, Borg dismissed an "older understanding" of Jesus and the Bible that believed that the "central events" of Christianity, the parting of the Red Sea, the Virgin Birth, or Jesus' walking on water, literally happened. This old understanding included the Nicene Creed as a regular part of worship, was "moralistic," focused on Jesus as the only way of salvation and was concerned about the afterlife. "We need to be clear and candid," Borg said. "The Bible is a human product." Ascribing it to divine inspiration leads to "massive confusion." He cited prohibitions against homosexual conduct as clearly "not God's law" but human inventions.

Borg recalled once believing in the Christmas story as literally involving a Virgin Birth, a "magic star" and wise men with gifts. He did so because he lacked the "mental equipment" when young to think otherwise. Most people develop the ability for critical thinking in late adolescence, he noted. "Fundamentalists" reject this route and instead uncritically cling to stories of Noah and the Garden of Eden. But maturity involves moving into "post-critical" thinking so as to accept Bible stories as not factual but still spiritually true in some mystical way, Borg affirmed. He related that his own spiritual development had rejected "supernatural theism" altogether in favor of panentheism. The former hails God as creator of the universe, while the latter acknowledges the universe as literally part of God. (This is slightly different from pantheism, which asserts that the cosmos is God in his entirety.)

The old supernatural theism, according to Borg, had described God as separate from the universe and occasionally intervening in it, making God "remote and irrelevant." But panentheism recognizes that "we and everything that is are in God. God is not something else. God is right here and all around us. We are within God." Panentheism, Borg claimed, is very "ancient" and was a "foundational element in the Christian tradition."

This panentheism allows us to pray to a "reality that is all around us," Borg affirmed. "The best way to refer to God is you, the you who is right here." He called himself a "happy agnostic" regarding life after death. "Salvation is something that happens in this life." He said, "I don't think God cares if we're Christian or Muslim or Buddhist or something not yet born. We're not talking about a divine requirement that we be Christian."

Borg distinguished between the pre-Easter and the post-Easter Jesus. The pre-Easter man was simply a great historical figure who fought for social justice. But the post-Easter figure, he asserted which the early church developed in its traditions, became a divine miracle-worker who was raised from the dead. Borg said Jesus could be viewed as the "decisive disclosure of God" without having to say he's the "only one or without even saying he's the best one." He described the Bible and Jesus as simply a helpful "lense" through which to view the sacred. "If we stop using the Christian lense then we cease to be Christian and that's not the end of the world. If humanity lasts 10,000 years then I expect that if Christianity lasts at all then it will be a tiny sect like Zoroastrianism. We're not going to last forever in the Christian tradition. The Christian lense will eventually fall into disuse."

According to Borg, "fundamentalism" has "reached its high water mark." He forecast a "very bright" future for mainline churches if they understand their traditions "metaphorically" and not literally. To be successful, churches will have to recognize that

Christianity is not the only way of salvation, he concluded. The Iliff audience received Borg's theology approvingly.

It's hard to validate Borg's claim that "fundamentalism," by which he really means traditional Christianity, has peaked. The denominations and seminaries, like Iliff, that share Borg's theologies have suffered decades of decline. And almost all thriving churches and seminaries in the U.S. and around the world share an orthodox understanding of Christianity. But undoubtedly Borg does speak for much of the elite of mainline Protestantism, wanting to remain "spiritual" and retain Christian language and symbols, while not bound to Christian doctrine or ethics.

One of the strongest attacks on Christian orthodoxy within our seminaries in recent years came from radical feminist theology, which dismissed the Scriptures as "patriarchal," i.e., male-dominated. It proposed the worship of new feminine images of God or even the exaltation of ancient goddesses. One of the most notorious episodes of goddess adoration occurred at a chapel service at United Methodist Garrett School of Theology on May 4, 1995. Its litany, called "A Psalm in Search of the Goddess," offered prayers to more than a dozen ancient goddesses, including Ishtar, Isis, Asherah, Cybele, Athene, Aphrodite and Astarte. Sophia and Gaia the earth goddess were also adored.

A few days after the service, Garrett professor Robert Jewett wrote that "praying to such deities should be repudiated as a fundamental contradiction of Christian faith." He called the adoration of "brutal deities in the name of liberation" an "unfortunate example of historical amnesia" and also a "violation" of Garrett's "deepest faith commitments." Radical feminist theologian Rosemary Radford Ruether had been the speaker at the controversial chapel service, although a student had introduced the litany. Responding to Jewett, she called the liturgy a "mistake in terms of audience and communication strategy" but "not theologically objectionable." She insisted that "true glimpses of the divine" have arisen in "many religions" and she warned against a "Christian parochial exclusivism."

Garrett's then president, Neal Fisher, in his first official response to the controversy, said the seminary encourages "inclusive" language for God but "had no desire to justify the use of the materials in question in our chapel or to condone their use in the churches." Later, he called the goddess litany "theologically objectionable." When IRD did a news release about the goddess litany and Ruether, Fisher complained of its distortion. In an August 23, 1995, letter to me, he wrote, "If you find it impossible to push your agenda without a sign of Christian charity, I hope you will at least consider yourself bound by the elemental respect for the facts and withstand the temptation to smear those with whom you disagree." But Fisher would not identify what "distortion" was in our news release.

In her own response to our news release, Ruether similarly "deplored" IRD's "campaign of misinformation" but she also declined to identify any specific inaccuracies. Nor would she disavow the goddess litany, calling its introduction into the chapel service "ill-advised," but seemingly only for pragmatic and not theological reasons. She asserted that we need to "consider larger issues of how we recognize positive elements in other religious traditions, as well as negative elements, such as racism and militarism, in our own traditions." Seven years later, Garrett was under new leadership, and Ruether retired.

Ruether's colleagues and fans gathered at Garrett in April, 2002, to celebrate her 25 years at the seminary. Attended by my then-assistant Chris Regner, the Ruether conference became a rally against the "patriarchal" systems against which Ruether railed and which supposedly drew their power from traditional Christian doctrines. Ruether herself recalled having embraced feminism at age eight when she was told she would "make a good wife," which provoked her "anger and betrayal" by its supposed denial of her own identity.

International theologians from different religions at Garrett hailed Ruether's work, which included *Gaia & God: An Ecofeminist Theology of Earth Healing*. This book ascribed to the earth (Gaia was the Greek earth goddess) divine attributes. Politically outspoken, Ruether responded by distributing her own self-written anti-Israel petition for her colleagues to sign. "[We] protest the continuing violence against the entrapped Palestinian people by the armed violence of the Israeli military and the policy of criminal acquiescence to this violence and destruction of the American government," she declared. Ruether demanded that the U.S. end all economic support for Israel, and she urged all countries to "break economic relations" with Israel. Since retirement from Garrett, Ruether has endorsed 9-11 conspiracy theories that claim the U.S. Government destroyed the World Trade Center.

Thankfully, Ruther's brand of radical feminist theology has mostly faded from popularity, even if her paranoid style of politics among seminary elites has not. A leading 9-11 conspiracy theorist is David Ray Griffin, a professor emeritus at United Methodist Claremont School of Theology in California. Griffin has written several books describing how the Bush Administration orchestrated the 9-11 destruction. Ruether even provided a supportive blurb for Griffin's *Christian Faith and the Truth Behind 9/11*, which claims that "the motives behind this false-flag operation were imperial motives, oriented around the dream of extending the American empire so that it is an all-inclusive global empire, resulting in a global Pax Americana."

Griffin is a disciple of Claremont's famous "process" theologian James Cobb, who asserts that God is constantly evolving and never complete, and with whom Griffin directs the Center for Process Studies at Claremont. Griffin rejects the idea that Jesus bodily rose from the dead, which he says was actually a doctrine that the church contrived decades after Jesus' death. Instead, Jesus had a spiritual "resurrection" over the demonic power of the Roman Empire. "For Christians in this country to denounce and work against the America empire will, of course, require courage, because we may be subjected to one of the many contemporary forms of crucifixion," Griffin has warned. "It is good, therefore, that we have our resurrection faith." Except this "resurrection" is, for Griffin, not a real thing, but merely a helpful political metaphor.

Nutty conspiracy theories are popular on some of United Methodism's most radical campuses, but homosexual causes are still far more popular. One of the most startling was in April 2007 at United Methodist Boston University School of Theology in a conference called "Queering the Church: Changing Ecclesial Structures." Speakers discussed "hardcore queer theology," "triadic unions," "erotic relation with the divine" and the "queerness of God."

One speaker at "Queering the Church" was Professor Mark Jordan from United Methodist-affiliated Emory University in Atlanta. He denounced the "exclusion of queer bodies" and the "long history of persecution, and facing condemnation from dominant theologies." Jordan called for Christians to go further in "exploring the present queerness of bodies in church—or the implications of enacted queer ritual." The professor warned, "When churches fail queer people, they fail the principle of incarnational theology. . . . It is a refusal to understand what incarnation means." There is an urgent "need to lift the ban on queer love," Jordan concluded. "The language of the queer church is a hot breath of desire."

Ray Nothstine, a former IRD intern and Asbury Seminary graduate, attended "Queering the Church" as an IRD reporter. During the event, his tape recordings of the event were snatched by a conference organizer. After Ray talked to a Boston University police officer, the organizer returned the tapes, which had been erased. The conference organizer then offered Ray $100 to turn over his written notes. When Ray asked why he was so eager to suppress coverage of the event, he charged that IRD's reporting was "biased."

In refreshing contrast to the outrageous behavior at the Boston seminary event, I had the pleasure of covering a symposium on Wesleyan doctrine sponsored by the John Wesley Institute outside Chicago, in February 2005. The featured speakers were then Garrett Seminary President Ted Campbell and Kansas Bishop Scott Jones, who formerly taught at United Methodist Perkins School of Theology in Dallas. Campbell previously taught at United Methodist Wesley Seminary in Washington, D.C., and both he and Jones are John Wesley fellows who emerged from AFTE.

"Doctrine is crucial for the existence of a religious organization, and we haven't done a good job," Jones declared. "How do we stay Wesleyan if we don't heed the *Notes and Sermons of John Wesley* in some way?" He addressed the responsibility of clergy to uphold the church's teachings. "You need to not preach your personal theology but preach the theology of the church," Jones said. "You are duty bound to be Wesleyan. Dissent from the church is important but must be done appropriately."

Campbell listed the essentials of Christian doctrine as described by John Wesley, which were the Trinity, the deity of Christ, the Atonement, biblical authority, original sin, justification by faith alone and regeneration by new birth. Wesley believed that the doctrine of the Trinity of Father, Son and Holy Spirit was a "fundamental belief" of Christian faith, according to Campbell. Sincere believers may not know the terminology and might even have mistaken opinions about it, he noted. But Wesley thought faithful and serious Christians must uphold the doctrine.

Wesley thought believing in the "complete divinity" of Christ was also "essential" to Christianity, as Campbell explained. Similarly, Wesley thought there was "nothing of greater consequence" than the doctrine of Atonement. Without belief in the Atonement, religion becomes merely deism, Wesley feared. Campbell said Wesley did not insist on "any particular understanding" of the Atonement but emphasized that "salvation was based on the whole life of Christ."

Campbell noted that Wesley was committed to the traditional Protestant doctrine of scripture alone as the final authority for the church. Likewise, Wesley affirmed the doctrine of original sin but modified the Augustinian and Reformed belief that God would damn persons for the sins of their ancestors. According to Campbell, Wesley leaned on Eastern Orthodox traditions by stressing that we are "liable for [our] own sins, not the sins of our parents."

Another traditional Protestant belief that Wesley thought essential was justification by faith alone, Campbell said. But Wesley's emphasis was slightly different because he insisted that faith cannot mean only assent but must engage the heart and affections. Wesley's seventh essential doctrine was regeneration through the "new birth," Campbell said. Methodism's founder warned against leaning on the "slender read of baptism," when salvation required being born again. Belief in the possibility of entire sanctification beyond regeneration was a distinguishing mark of Methodism, though Campbell said Wesley did not make that an essential Christian doctrine.

Campbell and Jones complained about United Methodist seminary education. "Modern seminaries fail our students by breaking down each book of the Bible," Campbell said. Seminaries used to teach only a "historical-critical" approach to the Bible, presuming that entering students knew the Bible's basic content, he recounted. But now students need to be taught both content and the critical approach, while also knowing that the church teaches that there is a unity to the biblical message.

Noting that the Kansas Area of which he is now bishop had suffered a 50 percent loss in Sunday school attendance, Jones complained of widespread membership decline. "The United Methodist Church has become more liberal and the culture more conservative and people have gone elsewhere," he said. "There has to be greater doctrinal discipline." Jones observed: "There is a bend-over-backwards, don't-offend-anybody attitude in the United Methodist Church that doesn't mention Jesus."

United Methodism's official seminaries are still dominated by liberal theology. But increasingly, John Wesley fellows like Jones and Campbell, who now teaches at Perkins Seminary, are more numerous and influential. Even more significant are the numbers of prospective United Methodist clergy who attend independent evangelical schools, Asbury Seminary foremost among them. Located in Wilmore, Kentucky, just outside Lexington, nearly one thousand United Methodists now attend Asbury, representing almost one third of the church's total seminary population.

Unfortunately, Asbury receives no official funding from our denomination, which channels about $1 million annually into each of the official seminaries, creating inordinate disparities. Boston University School of Theology, for example, has about 60 United Methodist students, only six percent of Asbury's total. That works out to more than $16,000 per student!

Will this disparity continue? Or do evangelical seminaries and evangelical professors represent the future of United Methodism?

CHAPTER THIRTEEN

GENERAL CONFERENCE 2004 – RENEWAL OR DIVISION?

At the 2004 General Conference in Pittsburgh, delegates over-whelmingly defeated attempts to overthrow or dilute the church's disapproval of homosexual practice. With the exception of one vote, the margins were greater than in 2000. But evangelicals were emotionally exhausted and astonished by the acrimony of the pro-homosexuality forces. Presiding Bishop Janice Huie's in-viting demonstrators to parade on the General Conference floor was especially galling.

Amid the tension, Confessing Movement President Bill Hin-son publicly suggested a formal division of United Methodism so as to end the draining battle. The suggestion, from the former pastor of United Methodism's once largest church, aroused inter-national headlines. In the end, Hinson's suggestion was dispelled by a symbolic General Conference vote affirming the church's unity. And when the dust had cleared, liberalism's hegemony over the church had eroded further. The conference reapportioned the composition of the church's agencies, increasing representation for the church's growing conservative areas in the south and re-ducing the often over-represented fast declining liberal areas of the West and Northeast. Conservatives retained a majority on the Judicial Council, the church's top court, but not before three liberals who oppose the church's teaching were elected.

Liberal caucus groups claimed that the 2004 votes on homo-sexuality had narrowed since 2000. This was incorrect with one exception. The Social Principles' affirmation that the church does not condone homosexual practice got 60 percent in 2004, down from 65 percent in 2000, and the same as in 1996. The difference may be attributable to the issue having moved from the more conservative Faith and Order legislative committee in 2000 back to the more liberal Church and Society committee in 2004. Even there the liberal side prevailed only by one vote, and only because an African delegate did not return to his seat in time to vote.

On all other homosexuality votes, the margins expanded in favor of the church's teachings. In 2000, 67 percent voted to prohibit actively homosexual clergy, increasing to 72 percent in 2004. In 2000, 69 percent voted to prohibit same-sex unions, increasing to 80 percent in 2004. In 2000, 80 percent affirmed celibacy in singleness and monogamy in marriage for clergy, increasing to 85 percent in 2004. The ban on funding for pro-homosexuality advocacy by general church agencies was approved by 70 percent in 2000, increasing to 99 percent in 2004.

The 2004 General Conference also reinforced the church's disapproval of homosexual practice in several other areas. By 77 percent, it endorsed laws in civil society that define marriage as the union of one man and one woman. (This resolution came from me and was unsuccessfully opposed by Thom White Wolf Fassett in legislative committee.) By 54 percent, it expanded the prohibition of pro-homosexuality advocacy by church agencies to include local annual conferences. By 51 percent, it specified that chargeable offenses include not being celibate in singleness or not being faithful in marriage, being a self-avowed practicing homosexual or conducting same-sex ceremonies.

Both in 2000 and 2004, numerous attempts at "compromise" language were rejected. In 2000, the closest "compromise" vote was a proposal to change "we do not condone" to "many do not condone" homosexual behavior. This weaker language was defeated by 54 percent. In 2004, a proposal that said The United Methodist Church does not condone homosexual practice, but recognizes disagreement on the matter, was defeated by 55 percent. The one attempt by an official United Methodist agency to change the church's stance on homosexuality came from the General Board of Church and Society, which proposed amending the Social Principles to read that "faithful Christians disagree on the compatibility of homosexual practice with Christian teaching." This proposal was rejected by 95 percent.

Despite these defeats, liberal caucus groups were intensely active in Pittsburgh. Having apparently realized that the demonstrations and arrests of 2000 were politically counter-productive, they instead focused on off-site rallies. One example was a Reconciling Ministries Network church service at a nearby Presbyterian church. The irrepressible Bishop Joe Sprague, wearing a rainbow stole, was an official "co-celebrant."

Former Nashville minister Janet Wolf, a prominent Reconciling activist, claimed the church was at a "crisis" point in which the "evil" of those who oppose the homosexual agenda "seems to reign." She urged rejecting "compromise . . . and cooperation with the powers and principalities" of evil. Wolf warned against "the man who appears to be the Lamb, uses the words of the Lamb," and "appears in the places where the Lamb might be, but is not the Lamb."

Resounding applause greeted San Francisco minister Karen Oliveto, who was the first United Methodist pastor to conduct a legally recognized homosexual "marriage" ceremony, when San Francisco temporarily recognized same-sex unions. Warning against a "restrictive definition of marriage," she denounced the "oppression" and "homophobia" of official church policy, bragging that "try as others may, they can't get rid of us." Oliveto left local church ministry before charges could be filed against her. Meanwhile, retired Bishop Leontine Kelly, speaking at a Methodist Federation for Social Action (MFSA) luncheon, equated approval of homosexuality with being "willing to take the risk of following Jesus." Kelly admitted feeling embarrassed to be a United Methodist and warned that the church was "at a point when a split is the intent of some." But she insisted: "You don't win a battle by leaving the battlefield. We're here to stay!"

Similarly, retired Bishops Jack Tuell and Joseph Yeakel addressed still another MFSA gathering, when they told of their role in the March 2004 acquittal of openly lesbian minister Karen Damman, whom a Seattle church jury refused to defrock by claiming the church had no clear policy. Tuell admitted there was "no skirting around the truth" and that the jury of 13 elders did find by a 13-0 vote that Dammann had participated in homosexual acts. Having been an expert witness at her trial, Tuell agreed with the verdict that the *Discipline's* prohibitions against homosexual behavior by clergy are not legally binding. He confessed that much of his "testimony focused on grammar, frankly."

Bishop Yeakel said that in his 26 years of being a bishop he never asked for the credentials of anyone who was honest about being homosexual, although some were motivated by their consciences voluntarily to step aside. He coyly suggested that heterosexual people should be asked when they chose their sexual orientation.

At MFSA's largest rally, with hundreds of supporters including many bishops, MFSA co-chair Joseph Agne praised Rev. Dammann, who sat in the audience. "She is someone to whom history called," Agne declared, "and she responded wonderfully." He hailed the church's Western region, which declined to convict Dammann, as the "rainbow jurisdiction." Applauding bishops included Beverly Shamana of California-Nevada, Fritz Mutti of Kansas and retired bishops Joe Wilson, Dale White, Don Ott, Roy Sano and Calvin McConnell.

During every General Conference, MFSA awards its Lee and Mae Ball Award to a noted "progressive" church activist. The 2004 recipient was the Rev. Gilbert Caldwell, a one-time civil rights activist who now champions homosexual causes. "He embodies the hopefulness of the Resurrection," chimed MFSA Executive Director Kathryn Johnson about Caldwell. "He has crossed boundaries of race and class and sexual orientation and gender." She added, to laughter from the audience, that Caldwell "turns out commentaries and articles faster than [UM*Action* Director] Mark Tooley."

Caldwell recalled his arrest at the 2000 General Conference during a pro-homosexuality rally. He insisted on the "inevitability of change" in the church and compared the civil rights movement for American blacks to today's homosexual cause. "Maybe 50 years from now those from the conservative movement in the church will thank MFSA," he suggested about MFSA's "justice" work. Caldwell, who was one of the early leaders of Black Methodists for Church Renewal, admitted that he is no longer active with that group, whose views on homosexuality disagree with his. "Sometimes I felt they were on one course and I on another," Caldwell noted. "But I still love that organization."

"All of us must change," Caldwell insisted. "There was a time in the church when there were concerns about folks who smoke and drink." But some of those smokers and drinkers were among Caldwell's most effective mentors, he recalled. "Similarly, there was a time when the church looked askance at divorce," Caldwell remembered. "Now look at the bishops!" he told a giggling audience, making light of the number of divorced bishops.

"I don't believe that delegates who are conservative, moderate or liberal want their grandchildren to know they were the ones who kept a separate place for gays and lesbians," Caldwell asserted. "Why would anyone want that on their record?" he asked. "Who would say, 'I am proud of that'?"

Caldwell alleged, "In the life of the church we are denying Jesus" by disapproving of homosexual practice. "There are folks who have been called," he said. "Some would deny them a visa into the United Methodist ministry. How empty! How unfaithful!" Caldwell claimed "to be estranged from one's own sexuality" was a great tragedy. "We are denying persons from being fulfilled in their relationships," he complained of the church's stance that sex is only for marriage. He wondered, "Will God open the hearts of hundreds of delegates? It's not too late."

But in fact it was too late for the pro-homosexuality cause in 2004. Once again, African delegates led the way in defending traditional Christian teachings. "We have received teaching from our missionaries on marriage," said Tshibang Kasap Owan from the Congo, who recalled African polygamy. "And the Christian teaching that we received taught that there should be marriage between one man and one woman. . . . We Africans, we accepted this teaching, and we became Christians." Tshibang warned, "Now we are hearing another message in this General Conference," speaking of homosexuality.

Another Congolese delegate, Yema Kasongo, agreed. "The church needs to speak with a clear voice" and not be "ambiguous," he said. "The church is not here to follow the will of every... person. It is [up] to the individual to follow God's will through the church's voice." Muland Aying Karribol from the Congo similarly warned against compromising the church's sexual standards. "If The United Methodist Church today is passing through a time of confusion, our children will live through a time of destruction in the church." He questioned whether it was "permissible to us to waste so much time speaking about sin."

Forbes Matonga of Zimbabwe reiterated: "When we are saying 'no' to homosexuality, we are not hating the persons . . . Like prostitution and everything else, it is not a person. It is about a practice." Liberian delegate Samuel Quire added, in language stronger than any U.S. delegate would have dared try, "I don't think The United Methodist Church can license people to go to hell . . . It is a sin that leads to hell."

After all the votes on homosexuality had been completed, Presiding Bishop Janice Huie announced that pro-homosexuality demonstrators would enter the General Conference arena. She did not consult with the delegates. She called the demonstrators "guests" who "come in peace as a witness among us." Two dozen bishops stood in solidarity with several hundred delegates as the demonstrators walked in a circle on the General Conference floor for 35 minutes. They were festooned with rainbow paraphernalia, and many carried placards denouncing the church's stance. They also placed a three-foot tall rainbow candle on the General Conference altar. The delegates watched in silence, with many believing that the altar had been desecrated.

Before this silent demonstration, an MFSA event had featured Baltimore-Washington delegate Mike McCurry, former spokesman for President Bill Clinton. Perhaps more accustomed to political realities, McCurry warned liberal activists against pushing too hard. He favored a "more inclusive" approach to homosexuality. "But now I find myself torn over the division in our denomination over this issue," he said, citing the many letters he had received warning against change in the church's stance.

"There are those who say we can never be silent [on homosexuality]," McCurry acknowledged. But constant polarizing debates on this issue are a "formula for gridlock and despair that exists in our political system." He said his wife and daughter marched in a recent pro-abortion rights demonstration in Washington, D.C. But he also urged caution, admitting that some abortion rights speakers may have been strident. "We have to be equally sensitive on issues where we represent the majority of most Americans," he said.

McCurry also wondered if the church should speak so prolifically on many political issues, referring to the several thousand petitions submitted to the General Conference. "We don't need to legislate on everything," he suggested. "Sometimes the church should just sit and be quiet." Delegates should ask: "Does the church need to pronounce itself on this issue?" He also urged: "We need to think evangelically about making new disciples."

"We are often incoherent on the left," McCurry admitted. "We are not as well organized and present ideas in ineffective ways." And he lamented that the "work and mission of the church is balkanized now." He also suggested that young people are not hearing "conversation that relates to them" and "a lot of these issues are generational." Before the church decides on issues, it should ask "if we are of one opinion," McCurry concluded. He also said that advocates of all sides must realize they need to "give some things up" if they are to remain at the table.

McCurry's call for restraint was not widely heeded by liberal activists in Pittsburgh. In typical fashion Board of Church and Society General Secretary Jim Winkler lashed out against critics of his agency at his lunch for international delegates. Rather than responding to substantive criticism, Winkler bewailed the "lies, attacks and hate" supposedly aimed at the board. "They are trying to persuade you that we are doing bad things," Winkler said. "Consider their claims with a critical eye and read between the lines."

Winkler denounced the war against terrorism. "I believe fundamentally that war is wrong," he said. "I'm concerned that this General Conference may not speak clearly against war and against the war in Iraq." He suggested a "common sense" approach to terrorism. Rather than striking directly at the groups committing terrorist acts, he favored a strategy centered on fighting poverty around the world. "For a fraction of annual spending on war, we can provide clean water, health care and food to all the people who don't have those now," Winkler said. "It should be obvious now that war on terrorism is fraught with danger," Winkler asserted. "This war will needlessly sacrifice young lives and will create a cauldron of young revolutionaries." Because of their "desperation and utter hopelessness," terrorists will vent their anger at the cost of their lives, Winkler warned.

Global Warming is a bigger threat to civilization than terrorism, Winkler claimed. Citing an unnamed British newspaper, he asserted that a "secret" U.S. Government report admitted that major European cities will "sink beneath the sea" because of "abrupt climate change" by the year 2020. "Will we trust in God or in military might?" Winkler asked.

Winkler's agency also hosted a banquet in Pittsburgh that featured United Methodist minister and old-time civil rights activist Joseph Lowery. Rainbow stoles of the pro-"gay" caucuses abounded throughout the crowd, as Lowery condemned U.S. economic and foreign policies while implying criticism of the church's stance on marriage and sex. Stressing that God was calling them to "take America down by the riverside," Lowery demanded that America's economic system be restructured, criticized U.S. trade policy, called for an increase in the minimum wage, asserted "we got to stop this war on the poor," denounced the war in Iraq and called inadequate health care a "weapon of mass destruction."

Lowery also claimed that the "re-segregation" of American society was attributable to "these judges appointed by [Presidents] Reagan and Bush." He pointed to the 2000 election in Florida as an example of people still being denied their voting rights, with the current president being "selected" rather than elected. He also lambasted the U.S. government's efforts in the War on Terror for allegedly eroding the freedom of Americans. Rather than making Americans safer, Lowery claimed, "[we] have done more to help bin Laden in his demagoguery than anything I know of."

After sarcastically asking if President Bush was a fellow United Methodist, Lowery responded to the audience's resounding disapproval by saying, "Don't blame me; I didn't let him in!" Lowery juxtaposed Bush with notorious civil rights-era segregationist, Governor George Wallace of Alabama. Although he praised the Board of Church and Society, Lowery lamented that his church is not even more politically outspoken, saying he sometimes is "ashamed to admit" that he is a United Methodist. About homosexuality, Lowery said: "I'm not an absolutist, but I know this much: I'm going to be on the side of inclusiveness, not exclusiveness!" Although he was not sure if he would perform same-sex "marriage" ceremonies, he expressed his disapproval of efforts in civil society to define marriage as being between one man and one woman.

It is predictably common for many liberal church groups not having better arguments to label opponents as "racist." So Winkler condemned the U.S. government for not providing visas to all international delegates. "It was a racist policy not to allow in delegates from central [overseas] conferences," he claimed. He conceded that overseas delegates to General Conferences had visa problems even before the tighter restrictions in the wake of 9-11.

Similarly, retired Bishop Marshall Meadors alleged that U.S. visa policies are "racist and unjust" at a press conference in Pittsburgh. "It was only delegates of color from Africa and the Philippines who were denied visas," Meadors complained. "We call for justice for these people who were mistreated." Of 189 international delegates who are supposed to be at the General Conference, 25 from Africa and the Philippines were not present because of visa problems. Seventeen others were denied visas but were replaced by alternate delegates who could obtain visas.

Bishop Felton May of the Baltimore-Washington Conference claimed, "Racism is no small part of this matter," noting that no European delegates had visa problems. About twenty percent of the international delegates are from Europe. "Our light-skinned brothers and sisters from Europe are not facing this," May said.

But a U.S. State Department spokesman denied the charge. "The fact that these are people of color is absolutely, completely irrelevant, but the question of their economic means may not be irrelevant," said Stewart Patt of the department's Bureau of Consular Affairs. Patt said U.S. policy requires that visa applicants must prove strong ties to their native country, such as jobs and property, to indicate they do not plan to remain in the U.S. beyond their scheduled visit.

Meadors still condemned such State Department policies for

fostering "economic injustice." He called for President Bush and Vice President Cheney, both of whom are United Methodist, to change U.S. visa policies in time for 2008. The bishops did not admit that possibly United Methodist officials in the U.S. were delinquent in providing documentation that international delegates needed for visa interviews at U.S. embassies. International delegates are mostly conservative, especially on homosexuality. Was the Board of Global Ministries, which was in charge of travel arrangements, less than enthusiastic about the presence of international delegates?

Despite some key conservative victories, General Conference 2004 approved the usual left-leaning political statements without much debate. Perhaps most egregiously, 57 percent of delegates affirmed continued membership in the Religious Coalition for Reproductive Choice (RCRC), the Washington-based lobby group that supported unrestricted legalized abortion on demand. As usual in the debates about RCRC, its defenders were not entirely candid about RCRC's mission. Beth Capen of New York, who is now a member of the Judicial Council, asserted that "the coalition does not do or advocate for anything which is inconsistent with that which we as United Methodists—since we are a significant contributor—have in our Social Principles." In fact, RCRC supports the legality of partial-birth abortion, which our Social Principles specifically oppose. Capen continued: "The coalition does advocate for free choice—for choice; and there are many of us who . . . hope that that continues so that we don't return to the desperate situations that existed prior to Roe v. Wade."

In other political action, delegates opposed all U.S. "unilateral first-strike military actions without UN collaboration," endorsed the Kyoto accord on Global Warming, condemned Israel, opposed "detrimental" privatization of resources around the world; supported a study of U.S. reparations for descendants of slaves; opposed the U.S. Patriot Act; opposed U.S. arms sales to all countries; supported removal of U.S. military from Okinawa; urged removal of U.S. sanctions against communist North Korea and Cuba and, surprisingly, endorsed freedom for political dissidents in Cuba.

Few of these statements caused any surprise. By far the big news in Pittsburgh was an unexpected speech by the Rev. Bill Hinson near the close of General Conference. Noting that he had consulted with members of the Confessing Movement, of which he was president, Hinson made clear he was speaking for himself when he suggested a formal division of The United Methodist Church. "All of us have poignant moments when deep sadness sweeps over our souls," Hinson began. "Mine is the last generation of United Methodist preachers who can remember when we were a growing movement."

Speaking at one of the daily breakfasts for delegates sponsored by Good News, Hinson lamented: Our friends in the Western Jurisdiction have left us. Our covenant is in shreds." He sadly observed that pro-homosexuality activists "feel disenfranchised, they feel we are doing spiritual violence to them . . . are seeking autonomy from the larger body . . . [and] garnered more than 300 votes in an attempt to do things their way with regard to ordination. . . ."

"There is a great gulf fixed between those of us who are centered on Scripture and our friends who are of another persuasion," he observed. "For many, truth is still evolving. They sincerely believe that the world has the wisdom we need and we should relativize the Bible so as to bring our thoughts into harmony with whatever the current worldly wisdom suggests. We on the other hand believe that Jesus Christ is the same yesterday, today and forever."

Hinson concluded: "Our people, who have been faithful and patient, should not have to continue to endure our endless conflict. I believe the time has come when we must begin to explore an amicable and just separation that will free us both from our cycle of pain and conflict. Such a just separation will protect the property rights of churches and the pension rights of clergy. It will also free us to reclaim our high calling and to fulfill our mission in the world."

The several hundred listening to Hinson responded with a rousing standing ovation. Everyone sensed an historic moment. "I'm so glad I got up early to be here this morning," religion reporter Larry Stammer of the *Los Angeles Times* told me. Conscious of the news value of Hinson's remarks, I asked for his text. He had relied only on notes. So he and I quickly went to a computer, and I helped transcribe what he had just said. And I made copies available in the news room of the General Conference. The Associated Press reported Hinson's remarks around the world, perhaps exaggerating their importance, and leaving many United Methodists with the impression that their denomination was about to split.

Some in the renewal movement discussed a possible resolution calling for formal consideration of a possible church division. An informal draft was even circulated by church liberals, who had been shown the draft during an informal dialogue. But after further consideration, and with Hinson's agreement, renewal leaders decided not to submit it.

Hinson addressed the full General Conference and again spoke to the Good News daily breakfast. He expressed regret for creating an unintentional furor. "I stand in amazement at the combustibility of a speech made at an early morning breakfast by someone who is not even a delegate," he said. "But those are my honest feelings, and I can't deny them for the cause of unity." Meanwhile, the General Conference overwhelmingly approved a resolution affirming the church's unity."

Some in the renewal movement were disappointed. The Hinson proposal was likely the fruit of emotional exhaustion by evangelicals drained by the homosexuality debates. Despite its struggles, the 2004 General Conference was one more significant step toward a renewed church, however haphazard. The pro-homosexuality arguments were decisively rebutted. Conservatives would have greater voice in the church bureaucracy, thanks to reapportionment of church agency board members. The Judicial Council's majority would still enforce church law. The General Conference had declined to issue an Iraq War condemnation but had, to the consternation of church liberals, made United Methodism the first mainline denomination to support laws in civil society defining marriage as man and woman. And the international delegates were becoming increasingly outspoken and were fast growing in numbers.

A formal split in The United Methodist Church is unlikely. Conservatives in large numbers would organize one only if the General Conference formally repudiated the church's teachings on homosexuality. Under current trends, this repudiation will not happen. And liberals almost never organize schisms or new denominations. Theological liberalism is mainly parasitic. It takes over already existing religious institutions, but it does not generate new ones. My personal dream of 20 years ago was for a reformed United Methodist Church, not a divided one. That remains not only my hope but also my strong expectation today.

The trends of the 2000 and 2004 General Conferences will continue, thanks to strong membership growth in Africa and the tragic ongoing membership implosion in the most liberal U.S. regions. God is renewing his church, at his own pace. If only we would be patient!

CHAPTER   FOURTEEN

TRANSSEXUAL MINISTERS?

United Methodists have debated homosexuality across four decades. But, in reality, the pro-homosexuality movement is pushing for more than acceptance of same-sex couples. They seek to overthrow Christianity and Judaism's understanding of marriage and of sexual identity, which are built around God's order of creation and the divine gift of maleness and femaleness.

In June 2007, The United Methodist Church got its first openly transsexual minister. The Rev. Drew Phoenix, formerly known as Ann Gordon, was reappointed to St. John's Church in Baltimore by Bishop John Schol after a surgical procedure that ostensibly changed Phoenix from female to male. Oddly enough, Phoenix was the second minister in the Baltimore-Washington Conference who had a sex change operation.

In late 1999, the Rev. Richard Zamostny of Rockville, Maryland, first told Bishop Felton May of the Baltimore-Washington Conference about his impending sex change operation. Zamostny was divorcing his wife, with whom he had three children, to adopt a female identity. He and the bishop agreed that Zamostny would take medical leave, and they would keep the impending sex change procedure a secret. Bishop May did not promise that Zamostny could return to the pulpit in his new female identity.

Zamostny had the operation in Thailand in May 2000. Meanwhile, the Baltimore-Washington Board of Ordained Ministry ultimately decided that "being transgendered does not in and of itself make a person unfit for ministry," its chairman told the *Washington Post* in July 2002. But this process was hidden from the public. The conference United Methodist Men's president, Morris Hawkins, heard about it and emailed the news to all the clergy and lay members of the annual conference in May 2001. Hawkins regretted that the "world's standard of moral conduct is higher than a majority of the leadership of the church." He also pointed to the picture of the former Richard Zamostny, now Rebecca Steen, in the conference pictorial directory, clearly adopting a female appearance.

Hawkins later told the *Washington Post*: "The bishop called me into his office . . . and dressed me down royally for an hour and a half, calling me disloyal and to stop sticking my nose into personnel matters." But Hawkins was understandably concerned that May would quietly appoint Steen to an unsuspecting congregation, with no open discussion at the annual conference. Instead, the bishop deferred the decision for another year.

Before the 2002 annual conference, I helped Hawkins get the word out by sending a news release about Steen's potential appointment to the newspapers, television and radio stations of Washington, D.C., and Baltimore. "This person, even though he uses a female name, in the sight of God is genetically still a man who has mutilated his body," the *Baltimore Sun* quoted me as saying. Dr. J. Philip Wogaman, the retired pastor of Foundry United Methodist Church, and Steen's official "advocate," was quoted in defense of transsexual clergy.

Our June 5, 2002, news release argued: "(1) Gender identity is not simply a mindset or an aspect of our physical appearance. It is predetermined genetically. More importantly, it is predetermined by the God who knew us before He made us. (2) A sex change operation is a deliberate physical mutilation of our bodies as God created them and therefore is a desecration of the temple in which

God's Holy Spirit dwells. (3) Someone who is so confused about his or her identity that he or she resorts to a sex change operation is likely not sufficiently stable emotionally, psychologically and spiritually to serve as a church pastor. (4) Persons who seek sex change operations need the church's ministry and compassion. They do not need church leadership thrust upon them. (5) The church should not compound the confusion of a transsexual by giving the church's blessing to an operation that is not likely to provide peace and happiness."

Eight evangelical pastors in Baltimore-Washington also released a "Renaissance Affirmation" on June 8, proclaiming, "We cannot affirm gender reassignment surgery as the proper medical treatment for gender identity disorder," and concluded that someone with "gender identity disorder" is not able to fulfill the "necessary requirements" to serve as a minister.

At the last minute, during the annual conference in June 2002, as media attention swirled around Steen, the bishop's cabinet filed a complaint against Steen that again postponed any church appointment. Steen was accused of "breaking" a covenant with the bishop and cabinet and also pressuring the conference for funds. A complaint from Steen's former church secretary also surfaced. On June 28, May announced that Steen had "voluntarily" resigned as a United Methodist minister. "There has been a parting of the ways because I don't think the church is ready for me, and I'm sad to say that," Steen told United Methodist News Service. "I will continue to seek to do the will of the Lord and to be active in ministry wherever God leads me."

In our news release, I responded by thanking the bishop for facilitating Steen's departure, adding: "But I wish Bishop May and other church leaders had used this situation as an opportunity to lift up traditional Christian teachings about gender identity. Unlike the ancient Gnostics, or the self-absorbed delusions of modern culture, Christians believe that gender is intrinsically determined by the bodies God made for us, not by our thoughts or feelings."

Unfortunately, Steen's situation had been handled legalistically and politically, with little reference to Christian teachings. It was assumed that our church's *Book of Discipline*, which never mentions trans-sexuality, is the only available guidance. Even more unfortunately, the 2004 General Conference also failed to ratify any legislation addressing sexual identity issues. Meanwhile, Steen seems not to have received firm guidance from the bishop or the church before getting the sex-change operation. What if the bishop, speaking more as a pastor than a supervisor, had strongly counseled Steen against the surgery?

Five years passed, and the Baltimore-Washington Conference's second transsexual minister emerged. In early May 2007, an anonymous caller to IRD reported that the Rev. Ann Gordon of Baltimore had undergone a sex identity change and had become Drew Phoenix. The name "Phoenix" refers to the ancient mythological creature that arises from the ashes of the old self. Reportedly, both the Board of Ordained Ministry and the bishop had approved, and Gordon/Phoenix would be quietly reappointed back to St. John's Church, which was a "reconciling", i.e., pro-homosexuality congregation. A few days later, we received the report of the Board of Ordained Ministry, which simply cited the Gordon/Phoenix name change without explanation.

Seeking confirmation, my assistant Rebekah Sharpe attended Phoenix's church. A fairly new employee recently arrived from North Carolina, where her father was a former United Methodist minister, Rebekah dutifully attended St. John's. Soon after arriving, Rebekah was greeted by a "very petite man with closely cropped ginger hair." It was Drew Pheonix, clearly now professing to be male, and no longer Ann Gordon. The anonymous phone tip was true!

In Phoenix's church, Rebekah observed the display of enormous, multi-colored butterflies, presumably symbolizing Phoenix' own figurative rebirth into a new creature. Several dozen worshipers were there. During the announcements, Phoenix asked for a

volunteer to help staff the booth of the local Reconciling Ministries Network chapter for the annual conference. And Phoenix
described the church's trailer in the upcoming Gay Pride Parade.
Prayers were said for a lesbian couple in the congregation soon
to be wed. Phoenix briefly referred to having recently met with
Bishop Schol, whom he likened to the Roman centurion in the
Gospels, i.e., a man under authority and bound by law.

In the end, Schol did not feel bound by historic Christian
teachings about sexual identity and the human body. His reap-
pointment of Phoenix was effusively announced a week later at
the Baltimore-Washington Annual Conference. I had already
alerted the bishop about our May 23, 2007, news release before-
hand, which said: "Gender and physicality, in Christian and Jewish teaching, are intrinsically linked to God's order of creation, as
first described in Genesis. The God whom we worship knew us as
male or female before He created us. Gender is not a choice but
a reality." The news release was quoted in the *Baltimore Sun* and
on local radio stations, helping to ensure that at least some of the
members of the annual conference had some warning.

Phoenix told the annual conference about having gone through
"spiritual transformation" since finding "my true gender identity"
and honoring God in the process. "It is my intention and hope
that by sharing my story that we commit ourselves as Christians
and as United Methodists to become educated about the com-
plexity of gender," Phoenix disclaimed. The pastor recalled always
having "felt like a boy," even though "society declared that I was
a girl." Apparently as a small boy, Phoenix's family had allowed
Phoenix to "let me be my boy-self" until puberty, when Phoenix
was pressured to "act like a female."

"The gender I was assigned at birth has never matched my own
true, authentic, God-given gender identity… how I know myself," Phoenix explained. "Fortunately, today, God's gift of medical science is enabling me to bring my physical body into align-
ment with my true gender." Phoenix reported being "even more

effective as a pastor" since the sexual identity change. And Phoenix regretted that "we have been steeped in an either/or, male/female-only understanding of gender," and noted the difficulty of believing "that our bodies do not tell the whole story about what we are." Many people in our churches are "suffering with the disconnect that I have felt," Phoenix lamented.

Meanwhile, a supportive Bishop Schol insisted: "This isn't an issue. This is a human being." The bishop also boasted that Phoenix had impressively "quadrupled" St. John's Church membership, though Schol did not mention the size of the still very small membership. "Many people would say let's just sweep it under the carpet, but in this conference, we're a people of integrity," the bishop further pronounced. But in fact, no time was permitted for discussion about transsexuality, and there had been no official advance warning for the members of the annual conference, who were presented with a fait accompli.

An announcement from the Baltimore-Washington Conference afterwards asserted: "A name change does not require that any formal action be taken by the church; and the *Book of Discipline*, which outlines church law, contains no policies that address transgender clergy." A spokeswoman for the Board of Ordained Ministry further explained: "There is nothing in the *Discipline* that prohibits, or even mentions, transgender clergy. If someone were to bring a charge against, or lodge a complaint, there would have to be action taken. But in this case there is nothing that questions Rev. Phoenix's ability to be a pastor."

According to the Associated Press, Schol reported that there had been no objections to Phoenix's appointment during a closed clergy session. But in fact, two pastors asked for a "ruling of law" about the propriety of Phoenix's appointment. The requests automatically meant the denomination's Judicial Council would have to address the issue. I made sure the *Baltimore Sun,* which published the story, knew this.

Liberal church caucus groups also responded warmly but

warily to Phoenix's appointment. Affirmation, a self-professed "independent voice of Lesbian, Gay, Bisexual, Transgender, and Queer people," congratulated Phoenix. But it also warned: "Opposition will continue to grow," noting the appeal to the Judicial Council and General Conference petitions from "conservative groups" to preclude transgender clergy. Affirmation quoted my interview on the May 29, 2007, Albert Mohler Radio Program, in which I said "This case of Rev. Phoenix now guarantees that the idea of transsexual clergy will be addressed in church law" at the 2008 General Conference.

Absent a clear *Disciplinary* prohibition, the Judicial Council was unlikely to rule about Phoenix. As expected, at its meeting in October 2007, the council declined to take a position on Phoenix's appointment, noting that at the time of the annual conference no formal complaint had been filed against Phoenix, whose standing as a pastor could not be challenged without due process. Interestingly, the council did specify that it was not ruling on "whether gender change is a chargeable offense or violates minimum standards" of United Methodism.

Of course, Phoenix was "elated" about the ruling, calling it a "historic day" for United Methodism and a "very important first step in opening the doors of our churches to the transgender community." Phoenix celebrated that the council's decision was a sign that Jesus' "love has, and will, overcome the fear so prevalent in our society." Naturally, Phoenix emphasized the issue as one of love for all people rather than the church's teaching on sex-change procedures.

Transgender and sex-change issues are increasingly paramount for United Methodism's liberal caucus groups. Amusingly, but also sadly, a transsexual shared a testimony at the "Hearts on Fire" pro-homosexuality rally at Lake Junaluska, North Carolina, over Labor Day weekend in 2005, as reported by my assistant John Lomperis. Reconciling Ministries Network board member Sally Sparks of Washington, D.C., recounted that 10 years before,

"I was a straight, conservative, evangelical, white male" and now is still white, but none of the others, as the audience chuckled. Even though now professing to be female, Sparks has remained with his wife, with whom he now apparently relates as a lesbian. "We as a couple went through that [transition] together," Sparks said, explaining that his sex change "was all about living in the truth."

The decision by United Methodist Lake Junaluska Conference Center to host a pro-homosexuality rally ignited enormous controversy throughout the church's Southeast Jurisdiction, which owns the facility. The convocation was organized by the Reconciling Ministries Network, whose purpose was to convene "United Methodists of all sexual orientations and gender identities that are called in faith to celebrate, ignite and empower the inclusive church of Jesus Christ!"

According to Lake Junaluska's guidelines at the time, "Groups using our facilities should have a mission compatible with Lake Junaluska Assembly and The United Methodist Church, its Discipline and Social Principles." Spokeswoman Joetta Rinehart defended renting to "Hearts on Fire," citing the United Methodist advertising slogan, "We believe our vision and mission encourage us to join the total church in opening our hearts, our minds, and our doors." She also said that "compatible" groups were "groups that are not in opposition to our mission of making disciples for Jesus Christ." Rinehart hoped that persons that use Lake Junaluska would leave "as more committed followers of Jesus Christ."

Lake Junaluska's executive director, Jimmy Carr, decided to host "Hearts on Fire" in consultation with Virginia bishop Charlene Kammerer, who chaired the Southeast Jurisdiction's Administrative Council, also called the Connectional Table. "How sad that Lake Junaluska generated this needless controversy by ignoring its own internal standards and renting itself to a group that opposes the church's teachings on marriage and sexual ethics," I said in a September 1, 2005, news release. IRD organized a petition campaign opposing "Hearts on Fire," gathering thousands of signatures, which we forwarded to Carr.

We mailed a July 2005 letter to more than tens of thousands of United Methodists in the Southeast, saying:

> Have you ever been to beautiful Lake Junaluska, the United Methodist retreatcenter in the mountains of Western North Carolina? It is one of the jewels of our United Methodist connection. But this September 2-5, the jewel of our church will be tarnished. Lake Junaluska, which is owned by the relatively conservative Southeast Jurisdiction of our church, is renting itself out to "Hearts on Fire!" a huge jamboree for homosexual activists and their supporters. Do you share my indignation over Lake Junaluska's decision to allow this? Are you willing to contact Lake Junaluska directly to register your protest? If so, please read on.

A revered retreat of spiritual contemplation and worship for much of the 20th century, hundreds of thousands of United Methodists have enjoyed its mountain tranquility across the decades. We received more reaction to our "Hearts on Fire" letter and petition than to any other issue during my 13 years at IRD. Seven bishops were scheduled to speak at "Hearts on Fire." Bishop William Willimon of North Alabama, along with his cabinet, wrote "a letter of concern" to Lake Junaluska, urging that the facility "examine more closely its practices and procedures regarding the groups hosted at its facilities." They said: "While Junaluska felt compelled to offer this group rental use of the facilities, this in no way changes the clear and frequently reiterated stance of the *Discipline*." Although other Southeast bishops reportedly shared these concerns, they did not speak out.

Bishop J. Lawrence McCleskey, then of South Carolina, wrote

an August 16, 2005, letter defending Lake Junaluska's "call to Christian hospitality and ministry." He was "aware that United Methodists hold strong and diverse opinions," which did not bother him. But "what does trouble me is the animosity and mean-spiritedness which persons on each side of the issue have expressed towards those who differ with them." He was praying "that the negative energy being expended around this event may somehow be transformed into positive emphasis on our primary mission to make disciples of Jesus Christ."

Meanwhile, Reconciling Ministries Network asked its supporters to rally behind Lake Junaluska, warning that the "independent conservative caucus Good News along with outside agitators—Institute for Religion and Democracy and the American Family Association—continue to attempt to stir up inhospitality to lesbian, gay, bisexual, and transgender United Methodists." These groups were trying to "intimidate" those who have "faithfully followed both the Gospel and United Methodist policies." Reconciling Ministries regretted that "such extremism ultimately fosters a climate of exclusion that violates the Gospel and harms the church." The e-mail alert saluted Lake Junaluska for "faithfully living its mission to serve all United Methodists in continuing to make disciples for Jesus Christ."

"As a people dedicated to justice, such intimidation only serves as validation of the clear need for our ministries to continue to open hearts, open minds, and open doors," the Reconciling email said. It urged pro-homosexuality supporters to contact Jimmy Carr and express their "support" for his decision. And it asked supporters to write letters to the editors of local newspapers around Lake Junaluska. According to Reconciling, Lake Junaluska's staff had "expressed thankfulness for the supportive notes they have received from reconciling people and continue their commitment to hosting a great event for our faithful group of United Methodists!"

Lake Junaluska's Jimmy Carr defended "Hearts on Fire" by citing the church's Social Principles and by describing the Reconciling Ministries Network as an "affiliated caucus" of the church, since it's listed in the *United Methodist Directory*, along with other causes such as UM*Action*. "We understand a majority of the participants in the conference will be heterosexual," Carr wrote, without explaining why that was significant. He also noted that the Southeastern Jurisdiction's Executive Committee had agreed with Lake Junaluska's providing "hospitality."

Meanwhile, the Southeastern Jurisdiction Administrative Council (SEJAC), also known as the Connectional Table, chaired by Bishop Kammerer, defended the hosting of "Hearts on Fire." It strangely quoted the church's constitution, which forbids discrimination based on "race, color, national origin, status, or economic condition." The Constitution makes no reference to homosexuality. SEJAC seemed tacitly to endorse the claims of pro-homosexuality caucus groups that "status" includes sexual practice. "We cannot exclude baptized professing members of The United Methodist Church from Lake Junaluska Conference and Retreat Center, which belongs to The United Methodist Church," SEJAC insisted, when nobody had asked Lake Junaluska to deny entrance to particular individuals. SEJAC, noting "heated controversy" and "stern criticism" over "Hearts on Fire," warned against any withholding of apportionments to protest the event.

While United Methodist bishops were largely silent about "Hearts on Fire," local Baptists were not. "To host such a conference is to promote open and unrepentant rebellion to the commands of the Lord Jesus Christ," declared the Baptist Association of Haywood County, where Lake Junaluska is located. "This conference has at least for one of its purposes the blatant promotion and practice of this sin of homosexuality." The Southern Baptists warned that "Hearts on Fire" would "prove harmful to the wholesomeness of our community" and would be "detrimental to the efforts of Evangelical Christians to reach out in love to all people in the name of Christ."

The Ku Klux Klan unfortunately joined the controversy. The *Asheville Citizen Times* broke the story that the Klan planned to demonstrate at "Hearts on Fire." Without permission, the Klan's website ran an article I had written about the event, which it had extracted from the American Family Association (AFA). AFA asked the Klan to remove the article, but it remained. Unable to find a functional phone number for the Klan, I e-mailed the various "wizards" and "kleagles" whose e-mail addresses were on the Klan site, insisting that my article be removed from the Klan site immediately.

I did not expect the Klan, not known for its courtesy, to respond. But within a few hours, the Imperial Wizard of the American White Knights of the KKK had responded. "The Christian thing for you to have done was to ask yourself if contacting me in the manner that you have would make you a hypocrite," the Wizard intoned. "I wonder how much of our website that you have taken time to study . . . or is it that you judge people by a name they use?"

The grand wizard also had advice for me. "Now pull off your pretty little tie and walk out of your pretty little office, and start doing God's work. Usually, the most good can be done in what some see as the lowliest of places." The wizard signed off with "In Jesus Name" and called himself a Baptist. The note seemed appropriately nasty and absurd. But the wizard did remove my article from his website.

Fewer than 20 Klansmen showed up for their protest, while 500 pro-homosexuality activists rallied for "Hearts on Fire." Seven bishops spoke, including Minerva Carcaño of Phoenix, John Schol of Washington, D.C., Sally Dyck of Minneapolis, Susan Morrison of Albany, and retired bishops Melvin Talbert and Richard Wilke. Also present was Bishop Scott Jones of Kansas, who spoke not as a supporter but to offer dialogue.

"I'm so frustrated with people who take a prejudice and then

find a Bible quote to support it," Bishop Wilke said. He likened
disapproval of homosexual practice to earlier defenses of slavery, discrimination against women and support for war. "Today
people are coming out of the closet, being honest with God and
neighbor about who they are," Wilke enthused.

Retired Bishop Melvin Talbert agreed. "I'm here to say that I
believe, as a bishop of the church, the position that our church
has on this issue is wrong, and I say that unapologetically!" he
declared.

Bishop John Schol of Washington, D.C., said that he was there
"to go give honor and glory to God" and also "to say 'I'm sorry'"
for the "times in my life" when he "found it easier to make fun of
or to make jokes about people that I didn't understand or people
that I didn't think I wanted to associate with." He said he was
making sure that "gay and lesbian, transgendered and bisexual
persons are also in leadership positions" in the Baltimore-Washington Conference.

Lamenting that the church has not done enough study about
homosexuality, Bishop Sally Dyck of Minneapolis said, "I believe
that fear is the original sin." She noted that she had been outspoken about affirmation of homosexuality for "quite some time."

Bishop Susan Morrison of Albany lauded the "gifts of the Denver 15" bishops who in 1996 publicly declared their opposition
to the church's teachings about sexual ethics. They "broke the
myth about the Council" of Bishops being composed of leaders
who "all agreed," she rejoiced.

As a supporter of the church's stance on homosexuality, Bishop
Jones urged going back to John Wesley, the church's doctrines
and the Bible for guidance. His remarks were received politely.

Perhaps most provocative was the Rev. Karen Oliveto, who in
2004 presided over a string of same-sex unions in San Francisco,
defying church law. She criticized St. Paul's casting a demon out
of a slave girl, as recorded in the Book of Acts. By depriving
the girl of her fortune-telling abilities, Paul did her "economic

injury" and made her "damaged goods," Oliveto complained. She urged a "progressive theology" guided by "pluralism," "feminism," "liberationism," "post-colonialism" and "ecological and environmental responsibility."

The audience gave a standing ovation to Lake Junaluska executive director Jimmy Carr. "Well, I thought I'd never run for General Conference again!" Carr smilingly responded. Speaking of his critics, he hoped they now "understand that 'open hearts, open minds, open doors' really does mean something!" Carr lamented Lake Junaluska's policy decades ago of not renting to black people, by implication equating disapproval of homosexual practice with racism.

Despite all the hullabaloo of "Hearts on Fire," the Southeastern Jurisdiction Administrative Council (SEJAC)/Connectional Table rejected a proposal that Lake Junaluska rent only to groups upholding "Judeo-Christian ideals." Meeting less than three months after the event, SEJAC debated the controversy, with Bishop Kammerer presiding. SEJAC's Property and Services Committee had recommended a new policy that said, "Lake Junaluska reserves the right to refuse or cancel any group, even after they have begun, if their program and/or philosophy is inconsistent with the Judeo-Christian ideals inherent in this purpose." But the Table voted nearly unanimously to remove "Judeo-Christian ideals," so that the policy said merely that renting groups must be consistent with the "mission, vision and purpose" of Lake Junaluska. The facility staff, consulting with SEJAC and its executive committee, would determine which rental applicants qualify. These were the same parties that had approved "Hearts on Fire." And the new policy seemed little different from the old policy, which said that "groups using our facilities should have a mission compatible with Lake Junaluska Assembly and The United Methodist Church, and its Social Principles."

Earl Peacock, a North Carolina lawyer providing unpaid legal counsel, argued strongly against the "Judeo-Christian" language, implausibly claiming it would place Lake Junaluska in "serious legal jeopardy." He said some have argued that homosexuality is an "immutable characteristic" and protected by North Carolina's civil rights laws. He also argued that Lake Junaluska, as a public facility, could not decline to rent to other religions. Bishop Michael Watson, as chair of the Property and Services Committee, explained that the "Judeo-Christian" language would keep Lake Junaluska from having to rent to groups such as Nazis. But Peacock dismissed that concern, ridiculously claiming, "The Nazi Party does not have any legal rights in this country."

John Sherrer of Alabama pointed to a higher authority than some interpretations of North Carolina laws. "We need to turn to the Bible for inspiration and holy living instead of to man's laws for intimidation," Sherrer said. "There's a cost for remaining faithful, and an even greater cost for not being faithful," he added. "Jesus Christ was not always tolerant," Sherrer said. "But he was uncomfortable on the cross for us." Sherrer rejected accepting homosexuality as an "immutable characteristic" which would "throw out" the Holy Spirit's ability to change people and would portray "God as an old man with a beard who is no longer effective."

In response, retired North Carolina pastor Rufus Stark declared that the "Hearts on Fire" event had been "one of the best spiritual events I've ever been to." He warned that homosexuality is a "polarizing" issue for United Methodists, who should instead seek a way "through the middle." Stark concluded, "Methodists are called to be bridge-builders." Agreeing with Stark, Kathy Fitzjeffries of Western North Carolina compared disapproval of homosexual practice to racism. "There was a time when African-Americans were not allowed here [at Lake Junaluska]," she said. "Scripture was used to justify the separation." She said she was "very proud" of Lake Junaluska's having hosted "Hearts on Fire."

Alabama clergy Lester Spencer disagreed. "We're opening ourselves up to spiritual darkness," he said, noting that "Hearts on Fire's" Reconciling sponsors, according to their website, promote acceptance of homosexual, bisexual and transgender behavior in the church. Spencer warned that Lake Junaluska's rental policy will be "tested again and again" and will set a precedent for other United Methodist facilities. "It's a poor witness" to rent to groups that go against scriptural authority, Spencer said. "I'm glad my children were not here," he observed of the "Hearts on Fire" event. He recalled that his own local church had turned down some groups that wanted to meet there, although all are welcome to attend worship services. "We have legal rights as a church," Spencer concluded. "It might be good [for Lake Junaluska] to take a stand."

But SEJAC accepted the vaguer language that omitted "Judeo-Christian ideals" which had been proposed by Ruth Wiertzema of the Red Bird Missionary Conference in Kentucky. After I had asked her for the spelling of her name, she approached to tell me several times that I did not have "permission" to quote her by name. I responded that at a public meeting her permission was not needed. Seemingly she had not originated the proposal herself and was uncomfortable being associated with it. But if so, who had composed it?

Thanks to "Hearts on Fire," Lake Junaluska took some financial losses, due to cancellations by objecting persons and groups. One was The Episcopal Church Missionary Community (ECMC), which typically attracted more than 1,000 people to its regular "New Wineskins" gatherings. ECMC relocated to nearby Ridgecrest, which is Southern Baptist-owned. As an advocate for evangelical missions within the Episcopal Church, which is splintering over homosexuality, the ECMC was determined to affirm traditional Christian teachings.

Meanwhile, the General Council on Finance and Administration, in a June 28, 2005 letter, warned the Council of Bishops about possible "questions" that would arise if bishops attending

"Hearts on Fire" spent annual conference funds, which the *Discipline* precludes from supporting "acceptance of homosexuality."

Despite SEJAC's rejection, under Bishop Kammer's leadership, of "Judeo-Christian" standards for Lake Junaluska, another "Hearts on Fire" seemed unlikely. Reconciling Ministries Network probably had hoped to be provocative by rallying in the relatively conservative Southeast. But their provocation only energized southern traditionalists, reminding them that the homosexuality issue could invade even tranquil Lake Junaluska.

Similarly, the transsexual issue will arouse further support for traditional Christian standards at the next General Conference. The seemingly limitless sexual boundaries of the liberal caucuses are not only disturbing but also, fortunately, self-defeating.

CHAPTER FIFTEEN

HOPE FOR THE FUTURE

Where did The United Methodist Church come from, and where is it going?

Most of us know where it came from, and many of us have deep family roots to Methodism's origins. My own ancestor, William Gilmore, was converted to Methodism in the wilds and rolling hills of southwest Virginia more than 200 years go. A child of the frontier, his mother had been kidnapped by Indians during the French and Indian War. Probably a nominal Presbyterian, Gilmore may have been converted directly by the preaching of Bishop Francis Asbury, who frequented the area and actually stayed in the home of another ancestor nearby. Gilmore was wealthy, and his conversion was so compelling that he freed his numerous slaves, personally escorting some of them to the free territory of Ohio and outfitting them with provisions for their new future, "in consideration of benevolent and Christian principles." He went on to become a Methodist preacher, and he fathered 21 children, three of whom would become Methodist preachers. Gilmore's tombstone was inscribed with Revelation 14:13: "Blessed are the dead which die in the Lord . . . that they may rest from their labors, and their works do follow them."

The story sounds exceptional now, but Gilmore's story was common in Methodism's early frontier days, when tens of thousands were converted, often dramatically. In just a few decades, the Methodist Church grew exponentially, from just a few thousand, to many hundreds of thousands and ultimately millions, becoming America's largest church. Rough-hewn circuit riding preachers, Asbury chief among them, shepherded this expansion, guided by the Holy Spirit. These early converts went on to build churches, initially log, and then timber, later brick, increasingly ornate, and occupying more central parts of their towns. Methodism became institutionalized into American culture, redeeming it, and sometimes corrupted by it. Methodists were zealous, organized and ambitious. They were converting America to Jesus Christ and expected to complete the work. Meanwhile, Methodist families transmitted the Christian faith across many generations, each generation uniquely affecting America for Christ.

My original Methodist ancestor died rich in faith. His son did not accept Christ until on his death bed. William Gilmore's grandson fell to his knees in prayer during the Civil War, asking God to heal his somewhat crippled legs. The legs got better, and he thereafter was a devout Christian and Methodist stalwart of his town. His son married a Presbyterian girl, but she became active in the Methodist women's movement. Their son, my grandfather, was also a churchman, but tragically killed in a car accident. His wife, my grandmother, would move to Arlington, Virginia, where she picked a Methodist Church based in part on its beautiful stained-glass windows. The church had also offered her its sympathy, and conducted the funeral, when her 24-year-old son died in a swimming accident.

The loss of a husband and son led to my grandmother living with my parents, my brother and me while I was growing up. She took charge of our religious education and took my brother and me to her Methodist Church. Often we resented the compulsory attendance! But I was indelibly shaped by those years of sitting in the pews, listening to the old hymns, reciting the prayers and creeds and listening to the sermons. The many young people with whom I grew up in the church gradually faded away, to other churches or religious non-involvement. But I would remain a Methodist. To this day, it seems not quite right to worship in some other denomination!

Charles De Gaulle once said that he was a Catholic for reasons of history and geography. In his aloof way, he was explaining that we are brought to faith by a centuries-long process of circumstances that, we trust, God has directed. I am a United Methodist, thanks to the exertions of my grandmother, but also to the faithful decisions of countless others before her. Some day I will meet all of these people and thank them!

Our denomination began to go astray, despite the faithfulness of so many, even before my grandmother was born. Nobleminded, trusting people granted virtual autonomy to the churchs' seminaries and assumed they would forever remain faithful, even without the church's direct oversight. John Wesley, no bubbly optimist about human nature, would not have been surprised by the tragic reality. It was not many years before the virtually autonomous seminaries, anxious for secular academic honors, became theologically liberal, leading thousands of clergy to proclaim a message increasingly dissimilar to the old faith. These theological liberals became bishops and church agency executives and seminary presidents. And they all successfully replicated their liberal theology across generations.

During these decades of liberal ascendancy and eventual control, most mainstream theological conservatives, at least among the laity, were blissfully unaware. They continued to worship and pray in their Methodist churches, to fund overseas missions, to sustain the seminaries, to revere their bishops and to trust their denomination. In 1964 our denomination recorded its very last year of growth in the United States. Starting in 1965, our church began losing what would eventually become three million members, even while the U.S. population increased from 195 million to more than 300 million.

United Methodists are fewer in number, but they are still generous and prosperous. So our church survives. In the congregation where I grew up, we largely relied on my grandmother's generation. Most of their children and grandchildren were not coming to Methodist churches. But that World War II generation was dedicated, keeping our church open, even when most people stopped coming. When I first began working for church reform, I relied on these robust older people for encouragement and support. They remembered a different United Methodist Church of decades ago, and they prayed that their church could be restored.

In my youth, I imagined that if only these older but still faithful United Methodists could be reached with the facts about our denomination's captivity to liberal theology, they would arise in mass to restore our church to its former glory. But the actual path of church reform has been more complicated and more wondrous. Thousands of United Methodists in the U.S. now are actively supporting church renewal. But much of our hopes for United Methodist renewal now depend upon millions of United Methodists who live far from America, in places with which most of us are unfamiliar, speaking often exotic languages, but worshiping the same Lord, and following the Wesleyan path, often more earnestly than we.

Three million United Methodists now live outside the U.S., most of them in Africa. There are 1.2 million United Methodists in the Democratic Republic of the Congo. By some counts, there are two million United Methodists attending a United Methodist church in the Congo on a typical Sunday. That number equals and may surpass the total number of United Methodist worshipers on average in the U.S. Even as United Methodism loses a thousand members or more EVERY week of every year in the U.S., the African churches are now increasing by that number, or faster. Perhaps it is providentially ironic that the number of United Methodists outside the U.S. is now equal to the total 43-

year membership loss of the church in the U.S.

My own United Methodist story is similar to so many in the U.S. I grew up in the church thanks to family that had been Methodist for generations. But compare our story to the Rev. Jerry Kulah, a district superintendent in Liberia. By his own account, his experiences included "raging storms, deep waters and blazing fire." Jerry was born to a polygamous family, in a Liberian village. He was among more than 25 children of one father and about seven wives, which meant a life of "competition, jealousy, hatred, and struggle for survival." An older half brother brought him to the capital of Monrovia but had little money and often was away on military assignments. On many days, Jerry went without food or stole to survive. At age 8, Jerry became a servant to another family with hopes of being provided before. Instead, he was introduced to child abuse and slave labor, to which he was subjected for 12 years.

But Jerry attended school, where he had Bible learning. At age 15, during a Bible study, he became affected by "the reality of my sin, hell and eternality." When he got home, he knelt on the floor and asked Jesus into his life. He became active in Christian youth activities but resisted the call to ministry, preferring a dream of material comforts. He earned a university degree in mathematics and got a well-paying job. In 1989, Jerry was planning a wedding with a young woman he had met in school, when Monrovia was besieged by rebels, starting a 14-year civil war, during which Jerry lost nearly everything.

The government declared Jerry's tribe to be enemies, and both Jerry and his older half brother, United Methodist Bishop Arthur Kulah, became hunted fugitives. While on the run, Jerry wore double layers of clothing, so as always to have extra clothes. When government troops finally captured Jerry, they accused him of being a rebel, thanks to his odd dress. The commander ordered a soldier to shoot Jerry, who pleaded his innocence while also praying. Amazingly, the soldier ordered Jerry to run for his life.

Several days later, Jerry again evaded arrest and likely death when compelled to give his identity card to a soldier. The soldier confusedly stared at the card while Jerry prayed the 23rd Psalm until the soldier returned the card and let Jerry pass. In 1990, Jerry recalls God telling him to escape to Nigeria. Jerry led evangelism in a refugee camp there while also attending seminary. His fiancée, Ruth, also escaped Liberia to meet Jerry in Nigeria, where they finally married in 1992. In 1994 they had their first child, whom they named Joshua. Finally, Jerry and his family returned to Liberia in 1997. He began pastoring a church in 1998, became evangelism director for the Liberian United Methodist Church in 2001 and became a district superintendent in 2007, supervising 34 churches and seven preaching points.

Today Jerry and his wife care for their four children, his mother and the five children of Jerry's brother, who died during the war. "God specializes in going into the interior of life and taking that which is inferior to make superior," Jerry has concluded. He also quotes from Jeremiah 29:11: "For I know the plans I have for you, declares the Lord, plans to prosper you and not to harm you, plans to give you hope and a future."

Like many African United Methodists, Jerry is a first-generation Christian, ministering among many first- and second-generation Christians. He works among fast-growing churches, where the gospel is proclaimed powerfully, and where there is no dispute about the authority of the Scriptures. His dynamic spiritual environment is not dissimilar to the upheaval and excitement of primitive Methodism in 18th-century and early 19th-century America. What is for most United Methodists in the U.S. a distant memory is a daily reality for many United Methodists in Liberia, Sierre Leone, Ivory Coast, Nigeria, the Democratic Republic of the Congo, Angola, Mozambique Zimbabwe and elsewhere.

Can the Holy Spirit-inspired United Methodists of Africa influence the U.S. church? They already are. Absent the African delegates, both their votes and their earnest arguments, phrased in New Testament syntax, United Methodism may well have compromised its teachings on homosexuality. Such a "compromise" could have led to a gradual Episcopal Church-style schism. Many conservative Episcopal congregations have left their U.S. denomination to affiliate with Anglican bishops in Africa. Fortunately, we United Methodists are an international church, which will help us avoid the Episcopal Church's disaster.

The increased representation of the Africans at the United Methodist General Conference over the years has been dramatic. In 1996, the Africans had 70 delegates, compared to the 62 delegates of the very liberal and fast-declining Western Jurisdiction of the U.S. In 2008, the Africans had 192 delegates, compared to 40 delegates from the Western Jurisdiction. In 1996, there were a total of 146 delegates from outside the U.S. In 2008, there were 286. In twelve years, the non-U.S. United Methodists have doubled their numbers. It is not unrealistic to assume that after another 12 years, by General Conference 2020, this rate of growth will have continued, and the international delegates will be more than a majority.

There are today more than 3.2 million United Methodists in Africa, more than one million alone in the Democratic Republic of the Congo. In our church's most liberal area, the Western Jurisdiction, there are fewer than 400,000, despite their region's including some of America's most populous and fastest-growing states, including California, Arizona, New Mexico, Nevada, Colorado, Oregon and Washington. Meanwhile, in relatively conservative Georgia alone, there are more than 480,000 United Methodists.

The delegate strength is even shifting within the U.S., where the somewhat conservative Southeast Jurisdiction is holding even in membership, while the more liberal Northeast and North Central regions are declining almost as quickly as the West. In 1996, the North Central Jurisdiction, including most of the Midwest, had

190 delegates. In 2008, it had 138. In 1996, the Northeast had 152 delegates. In 2008, it had 126. In contrast, the Southeast has remained stable, going from 264 delegates in 1996 to 252 in 2008. The South Central Jurisdiction went from 166 delegates in 1996 to 148 in 2008.

What does the church in Africa stand for besides opposition to homosexual practice? Jerry Kulah explained this in October 2007 at a conference called "A Hope and a Future Through Our Wesleyan Heritage," sponsored by United Methodist renewal groups, including IRD/UM*Action*. More than 100 recently elected General and Jurisdictional Conference delegates from around the United States and from every overseas region (Africa, Europe and the Philippines) of the United Methodist Church attended. In his "Africa Declaration," Jerry called United Methodists to scriptural faithfulness and effective ministry. The declaration was endorsed by the bishop and every district superintendent in Liberia as well as United Methodist leaders from other parts of Africa.

"We of the Central Conferences of Africa are deeply concerned that the global United Methodist Church is beginning to speak with different languages, and not with the common speech that presents Jesus Christ as the Good News of salvation, our only Lord, and only Savior," Jerry's declaration said. "As a result, the global witness of United Methodism is being threatened with the proclamation of different kinds of 'gospels.'"

Kulah noted that Africans are concerned that "some Euro-Western churches seem to be deserting the biblical path of church planting, disciple-making, of prayer, and evangelistic and missional endeavors to an inward focus," changing the "Great Commission" to the "Great Omission."

"We are saddened that some United Methodist Churches of the Euro-Western world have questioned over and over again the *United Methodist Book of Discipline's* biblical positions on such issues as homosexuality, abortion, and the authenticity of the Scriptures as the Word of God," Jerry said. "By such actions and attitudes toward the Gospel we are throwing both our adults and our children into confusion and, without words, telling them that Christianity does not have all the answers to their spiritual longing. We are afraid that the current unrestricted embrace of liberalism within the United Methodist Church is endangering the chances of our children to ever consider Christianity a possibility. It further creates a breeding ground for the rapid spread of other faiths amongst our future posterity."

Jerry's declaration cited as essentials that God is the creator, that humanity has sinned against God, that Jesus Christ is the "sacrificial offering" for sinful humanity, that Jesus was "wondrously born of a Virgin," performed "countless miracles," and "arose literally and physically from the dead," that Jesus will "literally" return to reign with his church, that all who confess Jesus will be saved and resurrected like him to live forever, that the "children of Israel" are a "holy tree into which now we as believers in the Jewish Messiah, have been grafted as branches," and that the Word of God calls us to "to chastity, temperance, charity and forbearance."

The Africa Declaration called for United Methodism, which collects more than five billion dollars a year in the U.S., to shift away from spending tens of millions on church agencies to confronting the "devastating poverty, disease and mortal suffering of our United Methodist brothers and sisters around the world." The church should affirm "on behalf of our impoverished brothers and sisters worldwide, life-giving freedom, rule of law, economic development, trade and property rights, electrification, industrialization, irrigation, transportation, basic health care and improved agricultural development." It called for support of seminaries in Africa and ensuring that the seminaries everywhere adhere to God's Word. United Methodism's Ministerial Education Fund, which distributes about one million dollars to each of the church's official U.S. seminaries, gives almost nothing to seminaries outside the U.S. The declaration also called for "just and proportionate representation" on church agency boards. Currently, non-U.S. United Methodists comprise only 10 percent of church agency boards, even though they represent more than 30 percent of the global church.

Jerry's declaration called for commitment to the Great Commission, the affirmation of marriage as "lifelong marriage between man and woman," for church leaders to model Christian behavior, for clergy, especially the bishops, to uphold the church's standards, and for the church's schools and publishing agencies to teach Scripture-based beliefs. The church's missional priority should be fighting deadly diseases, ensuring clean water, protecting the environment while improving the standards of living for the world's poor, declaring solidarity with persecuted Christians everywhere, affirming the "providential role of the family in God's order of creation, "defending the sanctity of all vulnerable human life, including the poor, the elderly, the terminally ill, the disabled, and the unborn," guarding the God-given dignity of all persons and advocating "voluntary charity, individually and corporately, around the world."

"When the baby Jesus was threatened by a vengeful King Herod, the Holy family fled to Africa for sanctuary," Jerry's declaration concluded. "Today, the Church in Africa offers itself as a sanctuary for God's Word for the renewing of his Church around the world. Will the United Methodist General Conference of 2008 and 2012 respond to this call for faithfulness from the church in Africa?"

When I first began working for reform within United Methodism 20 years ago as a recent college graduate active in my northern Virginia church, the power of the entrenched liberal church bureaucracy seemed forbidding. Theological liberalism had been ascendant for 80 years or more. Conservatives had almost no voice on the staff or leadership of most church agencies. The official seminaries were almost uniformly liberal. Most lay people remained conservative, but they were uninformed about the church beyond their local congregation. Pastors were usually more liberal than lay people though less radical than national church bureaucrats. But pastors often were professionally intimidated from even sharing information about the national church with their congregations, much less openly questioning the national church. Even conservative district superintendents and bishops frequently subsumed their own beliefs in obeisance to the church's national liberal culture.

"Nobody cares about this but you and Mark Tooley!" my fairly conservative district superintendent exclaimed in 1988 to a lay woman from another Northern Virginia church who was disturbed by the mission board's funding of left-wing and Marxist groups. My bishop at the time wondered if the concerns about the missions board were limited to former and current employees of the U.S. Defense Department and other security related agencies, of whom there were many in Northern Virginia churches. They were missing the point, obviously. Should not the missions board focus on spreading the gospel of salvation and new life in Jesus Christ and not a political message?

My district superintendent and bishop were merely reflective of United Methodism's liberalized, institutional culture, which portrays the general church as a smorgasbord of contending political, ethnic, regional and professional interest groups. Feminists, liberal theologians, homosexual groups and political activists of the left have for decades demanded and received patronage within United Methodism under the banner of diversity. United Methodists who simply expect the church to uphold historic Christianity are portrayed as just one more special interest group, motivated by their own economic or political concerns. Commonly, IRD's liberal critics portray us as a political response to United Methodism's "progressive" political advocacy on behalf of the downtrodden. In their caricature of us, conservative foundations fund the IRD because they are purportedly threatened by mainline Protestantism's "prophetic" message.

The liberal caucus groups and church agencies are deluding themselves. Liberal mainline Protestantism is no longer politically influential. Once the pillars of American religion, mainline Protestant church members now account for fewer than 15 percent of American church members. And the political pronouncements and lobbying of mainline officials, United Methodists above all, are widely discounted by the U.S. Congress and other policymakers, who know these statements represent only a minority of church members. More than 80 years ago, Methodism's Board of Temperance was truly a potent force on Capitol Hill. Methodist bishops in every region of America were formidable religious leaders. The Methodist clergy were prominent in their communities. General Conferences and other major Methodist governing councils routinely made national headlines. This is rarely true any more.

United Methodism is important not because of its potential political significance but because of its spiritual significance, to the global body of Christ, to America and the world. Amazingly and providentially, Methodism has remained alive, and even vibrant in some pockets, over many decades of liberal hegemony. The evangelical, populist spirit of early Methodism was already encased in the DNA of too many Methodist persons and congregations to be extinguished. The old hymns and liturgy preserved the faith among millions of lay people even when modernist ministers preached a different message. And increasingly, the competition of successful evangelical denominations and independent churches has compelled United Methodists to adapt. Forty years ago, liberal church agencies confidently spoke as the supposed voice of America's largest church. After 50 years of evangelical resurgence in America, coinciding with more than 40 years of mainline Protestant decline, United Methodist officials and clergy are adapting to a new reality.

Successful United Methodist clergy with growing congregations are more likely to replicate the techniques of evangelical churches in their communities as they heed the direction of United Methodist agencies. Not only are these pastors responding to failed theological liberalism, but also they realize that Americans under the age of 50 are mostly indifferent to denominational labels. Most United Methodists no longer feel the tug of their grandparents' denomination. Younger American church goers will go to churches where they are spiritually nourished. Stale churches, whatever their label, will not long retain more than a few steadfast and increasingly aging denominational loyalists. I knew many and cherished loyal institutional United Methodists as I grew up, and many of them strongly encouraged my early church reform efforts. Most are now deceased or elderly, unlikely to be replaced by equally fervent United Methodists.

Over the last 20 years, especially during my 15 years at IRD, I have routinely attended United Methodist church agency board meetings, Council of Bishops' meetings and General Conferences. The climate has definitely improved since the late 1980s. Liberals who once spoke confidently of implementing their agenda for the church and America, now complain of being besieged and unappreciated. Liberal church agency staffers are more prone to avoid controversial issues. Bishops speak more of fostering church agency than promoting "prophetic," i.e., liberal political causes. At the 1992 General Conference, a very liberal delegate from New York scoffingly derided one of our resolutions from Virginia about reforming the missions board, based exclusively on the name of the submitter: "United Methodists for More Faithful Ministry." It sounded suspicious, he surmised!

The formal investigations and secret study groups and papers once commissioned by church agencies against the renewal groups, including IRD, are now rarer. Even most liberal church agencies realize that the church is evolving in a more evangelical and international direction. They are cautiously trying to adapt to this new reality, ideally wanting to stop it, but realizing that at best they will have to accommodate to it.

They may not realize it yet, but these liberal church agencies will have to do more than accommodate. In 20 years, and probably in 10 years, they will no longer be recognizably liberal. With their boards overwhelmingly comprised of Africans or evangelicals predominantly from the U.S. South, their programs and staff will more accurately reflect the church as it really is, not as liberal elites have imagined it.

"Wake up, and strengthen the things that remain, which were about to die; for I have not found your deeds completed in the sight of My God," are God's words to the Church at Sardis, from Revelation 3:2. This Scripture I quoted in all of my speeches and sermons over the last 15 years. The United Methodist Church has slumbered almost to the point of death. But the Holy Spirit never left it, and God's work continued within it, despite the obstacles. Now, we must awake and enlarge what God has given us, that he might use us powerfully once again. The United Methodists in Africa, among others, are God's instruments in this process of reviving his church around the world.

Working with our friends across the seas, especially United Methodists in Africa, we must strive to complete what God has commissioned us to do. We celebrate the honor that he has bestowed upon us to serve him in so momentous a project as restoring The United Methodist Church.

ED JOHNSON AND GENERAL CONFERENCE 2008

Sometime in 2005 a long-time United Methodist friend in Virginia phoned me. His recently removed pastor was the Rev. Ed Johnson, who had become virtually the most famous clergy in United Methodism. Virginia Bishop Charlene Kammerer, often liberal agenda driven, had removed Johnson from his pulpit for not granting membership to an active homosexual in his congregation. Later, the United Methodist Judicial Council overruled Kammerer, restoring Johnson to his pulpit.

How my friend described his beloved pastor was considerably different from the liberal mythology. This stereotype claimed Johnson had spitefully refused church membership to a homosexual who worshipped at his South Hill United Methodist Church in southern Virginia. The mythology further asserted that United Methodism's top court, ruled by evangelicals, had essentially approved a ban on church membership for homosexuals. This myth, first launched by the Johnson case, would come to dominate much of General Conference 2008.

Johnson, whom I would later meet, is a low-key, quiet and personable evangelical pastor generally averse to controversy. He had been counseling a homosexual who sang in the South Hill Church choir and who was known to be sexually partnered with another man in town who did not attend the church. Johnson was welcoming to the homosexual man but had decided he was not yet ready for church membership.

United Methodism has no specific church law on homosexuality and church membership. The church officially decries homosexual practice, affirms sex only within marriage, prohibits ordination to practicing homosexuals and anyone else sexually active outside marriage, and forbids same-sex unions. New church members, in their vows, pledge to uphold the church's beliefs and to seek holiness. But after 45 years of continuous membership decline, not to mention a century of theological liberalism, typical United Methodist clergy are more than happy quickly to enroll any applicants into church membership.

Johnson, unusually and commendably, took his church's membership vows more seriously. According to my friend at Johnson's church, the homosexual man was not particularly chagrined and retained his high regard for Johnson. But the associate pastor, who was more liberal, essentially informed on Johnson to Bishop Kammerer, who never misses an opportunity to advance liberal causes, especially homosexual advocacy.

Kammerer demanded that Johnson install the homosexual man into immediate church membership. Johnson replied that he could not in good conscience comply, knowing full well the likely consequence for him. Kammerer removed Johnson from active ministry and successfully asked the clergy session of the 2005 Virginia Annual Conference to ratify her decision without providing many details. A pastor serving as counsel to Johnson asked for a "ruling of law" during the clergy discussion, ensuring the issue went before the Judicial Council at its October 2005 meeting.

The Judicial Council, led by evangelicals elected by the 2000 General Conference, did not rule on homosexual practice and church membership. It did rule that local pastors have discretion regarding readiness for church membership, and that Bishop Kammerer had improperly pressured and removed Johnson. Headlines about the church court's decision sometimes inaccurately implied that the court had banned the homosexual man from church membership. I was even personally interviewed on the "gay" themed *Logo* cable network about the Johnson case, and I strove to correct this misimpression.

Coincidentally, the Council of Bishops was meeting when the Judicial Council's Johnson decision was released. Likely motivated partly by liberal notions of unlimited inclusiveness, as well as self-protection regarding its own authority, the council reacted angrily. The bishops' "pastoral" response, ostensibly ratified unanimously, condemned the Judicial Council ruling in an almost unprecedented fashion and strongly implied that church membership must be automatically extended to all applicants, almost by right.

Thanks to the bishops, and liberal pressure groups like the Methodist Federation for Social Action and the pro-homosexuality Reconciling Ministries Network, "open" church membership became a rallying cry for General Conference 2008. Reportedly, Bishop Kammerer promised that the Judicial Council's errant ruling would be "fixed." As is often the case, Kammerer's aggressive, and not always transparent, promotion of her agenda would ultimately backfire politically. But liberals ambitiously exploited the Johnson case to enlist moderates in their campaign to depose the evangelical majority on the Judicial Council, to mandate open church membership and to diminish if not overturn United Methodism's disapproval of homosexual practice.

Mitigating against the liberal juggernaut for a more "open" and permissive United Methodism was the growth of international delegate numbers at the 2008 General Conference. Nearly 30 percent of all delegates came from outside the U.S., two thirds of them from Africa. The Africans were overwhelmingly conservative. And liberals, to prevail, had to win without almost any of the nearly 200 African delegates. At the same time, U.S. evangelicals increasingly were aware that the church's future rested with the Africans, which was a cause for hope and inspiration. Liberal institutionalists strove to limit African influence at General Conference 2008 by complex parliamentary procedures, poor translations and keeping Africans out of legislative leadership. Evangelicals concurrently tried to enhance African influence by helping them overcome communication obstacles.

Seeking better communication, the evangelical coalition at General Conference, which included IRD/UM*Action*, ignited enormous controversy by distributing cell phones to all international delegates at the 2008 General Conference in Forth Worth, Texas.   Bishops and liberal pressure groups loudly insisted that U.S. evangelicals were trying to "buy" African votes. They failed to explained why U.S. evangelicals would need to "buy" African votes when Africans were already, by their own choice, very conservative and largely in sync with the theological goals of U.S. evangelicals.

Retired Bishop Ken Carder complained that the cell phones had violated "boundaries of what is appropriate in this kind of community, and I hope that it would cease." Long an angry critic of evangelical groups, especially IRD/UM*Action*, he insisted: "This seems to be an undue influence and violates the very essence of what it means to be Christian community."

Even more laughably, a "joint monitoring team" from the Commission on the Status and Role of Women (COSROW) and the Commission on Religion and Race (CRR) ominously warned: "Whenever there is an imbalance of power relationships with the expectation of reciprocity, this behavior gives the appearance of paternalism, manipulation, exploitation and of course, racism." COSROW, at church expense, dispatched prying observers to General Conference to monitor any discrete signals of perceived sexism or other political incorrectness.

CRR's top bureaucrat further trumpeted the racism card. "My hope is that the white leadership of the church would be mindful of the actions in light of the history of exploitation of people of color in this church," simmered Erin Hawkins. "This action of giving cell phones to buy or manipulate people can be interpreted as a return to that sort of racist behavior."

The Board of Church and Society's Jim Winkler similarly warned that United Methodist renewal groups were "providing deliberately distorted and inaccurate information to African United Methodists." The cell phones were part of a "pattern of manipulation of the African delegates." Unmentioned by church bureaucrats like Winkler was that liberal church agencies had a long tradition of providing gifts and meals to international delegates on behalf of their own agenda. What was really troubling to the church agencies was the possibility that Africans and other internationals could actually communicate and organize on their own, without control by the U.S. church bureaucracy.

Nearly every single international delegate appreciatively claimed one of the cell phones. Even *United Methodist News Service* quoted mostly words of thanks from African delegates. "It is a great help for me," declared one Liberian delegate. "We were told that the phones are to be used for local connections in the United States and to contact my fellow delegates."

But the head of a U.S. ethnic caucus excoriated the cell phones as "vote-buying" and "bribery." And COSROW chief Garlinda Burton intoned: "The hospitality that we offer should be the hospitality that is offered to everyone." That may sound highminded. But the international delegates, especially the Africans, sometimes spend several days traveling to General Conference, with no time for rest, with little knowledge of the English language or parliamentary procedure and cannot operate as equals in the General Conference without special communication and translation assistance.

Liberals want to keep international delegates passive and uninformed. The brouhaha over the cell phones wonderfully illustrated liberal fears over the emerging and empowered African

United Methodists, who can quite capably think and speak for themselves. Increasingly realizing the threat, liberals proposed a solution at the General Conference 2008: creating a new U.S. only General Conference that would exclude the internationals.

This "global segregation" plan, along with the church membership controversy, dominated much of General Conference 2008. Seeming liberal victories at General Conference on these issues, in the form of proposed church constitutional amendments, accompanied by defeats of evangelicals on the Judicial Council, probably persuaded many liberals that they could out-maneuver the growing evangelical-African majority. The votes at annual conferences around the world on global segregation and open church membership constitutional amendments in 2009 would showcase the limits of liberal manipulation.

Liberal direct assaults on United Methodism's scriptural affirmation of marriage and sexual ethics were directly defeated at General Conference 2008. An effort to soften the marriage stance by suggesting a "new insight" on sexuality was rejected. It was replaced with even stronger language in United Methodism's *Social Principles* affirming the "covenant of monogamous, heterosexual marriage." The margin on the closest vote was 501-417, meaning a shift of only 43 votes could have given liberals an enormously symbolic victory. This margin would not have been possible without the nearly 200 African delegates. In fact, just the increase of 84 delegates in the African delegations from 2004, when they had only 108 delegates, accounted for this victory.

Margins on the church's prohibition against actively homosexual clergy and same-sex unions were larger, sometimes surpassing 70 percent. But a loss on the "incompatible" phrase, which dates to 1972, likely would have ignited a conservative exodus from the denomination. When an African bishop was thanked for the support of his delegates, he replied, "That's why I brought them here." Liberals did not fail to notice the African impact. "We have feared this for years," reported a spokesman for "Reconciling Ministries Network," complaining that international delegates are in "clear alliance with the most conservative elements" of the U.S. church. "As some of us heard in speeches from the floor from some of these international delegates, they are far more conservative than even the average American conservatives, on a wide range of social issues."

Many U.S. liberals resented the growing African presence. Some African delegates reported receiving intimidating notes and pictures on their desks. One African delegate was angrily told by a liberal U.S. delegate: "Remember, the money for your conference in Africa comes from our conference here." Some African delegates had been given plane tickets mandating their departure before the end of General Conference, and they were not present for many important votes on the last day. And African delegations, unlike the U.S., could not afford to send alternate delegates.

Also unlike U.S. delegates, most African delegates only received General Conference legislation after arriving in Fort Worth. Official daily updates about legislation were published only in English, which about half the African delegates do not speak. Display screen instructions for delegates appeared only in English. During the crucial debate on major constitutional amendments, the simultaneous French audio translation stopped completely. Some overseas delegates said translations were of poor quality or tainted by the translator's biases. Elections to the Judicial Council and University Senate resulted in no African members, effectively disenfranchising one third of the church's members.

The exclusion of Africans from the important Judicial Council was especially outrageous. Five new members, with support from liberals and the Council of Bishops, were elected to the Judicial Council. They did not even bother nominating a single African, ignoring more than 3.2 million United Methodists in Africa. But of course they successfully elected a member of the ultra-liberal and fast declining Western Jurisdiction, with fewer than 400,000 members. Thanks to the Ed Johnson case, and other rulings that affirmed United Methodism's disapproval of homosexual practice, liberals had fiercely targeted the council's evangelical incumbents. The Council of Bishops unusually, but nor surprisingly, refused to re-nominate a single incumbent on its own slate. Liberal caucus groups supported the bishops' candidates and distributed its suggested ballot on the floor of the General Conference immediately before the vote. Ostensibly their candidates were centrist, compared to the purportedly extremist incumbents and others backed by evangelicals, including a distinguished district superintendent from Liberia.

The new, liberal-backed majority on the Judicial Council created doubts about the church court's willingness to vigorously uphold church law about sexuality, ordination and marriage. But so far, the majority has carefully upheld church law and precedent and shows little sign of radically changing the church's standards, as liberal caucus groups had hoped. In 2009, the new council even invalidated a pro-homosexuality stance by the liberal-dominated Baltimore-Washington Conference.

Somewhat promisingly, the General Conference nudged the church in a slightly more pro-life direction, but barely failed to end United Methodism's ties to an abortion rights lobby group, Delegates voted to:

• "Affirm and encourage the Church to assist the ministry of crisis pregnancy centers and pregnancy resource centers that compassionately help women find feasible alternatives to abortion."

• Replace language about "devastating damage" from "unacceptable" pregnancies with the affirmation that "we are equally bound to respect the sacredness of the life and well-being of the mother and the unborn child."

• Oppose abortions done for "trivial reasons."

•Describe abortion as "violent."

•Call for action against the global problem of sex-selective abortions.

•State our church's concerns about eugenics, including opposition to fertility treatment practices that selectively kill embryos with undesired genetic traits.

•"Reject euthanasia and pressure upon the dying to end their lives."

Sadly in contrast, General Conference 2008 continued United Methodist membership in the Religious Coalition for Reproductive Choice (RCRC) by 52-48 percent, the narrowest margin ever. RCRC opposes any restrictions on abortion. While RCRC prevailed by just 32 votes (out of 800 cast), the vote was scheduled on the conference's last day, when more than 100 African delegates (who tend to be more pro-life) were absent.

RCRC made a huge effort to woo delegates but almost certainly would have faced defeat if the vote had been taken earlier in the conference. The close vote was also influenced by misleading statements. An RCRC-produced flyer asserted that the group had "never" "supported the use of partial-birth abortion." Bishop Beverly Shamana of San Francisco also claimed: "RCRC does not support late-term abortion." In fact, RCRC has since the mid-1990s consistently lobbied against all partial-birth abortion limits (working against the United Methodist official opposition to these abortions). RCRC's defenders disingenuously but cleverly emphasized RCRC's supposed initiatives against AIDS in Africa while avoiding RCRC's aggressive abortion rights advocacy, which is RCRC's chief purpose.

United Methodism's tragic continued membership in RCRC became especially significant when, during the Obamacare debates of 2009-2010, RCRC strongly affirmed government funding for abortion in any government directed health care plan. Of course, the United Methodist Board of Church and Society enthusiastically backed this stance. Promisingly, Kansas Bishop Scott Jones, speaking to the annual service for pro-life United Methodists in early 2010, specifically condemned government funded abortions.

"We need to recognize that access to an abortion is not a right," Jones declared. "While we believe that persons have the right to health care, abortion is not normally a health care issue. Rather it is a sinful behavior." He further insisted: "Proposals in the recent health-care debate to provide tax funding for abortions are very misguided. What you fund with tax dollars will increase." Willingness by some bishops to dissent from RCRC's perspective, and the close vote at General Conference 2008, along with significant pro-life resolutions, indicate that time is on the side of United Methodist pro-lifers.

There was other good news at General Conference 2008, which:

•Defeated a *Discipline* change requiring pastors to grant immediate church membership and eligibility for congregational leadership to all applicants. This directly rebuffed the Council of Bishops, especially Bishop Kammerer, in the Ed Johnson case.

•Overwhelmingly rejected anti-Israel divestment proposals, which came primarily from the Board of Church and Society.

•Strengthened United Methodism's recognition of divorce's negative consequences.

•Called for "assurances" that the politicized National Council of Churches (NCC) would "remain faithful" to its purpose of making "visible their unity given in Christ" through proclaiming

"Jesus Christ as Savior and Lord."

•Condemned sexual exploitation and abuse committed by United Nations personnel. The United Methodist Women's Division and the Board of Church and society have long reflexively touted the U.N.

•Approved a constitutional amendment to allow non-ordained local pastors to vote for General and Jurisdictional Conference delegates. Most of these local pastors serve small churches and typically are more conservative than ordained clergy.

•Elected three evangelical United Methodists to the University Senate, which oversees the seminaries.

•Voted $2 million for theological education in Africa.

•Required that Ministerial Education Fund payments to United Methodist seminaries "only be used for" the benefit of United Methodist students (rather than general operating expenses). Some of our seminaries have non United Methodist student majorities.

•Reduced the number of U.S. Bishops by 4 (from 50), beginning in 2012.

•Preserved the right of individual United Methodists to submit petitions (proposed legislation) to General Conference.

•Adopted a UM*Action* resolution urging restraint in church political involvement, including a call for Christians "to have the humility to be cautious of asserting that God is on their side with regard to specific public policy proposals."

•Overwhelmingly rejected resolutions to condemn UM*Action*.

Amusingly, an ad hoc liberal caucus from Oklahoma called "Mainstream United Methodists" distributed an 8 page newspaper at General Conference 2008 exclusively attacking IRD/ UM*Action*. It even included anti-IRD cartoons. One showed the United Methodist Church as a Titanic about to hit an IRD iceberg, which was odd and revealing symbolism. Another showed an IRD snake hissing at a Methodist circuit rider on his horse. Even more unusually, a third showed IRD as an armored knight with sword and ball and chain, confronting a Methodist preacher in the pulpit. The final cartoon showed an IRD locomotive steaming angrily towards a bound Methodist preacher on the tracks.

This "mainstream" newspaper decried IRD as a cabal of "neocon Roman Catholic leaders" and "wealthy millionaires [redundant?!] who control billions of inherited tax-free trust dollars." Aiming to "discourage and confuse United Methodists," IRD's "accusations of Marxist support and sexual laxity of Methodists have been proven false," they claimed. They further bewailed that IRD aims to force United Methodists away from "protecting the environment" and the "living poor," while protecting "big corporations in areas of human slavery and child labor." In typical fashion, this critique of IRD was superficial and ham-handed. But it did flatter us with its effusive attention and generated a lot of laughter, which was much welcome during a grueling 10-day convention.

Less laughable, but nearly just as ham-handed, was the usual litany of left-wing and un-thoughtful political resolutions that General Conference 2008 approved. They included supporting "sanctuary churches" and amnesty for all past and future illegal immigrants; opposing hand guns; affirming the defunct Kyoto treaty on Global Warming; demanding the U.S. military welcome openly "gay, lesbian, bisexual or transgender" soldiers,

flyers, marines and sailors; called imprisoned Puerto Rican terrorists "political prisoners" and urged their release; lamented the
"colonialism" of Puerto Rico's commonwealth status; demanded
an end to U.S. military aid to Israel; endorsed a recent "Mission
Study" from the United Methodist Women's Division likening
Israelis to Nazis and terrorists; urged cooperation with the International Solidarity Movement, which is devoted to "nonvio-
lent, direct-action" for the Palestinian cause; accused the U.S. of a
"global economic agenda that is of, by, and for transnational corporations;" affirmed "progressive income taxes," and condemned
free trade agreements.

Fortunately, most United Methodists will remain blissfully unaware of their church's official political stances. Unfortunately,
the Board of Church and Society will cite these stances as validation for their Capitol Hill lobbying. Of far more serious consequence were proposed constitutional amendments that General
Conference 2008 approved. One directly responded to the Ed
Johnson case and would have required that "all persons" were
eligible for church membership "upon taking vows declaring the
Christian faith and relationship in Jesus Christ." Potentially this
would have mandated automatic membership and rejected any
pastoral discretion. It ultimately could have voided any official
United Methodist disapproval of homosexual practice, especially
if a liberal-controlled Judicial Council chose to exploit it for a
larger agenda. Revealingly, the amendment came from a Texas
clergy group "seeking full inclusion of gays and lesbians."

More complicated were 23 Constitutional amendments that
would have created a new U.S.-only "regional conference" excluding overseas delegates. Liberals opposed to United Methodism's biblical stance on marriage strongly supported these "global
segregation" amendments because they obviously would have reduced the influence of conservative Africans and other non-U.S.
United Methodists. The pro-homosexuality Reconciling Ministries Network naturally hailed these amendments as "a positive

development."

Ironically, but almost certainly not coincidentally, Bishop Kammerer, the originator of the Ed Johnson controversy, presided over the General Conference 2008 debate over the open membership amendment. An initial vote failed to garner the needed two thirds. But Kammerer cited a technical glitch and convened a second vote, which barely got the additional needed votes. Her exertions ultimately failed, fortunately. Annual Conferences in 2009 rejected the open membership and global segregation amendments, often by decisive majorities. Open membership got only about 50 percent of the vote in the U.S. and was rejected nearly unanimously by the African annual conferences. Global Segregation got less than 40 percent in the U.S. And Africans, seeing through its true agenda, also rejected it nearly unanimously. The total vote was 52-48 percent against, when two thirds was needed for passage.

More than 50,000 annual conference members voted on these amendments, and their rejection repudiated the Council of Bishops and, at least partly, the General Conference. When allowed voice, local churches are almost always far more traditional than church elites, including most General Conference U.S. delegates. Pleasingly, the constitutional amendment allowing non-ordained local pastors to elect General and Jurisdictional Conference delegates was easily approved. This reform hopefully will help to make General Conference more truly representative of most United Methodists.

The liberal gambit to separate the U.S. church from the Africans failed, as did the covert attempt to undermine United Methodism's strong stance for marriage. While liberals still firmly control nearly all United Methodist general agencies and most of the seminaries and command loyalty from most U.S. bishops, their future remains bleak. Liberal U.S. annual conferences continue to hemorrhage members, and their representation at General Conference will continue to shrink, compounded by the growth of the African churches, and more moderate growth by some conservative-leaning, southern U.S. annual conferences.

One growing U.S. annual conference has been North Georgia under the leadership of Bishop Lindsey Davis. During his 12 years, the North Georgia Conference became the largest conference in United Methodism, with more than 350,000 members, one of only about a dozen growing U.S. conferences, all of them southern. The declining Virginia Conference was previously the largest, its decline accelerated by Bishop Kammerer's often fickle and certainly liberal direction. In 2008, the theologically conservative Davis transferred to the Kentucky Conference, where he will continue his focus on evangelism and church growth.

In a sermon he gave before leaving North Georgia in 2008, Davis decried growing secularism in society: "There is a strong movement in the United States and in Europe, by those who want a very secular culture, to put the Christian voice on the sidelines—to not allow the Christian faith and the Christian witness to have to have its proper place in the public arena, in the public square, or in the marketplace." He warned against this effort to "sideline our Christian witness, so that we will be weak." He emphasized that the church must proclaim the "whole gospel story." Often churches in America today want to "spend all of our time talking about grace and redemption and salvation," all of which are an important "part" of the story, Davis said. "But it's also important that we tell the rest of the story — that we tell about sin and the consequences of sin, and that we talk about redemption and the need for redemption, so that then the stories of grace and salvation make sense to those who come after us."

Such words are rare from U.S. United Methodist bishops. But Davis represents United Methodism's future, while failed 20th century liberalism represents its past. Meanwhile, the Rev. Ed Johnson, despite Bishop Kammerer, is doing fine. She moved him from his South Hill, Virginia church in 2006, in an obvious gambit to outmaneuver the Judicial Council's ruling. Johnson and his new church seem to fit each other well. Meanwhile, his successor, though ostensibly evangelical, did accept the disputed homosexual man into membership, as Kammerer fervently hoped. But the homosexual man stopped attending South Hill Church, and the congregation has declined. It was a typically empty "victory" for liberals like Kammerer, who cherish their narrow agenda over the wider church's spiritual health.